Sawtooth
National Recreation Area

A guide to trails, roads and waters in Idaho's Sawtooth, White Cloud and Boulder mountains.

by Luther Linkhart

Photographs (except for a few that are credited to others) are by the author. Design is also by the author.

OPPOSITE: Spur ridge behind unnamed Lake 8733 on the east side of the Sawtooth Range below Mt. Cramer. Trees at timberline are whitebark pines and subalpine firs.

FRONT COVER: Upper meadow in Boulder Basin, in the heart of the Boulder Mountains. Foreground flowers are shooting stars.

This book was produced with the help and guidance of the Forest Service, U. S. Department of Agriculture, administrative agency for the Sawtooth National Recreation Area. No endorsement of this book is granted or implied by the Forest Service.

 Wilderness Press   Berkeley

Acknowledgements

This book is dedicated to David Lee, former backcountry zone manager of the SNRA, who lived all of his life among and for these mountains.

My wife, Virginia, heads the list of wonderful people without whom this book could never have been completed. She backpacked and skied the trails with me, planned the food and cooked most of the meals, transcribed the trail notes, typed and retyped the manuscript and never doubted that the book would someday be finished and, later, revised.

Ruth Murray walked more of the trails with us than anyone else and was of inestimable help in identifying flora and providing car-shuttles.

Our longtime friend, Marshall LeBaron, gave us the use of his beautiful second home at Ketchum as a base and sanctuary, as well as providing some of our transportation.

Roger Denney, trail and fishing companion and professional editor, read the manuscript and helped me through the minefields of style and grammar, as did Thomas Winnett, editor and publisher of Wilderness Press.

David Lee, Sandra Brown, Kenneth Britton and "Butch" Harper of the U.S. Forest Service cheerfully answered questions, volunteered information and reviewed most of the manuscript.

Others who walked with us, provided information, transported us and were just generally helpful are: Barbara and Bruce Brink, Delvan and Virginia Dean, L. Jacqueline Denney, Pamela Denney, Charles Ebersole, Michael LeBaron, Joe and Sheila Leonard, Edward and Lyda Linkhart, Richard and "Peg" Linkhart, Robert Linkhart, 'Stina Linkhart, Isabelle Miller, Mary Naylor, Leif Odmark, Bob Rosso, and Barbara Tucker.

Many other people, too many to list here, contributed unselfishly to the making of this book. To all of them, I am most grateful.

Copyright © 1981, 1988 by Luther Linkhart

Pocket map is reproduced by permission of the Forest Service, U.S. Dept. of Agriculture

Library of Congress card number 87-34073

ISBN: 0-89997-085-0

Manufactured in the United States

Published by
Wilderness Press
2440 Bancroft Way
Berkeley, CA 94704
(415) 843-8080

Write for free catalog

Library of Congress Cataloging-in-Publication Data

Linkhart, Luther.
   Sawtooth National Recreation Area : a guide to trails, roads, and waters in Idaho's Sawtooth, White Cloud, and Boulder mountains / by Luther Linkhart. - - 2nd ed.
      p.   cm.
   Bibliography : p.
   Includes index.
   ISBN 0-89997-085-0 : $14.95
      1. Outdoor recreation--Idaho--Sawtooth National Recreation Area--Guide-books. 2. Sawtooth National Recreation Area (Idaho)--Guide-books. I. Title
GV191.42.I2L56 1987
917.96 '0433--dc19   87-34073
                                                            CIP

Table of Contents

Table of Contents

Introduction

You are never quite prepared for it, no matter how many times you've driven up the Salmon River canyon to Stanley —as you round the last turn, the somber walls of the canyon open up like theater curtains to reveal an incredible tableau. Stop on the hump below Lower Stanley to drink it all in. Below on your left, the sparkling clear Salmon River flows swiftly but silently, bordered by the greenest of meadows. A mare and her foal arch their graceful necks to watch a flyfisherman perform his ritual in the shallows. Beyond the few rustic roofs of Lower Stanley, more meadows and bands of gray-green sagebrush lead up to the toylike log buildings of Stanley, overwhelmed by the bold sloping lines of the benches and foothills beyond. Above the foothills, breathtaking peaks and ridges fill half the sky with vertical mauve and purple granite, accented by many snow fields. The serrated crests are silhouetted against the intensely blue sky like the teeth of a saw. You are looking at the Sawtooth Mountains in the Sawtooth National Recreation Area.

The Sawtooths are just one of the many wonderful things to see and experience in central Idaho's Sawtooth National Recreation Area (SNRA). At 1,178 square miles, the SNRA is almost as big as the state of Rhode Island — some wags suggest that it would be bigger than Rhode Island if it were ironed out flat, heaven forbid. Within the SNRA boundaries are three mountain ranges with peaks between 10,000 and 12,000 feet, the headwaters of four major rivers, innumerable smaller streams, five large lakes and hundreds of smaller lakes. You can hike, climb peaks, sightsee in your car, camp, backpack, ride horses, trailbike, raft down rivers, kayak, sail, waterski, swim, fish, hunt, pan for gold, cross-country ski, snowshoe or snowmobile here (just to name a few of the possible activities).

The irregular boundaries of the SNRA fit roughly within a 40-mile square, with a few points sticking out. Stanley and Lower Stanley are just inside the north side of the square, a little

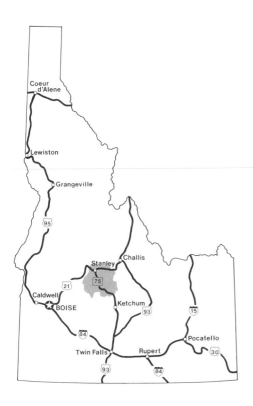

west of center. Ketchum and Sun Valley are 8-9 miles south of the southeast corner. From Ketchum, Twin Falls is 83 miles south and Boise is 153 miles southwest.

The Sawtooth Range fills most of the west side of the square, giving way to the Smoky Mountains in the southwest corner. North of the Boulder Mountains, which are piled up in the southeast corner, the remote White Cloud Mountains form a series of ramparts along the east side. Castle Peak in the White Clouds, at 11,815 feet, is the highest peak in the SNRA. Some people argue that seldom-seen Ryan Peak in the Boulder Mountains is higher, but the U.S. Geological Survey does not agree.

The 25-mile-long trough of Sawtooth Valley, cradling the Salmon River, runs north through the center of the square to meet the wide expanse of Stanley Basin, partly within the north boundary. From Stanley, the deep, crooked trench of the Upper Salmon River Canyon runs along the north boundary to the northeast corner.

Two forks of the Boise River, the Queens and Little Queens rivers and the South Fork of the Payette River originate in and drain west and south from the Sawtooths. The Salmon River and its East Fork drain the east slope of the Sawtooths and the White Clouds. The source of the Big Wood River is on the south side of Galena Summit, the divide at the south end of Sawtooth Valley. The Big Wood flows southeast, picking up water from tributaries in the

Boulders and the Smokies, and exits the southeast corner of the square.

Highway 75, the "Sawtooth Scenic Route," is the principal access to the SNRA. It runs north from Shoshone through Hailey and Ketchum to enter the SNRA at the southeast corner. From the SNRA headquarters at the confluence of the Big Wood River and its North Fork, the highway follows the Big Wood northwest almost to its source, then climbs over Galena Summit to follow the Salmon River through Sawtooth Valley and past the narrows near Redfish Lake to Stanley. Highway 21, the "Ponderosa Pine Scenic Route," branches west from Highway 75 at Stanley and makes a wide loop northwest around the north end of the Sawtooth Range on its way to Lowman and eventually Boise. Highway 75 follows the Salmon River as it flows east from Stanley through its upper canyon, and then north to Challis.

Man has not altered the magnificent scenery of the SNRA much since trapper Alexander Ross first saw it in 1824. We can thank the remoteness of the area and the lack of any large amount of merchantable timber or minerals for that fortunate circumstance. Grazing, tourism and a small amount of mining are the only activities currently affecting the natural order. Establishment of the Sawtooth National Recreation Area by an act of Congress in 1972 is controlling real-estate development and will preserve this precious asset for future generations.

Sun Valley, Ketchum and Bald Mountain at the height of the ski season

WHAT THE SNRA IS AND HOW IT WORKS

The criteria established by Congress for a national recreation area are: "an area containing outstanding combinations of outdoor recreation opportunities, esthetic attractions, and proximity to potential users. The area must be of national significance." Although there might be some small doubt about its "proximity to potential users," the SNRA is definitely overqualified in all of the other criteria.

Public Law 92-400, enacted by Congress in August 1972, reads in part: ". . . in order to assure the preservation and protection of the natural, scenic, historic, pastoral and fish and wildlife values and to provide for the enhancement of the recreational values associated therewith, the Sawtooth National Recreation Area is hereby established."

The congressional act also reclassified the former 216,000-acre Sawtooth Primitive Area to designated Sawtooth Wilderness and appointed the U. S. Forest Service as administrator of the SNRA as a subunit of the Sawtooth National Forest under the direction of a superintendent.

Mining and Logging—Except for valid existing rights, all lands within the SNRA are closed to mineral exploration, location, entry and patent, and mining of existing claims is subject to regulations for the protection of natural, scenic and recreational values. Further, the Secretary of Agriculture (under whose jurisdiction the Forest Service operates) has the right to acquire mineral interests in the SNRA, with or without the owner's consent, in order to further the stated purposes of the recreation area. Logging within the SNRA, since its establishment in 1972, has been limited essentially to fence poles, posts, firewood and building logs for local construction.

Grazing—Cattle and sheep grazing continues on suitable lands within the SNRA. Careful control of grazing is exercised to protect scenic, wildlife and recreational values.

Motorized Travel—No motorized equipment of any kind may be operated in the Sawtooth Wilderness. Wheeled and tracked vehicles are restricted in the remainder of the SNRA to specific roads and trails designated on Motorized Vehicle Maps posted at trailheads and information points. Except for snowmobiles in authorized areas, all cross-country travel by motorized vehicles is prohibited. Aircraft are allowed to land only at established airfields (Smiley Creek and Stanley) without a written permit for other locations from the area ranger.

Private Land—Over 25,000 acres of the approximately 754,000 acres of the SNRA are still in private ownership and will remain so within the foreseeable future. Most of these private lands are ranches in the Sawtooth Valley and Stanley Basin and townsite lots in Stanley, Obsidian and Sawtooth City. The SNRA has established use and scenic regulations that apply to all private lands in the recreation area. Some small holdings that did not comply, or that were needed for public access or recreation use, were bought on most of the larger holdings to compensate the owners for any loss of value due to the restrictions.

All subdivision for resale is controlled by SNRA land-use regulations. Ranching operations that comply with the regulations are encouraged.

The regulations, scenic easements and a few purchases have done much "to assure the preservation and protection of the natural, scenic, historic, pastoral and fish and wildlife values." Most of the remaining landowners are on good terms with the SNRA.

Visitors should be aware that private land within the SNRA is no different from private land elsewhere, and that the scenic easements generally do not include public access. Please respect private property.

Additional Wilderness—Congress, in the enabling act PL 92-400, directed the Secretary of Agriculture to review undeveloped portions of the SNRA as to suitability for inclusion in the National Wilderness Preservation System. So far the RARE II studies have recommended additions north and south to the Sawtooth Wilderness. The White Cloud Peaks and Boulder Mountains have been recommended for Wilderness designation in the "Preferred Alternative" of the Sawtooth National Forest Plan.

Human History

A Haskett-point spear blade found in an archeological dig near Redfish Lake indicates that humans may have been here as long as 10,000 years ago. There never was a large population of Indians in the present SNRA area, however, and evidence suggests that they were primarily summer visitors, as their successors are now.

Small bands of Bannocks, Shoshoni and Lemhi probably came to the Sawtooth Valley and Stanley Basin during the summers to catch salmon and hunt deer, elk and mountain sheep. They in turn were occasionally pursued by grizzly bears. Indians seldom entered the higher mountains because they had no reason to — travel was extremely difficult there and food was scarce. At the first sign of winter, the Indians moved down to more comfortable quarters along the Snake River and the lower Salmon. Only renegades or outcasts would consider enduring the awful winters in the Sawtooth country.

THE FUTILE SEARCH FOR BEAVER

John Colter, discoverer of Yellowstone, was known to have traveled west of the Teton Range and may have seen the Sawtooths before 1810. If he did, he left no record. The first known white visitor was a Hudson's Bay Company fur trader, Alexander Ross, who climbed to the top of a peak somewhere near Galena Summit on September 18, 1824, and later wrote in his journal, "The view we had enjoyed repaid us well for our troubles."

Ross and his men didn't linger long. Beaver were scarce and they were anxious to get to their winter camp at Canoe Point, farther down the Salmon, before the weather got any colder.

Later fur traders, including Captain B.L.E. Bonneville (on leave from the U. S. Army) and another American named Warren Ferris, who visited the Sawtooth Valley in the 1820's and 30's, didn't find any bonanza of beaver either, so interest in the area waned for another 30 years or so, until another kind of bonanza was discovered.

THE SOMETIMES SUCCESSFUL SEARCH FOR GOLD

In the Summer of 1863 a party of 23 prospectors lead by "Captain" John Stanley climbed over the mountains from the South Fork of Payette River and eventually made their way into what is now Stanley Basin. They found some gold in the sands of Valley and Stanley creeks, but shortages of supplies and dubious relations with visiting Indians forced them to return to more settled territory as winter approached. Stanley's name stayed, though, on several landmarks and eventually on the town that was founded many years later.

Stanley and a larger party of prospectors came back to Stanley Basin in 1864, but apparently Stanley didn't stay — his name is connected with the discovery of the Atlanta Lode on the other side of the Sawtooths that same year. Gold mining continued around Atlanta well into the 20th century. Not even the Bannock Indian War interrupted the digging there — presumably because Atlanta was so remote that the miners didn't hear about the war until it was over. Atlanta is still about as far away from anything as you can get, but rumors of a new mining boom circulated in 1986.

Prospectors continued to poke around the east side of the Sawtooth Mountains and the Big Wood River Valley for more than a decade before finding much of any importance, and what they finally did find was silver and lead, not gold. The Bannock Indian War (which the U. S. Government and the U. S. Army would like to forget) kept miners out of the area in 1877 and 1878. In 1879 Levi Smiley and T. B. Mulkey filed a number of claims near the headwaters of Smiley and Beaver creeks, and by 1880 the rush was on.

Sawtooth City, Vienna, Galena, Bullion, Hailey, Ketchum, Bellevue and Boulder City mushroomed and collapsed before the end of the century, all based on the mining and smelting of silver and lead, with a small amount of gold as a byproduct. Hailey, Ketchum and Bellevue have had a resurgence for reasons other than mining, but the rest of the towns are only memories.

Stanley Basin never produced a lot of gold, although miners continued to dig there for almost 100 years. However, Stanley Basin and Sawtooth Valley did produce a lot of beef, mutton and hay to supply the more successful miners at Bonanza, Custer, Joe's Gulch and Seafoam. Stanley is still a supply base and road center today, while the gold-mining towns have been reduced to ghost status.

McGOWN AND McGOWAN

The early history of Stanley, and later naming of landmarks in the SNRA, is confused by the coincidence of the very similar surnames of early settlers Arthur McGown and George McGowan. It's generally conceded that Arthur McGown, Sr., and his family were the first permanent residents of Stanley, but George McGowan was certainly around about the same time. The U. S. Forest Service and the U. S. Geological Survey have opted for "McGown Lakes" and "McGown Peak" on their maps,

but that has by no means settled the argument among old timers.

NATIONAL FOREST AND NATIONAL PARK

In May 1905 President Theodore Roosevelt established the 2-million-acre Sawtooth Forest Reserve despite the vehement protests of central Idaho's cattle, sheep, mining and timber interests. The reserve was increased to more than 3 million acres in 1906, including most of what later became Sawtooth, Boise, Challis and Salmon National Forests. Emile Grandjean was the second supervisor of the Sawtooth Forest Reserve. Other supervisors and rangers whose names are perpetuated on present-day maps were M. S. Benedict, William H. Horton and John L. (Jay) Sevy.

Central Idaho's women had different views from their men about preserving scenery and natural resources. As early as 1883, Mrs. W. H. Broadhead, wife of a Sawtooth City lawyer and mining executive, extolled the beauties of Lake Tahoma (Redfish) in the *Salt Lake Tribune* and suggested preservation of the area. Idaho women's clubs were instrumental in getting Sawtooth National Park bills introduced in Congress in 1913, 1916, 1935, 1960 and 1966. All the bills were defeated, but a small victory was achieved when the Sawtooth Primitive Area was established by the Forest Service in 1937.

The defeat of incumbent Idaho Governor Don Samuelson by Cecil Andrus in the election of 1970 had a great deal to do with establishment of the SNRA in 1972. Samuelson supported the development of a large open-pit molybdenum mine at the base of Castle Peak, jewel of the White Clouds; Andrus opposed the mine. The electorate had its say, and it became evident to Senators Church and Jordan in Washington that the people of Idaho wanted the Sawtooth area preserved. Timber and mining interests, as well as local landowners, were still adamantly opposed to a National Park, so the Sawtooth National Recreation Area, administered by the Forest Service, developed as a compromise after years of public hearings and congressional debates.

Isabelle Miller, operator of the Clark-Miller

McGown Peak anchors the north end
of the Sawtooth Range

Miner's cabin of fairly recent vintage
in Washington Basin

Guest Ranch and Grand Dame of the Sawtooth Valley until her death in 1986, reflected the opinions of most of the local residents as follows:

"I think the SNRA is great! Senator Church wanted this to be a National Park and I fought that idea very hard. With the cooperation of the Forest Service we got together an organization of local people who lobbied strongly against the establishment of a National Park and for the establishment of the SNRA as a more accep-table alternative.

"Of course, I really would have preferred that things could have stayed just as they were 20 or 30 years ago, but realized that with the pressure for development this could not be. We became painfully aware of this when land just south of Clark-Miller was sold and subdivided in the early 1960's. That subdivision is gone now, and the SNRA is preserving our valley as it should be."

Natural History

GEOLOGY

Glaciers that began to form 2 million years ago (a short time on the geological scale) molded the landscape we see today in the SNRA. These glaciers carved the Sawtooth and White Cloud peaks, scooped out the hundreds of basins that are now beautiful lakes, and filled the floor of Sawtooth Valley. The ice receded 10-15 thousand years ago, leaving behind enormous amounts of rock torn from the Sawtooth Ridge and deposited in giant moraines a few miles away on the west side of the Sawtooth Valley. The largest moraine, just south of Redfish Lake, dammed the valley and formed a large lake which, over several thousand years, filled in and then broke through the dam to expose the terraces and flat valley floor we see today.

The White Clouds glaciers never extended into the Sawtooth Valley, but did fill in the valley of Warm Springs Creek, now known as "The Meadows," in much the same way that the Sawtooth Valley was filled. Tributary streams of the Salmon River, rising in the White Cloud Peaks and flowing in-to the east side of the Sawtooth Valley, carried glacial debris and deposited it in huge alluvial fans, spreading from the mouths of the canyons to the center of the valley in some instances.

The Boulder Mountains were also glaciated, but except for Boulder Basin the effects are not as spectacular as those in the Sawtooths and White Clouds. Only the highest peaks and basins of the Smoky Mountains were affected by glaciers — quite dramatically in some places.

Some 350 million years ago, the area that is now the SNRA was covered by an inland sea. During the next 250 million years the land was lifted up, exposing thousands of feet of sediments left by the receding sea. These sediments, now transformed into rock, were deeply eroded over the eons, then folded and faulted by tremendous upheavals about 100 million years ago that began to form the mountain ridges we see today. The ancient sedimentary and metamorphic rocks are still quite evident in the White Clouds and Boulders, but are seldom seen in the Sawtooths.

During the period of upheaval, the Idaho batholith, a huge body of gray granite with outcrops over a 16,000-square-mile area of central Idaho, intruded through the older rock strata. It can be seen today in the Sawtooth and White Cloud Mountains. Later (only 40 million years ago), the pink granitic Sawtooth batholith intruded through the Idaho batholith and raised the ridge that is now the Sawtooth Mountains. Sawtooth granite fractures more easily than Idaho granite, allowing the glaciers to carry more of it away and to carve the jagged Sawtooth crests.

Massive volcanic activity beginning about 50 million years ago, and later uplifting, built up the Smoky Mountains. Other volcanic erup-tions occurred later on the east slopes of the White Clouds and the Boulders. The many hot springs throughout the area indicate that there are still some hot rocks not too far below the surface.

The most apparent present-day geological activities in the SNRA are avalanches and rock slides. In 1883, some miners claimed to have seen a volcanic eruption from Castle Peak. Geological evidence does not bear them out, and the consensus is that they probably witnessed a gigantic rock slide, possibly triggered by an earthquake. A number of faults run along the east side of the White Cloud Mountains, and a major earthquake, centered on Challis, occurred in 1982.

Fractured crest of Sawtooth granite, footed by talus slides, rises above Profile Lake in the Sawtooth Wilderness

CLIMATE

Warm, sunny days with highs in the 80's and cool, crisp nights with occasional frosts are typical of the summer weather in the SNRA. Precipitation is moderate overall, and a large part of it falls as snow from October to May. Frequent thunderstorms build up over the mountains during July and August, but seldom last very long. Rain from these storms can be heavy, but is usually limited in area.

The SNRA straddles the 44th parallel, which puts it a little farther north than Portland, Maine. This latitude, high elevations (6,000-11,000 feet) and intermountain isolation combine to produce long, cold winters. Low humidity and usually calm air help to make subzero temperatures bearable, however. The winter climate is covered in more detail in the chapter on Winter Activities.

The U. S. Environmental Protection Agency has established the air quality at Craters of the Moon, 55 air-miles southeast, as the national standard for clean air. There are very few days when air quality in the SNRA doesn't meet that standard. One hundred-mile visibility is common.

A subalpine creek breaks its winter bonds in mid-July

PLANTS

The plant communities most often observed by SNRA visitors are the riparian (streamside), meadow, sage and montane-forest communities. Transition to subalpine environment can be seen along Highway 75 at Galena Summit, and a few truly subalpine communities are accessible by trailbike and four-wheel drive, but the majority of subalpine and alpine areas can be reached only by horse or foot travel.

Typical riparian habitat, marked by willows and cottonwoods, borders the Big Wood and Salmon rivers at 6,000–7,000-foot elevations. Higher up, cottonwoods give way to quaking aspen and Engelmann spruce, but willows continue all the way to the alpine zone, above where aspen or spruce can grow.

Meadows are everywhere in the SNRA — they spread for lush miles in the wide valleys and basins, and appear as brilliant green jewels among the high peaks and cirques, contrasting spectacularly with the bare rock and snow. The meadows are also home to the showiest concentrations of wildflowers. In June, for example, Elk Meadow, northwest of Stanley, is a sea of shooting stars, buttercups, dandelions and marsh marigolds. Other meadows in Stanley Basin are carpeted with blue camas shortly after the snow melts.

Higher up, the smaller meadows turn green as the snow retreats, then burst into flower in the supreme effort to produce seeds during the short growing season. Alpine buttercups, gentians, elephant heads, mountain avens, globeflowers and alpine asters are especially prolific in the high meadows.

Along the lower reaches of the Queens and the South Fork Payette rivers, between 5,000 and 6,000 feet elevation, the meadows have a longer growing season and are decorated with a different group of wildflowers including lupines, goldenrods, sunflowers, yarrows, mariposa lilies and white field daisies. Huge ponderosa pines grow in the wooded areas of these canyons and in the Salmon River canyon near the confluence of the East Fork. The ponderosas seldom grow above 6000 feet in the SNRA, so they are not found anywhere else.

From an automobile on Highway 75, the dull gray-green sagebrush flats and slopes of the Big Wood River and Sawtooth valleys appear to offer little of interest. A closer inspection can be very rewarding—myriad wildflowers nestle among the bushes. Early in the season, lupines reflect the color of the sky. Later on, blue, purple and red penstemons appear along with yellow sulfur flowers and deep burgundy phacelias. After a summer shower, broadfruit mariposa lilies pop up as if by magic.

Montane forest, covering much of the mountains and foothills from 6,000 to 8,000 feet elevation, occupies a larger area of the SNRA than any other plant community. The predominant tree in this forest is the lodgepole pine. Pacific Coast states residents will be surprised to see large stands of Douglas fir, accompanied by kinik-kinik, Labrador tea and mahonia in the understory, growing up to 8,000 feet elevation on sheltered, moist, north-facing slopes. Subalpine firs appear at about 7,500 feet and predominate between 8,000 and 9,000 feet. Open groves of whitebark pines can be found in some of the same area, but the whitebark is more often seen as a gnarled frieze atop the most exposed, wind-blasted crests where no other tree could possibly grow. A difference of opinion exists as to whether the limber pine, a very close relative of the whitebark pine, appears in the SNRA.* The general opinion seems to be that if there are any limber pines, their distribution is very limited.

Engelmann spruce and quaking aspen grow in boggy areas and along streams and lakeshores throughout much of the montane forest. Common juniper grows primarily as a low shrub on poor, rocky soil in all the life zones.

Arrowleaf balsamroot, arnica, wyethia and lupine bloom in profusion on more open, south-facing slopes of the forest. In deeper shade and along watercourses, monkshoods, mountain bluebells, delphiniums and monkeyflowers flourish. As the snow melts and after summer rains, many varied species of mushrooms push up through the duff in the thickest forest.

The transition from the montane forest to the subalpine zone begins above 8,000 feet, but forest extends to 9,000 feet on some of the peaks. In the subalpine zone, only the white-

bark pines continue to grow as upright trees. Willows, junipers and heather grow in flat mats. Alpine sunflowers bloom at the base of talus slopes, and dwarfed shooting stars and intense magenta Indian paintbrushes have their short season in tiny meadows.

At the crests of the ridges and near the tops of the peaks, around 10,000 feet, the alpine zone begins. Even the whitebark pines can't stand erect here, and vegetation in the pockets of soil among the rocks is limited mainly to sedges and mats of pink-blooming moss campion and heather. Here and there the brilliant purple blossoms of Townsendia rise an inch or two above the surface of the mats. Above this elevation only lichens survive, clinging to the rocks.

*Being unable to differentiate between whitebark and limber pines, I have arbitrarily classified all five-needle pines in my descriptions as whitebarks. There are no western white pines or sugar pines in the SNRA.

Alpine buttercup pushes through the snow

Later and lower, a water lily decorates a small tarn

ANIMALS

Big-game animals that were once plentiful — mule deer, elk, bear, mountain goats and big-horn sheep — are now scarce in the SNRA. More than 100 years of hunting and occupation of their winter range by ranchers has made it difficult for the animals to survive. Since the establishment of the SNRA, deer and elk herds have been recovering slowly with the help of reserved winter ranges and better supervision of hunting, but bands of mountain goats and big-horn sheep are still endangered.

Grizzly bears once roamed the area, but they have not been seen here for 40–50 years. Black bears never did frequent the high country much. They have always been around Grandjean and Atlanta, however, and beginning in 1985, a few have shown up to annoy campers at Redfish and Alturas lakes.

The only remaining large predator is the mountain lion (cougar). Seeing the cougar's large, clawless, flowerlike footprints in the dust of a backcountry trail is a rare thrill today. Although they are protected now, the big cats have been decimated by years of ill-advised bounty and trophy hunting. Two smaller cats, the bobcat and the Canadian lynx, are more plentiful, but they are shy, nocturnal hunters and people seldom see them.

Raccoons seem to be summer visitors only in the lower valleys, returning to warmer climes for the winter. Short-tailed weasels are common and are often observed by visitors, as are striped skunks, because of their innate curiosity. The weasel's larger relatives — martens, wolverines and river otters — are both shy and rare. If you ever have the opportunity to watch river otters at play, you will see an unforgettable comic opera — they do pratfalls into the water from riverbank slides, chase, wrestle and clap hands — better than Disney.

Coyotes are increasing in numbers and range in the SNRA in spite of still being shot on sight by some ranchers and sheepherders. They are often seen hunting for mice and ground squirrels in the sagebrush and meadows. Coyote nightsongs are a thrilling addition to backcountry experiences. Red foxes are also doing well in the lower forests and valleys, since they are no longer trapped very much for fur.

The most populous animal group in the SNRA is the rodent family. Rodents vary in size from beavers, porcupines and rock chucks on the large end of the scale to tiny voles that weigh only an ounce or two. Porcupines range throughout the montane forest and are quite visible, since they have little fear of man (or anything else, for that matter). Painted and chemically treated wood is a gourmet delight to porcupines — trail signs, picnic tables and pit toilets bear constant evidence of their appetites. They also are quite partial to hikers' boots, sometimes leaving only the hard rubber soles. There is no record of any boots being eaten while on the hiker's feet, however.

Golden-mantled ground squirrels and chip-

A pika in its normal habitat

Irrepressible chickaree or pine squirrel

munks are quite common in the forests, but the hiker's constant, very vocal companion is the pine squirrel (chickaree). This feisty little fellow warns everything that moves to get out of his territory, but then can't resist coming down from the trees to get a closer look at the intruder.

Beavers, although never really plentiful (see Human History), are hard at work on a number of streams in the SNRA. Some good examples of their hydraulic engineering can be seen along the Big Wood River below Russian John Guard Station and along the upper Salmon River at the head of Sawtooth Valley.

The rabbit family is well represented by snowshoe hares, cottontails and everyone's favorite, the pika (cony, or rock rabbit). Colonies of pikas live in talus slides above 7,500 feet in all the mountain ranges of the SNRA. These tiny, short-eared, tailless rabbits whistle constantly as they go about their work of storing hay for the long winters. You don't have to travel to the backcountry to see pikas — a colony lives in the broken rock just below the Galena Summit Overlook.

During hard winters with deep snow, porcupines gnaw bark at snow level

BIRDS

Nearly 200 species of birds, most of them summer visitors, have been counted in the SNRA. The most conspicuous bird is the rare greater sandhill crane, which nests in the Sawtooth Valley. The startling size of this largest crane is obvious when you see one standing shoulder-high to a cow in a riverside pasture.

Golden eagles and red-tailed hawks nest in the backcountry, and bald eagles and ospreys are sometimes seen along the rivers. A few species of smaller hawks and a number of owls make up the rest of the raptor population.

Idaho's State Bird, the mountain bluebird, is sometimes seen in scintillating flocks during spring and fall migrations. The orange, yellow, black and white western tanager adds a quite different dash of color to the woodland scene. Several species of woodpeckers are not quite as visible, but make themselves just as noticeable by persistent drumming.

Although ravens are very noisy at times, the loudest bird in the SNRA has to be the Clark's nutcracker. The raucous calls of this large gray, white and black member of the jay family can be heard for miles from its perch on the highest snag in the area. By contrast its cousin, the gray or Canada jay, is so quiet that it can be on your picnic table stealing your food before you know it's around. That's how it came to be nicknamed "camp robber." The two jays, grouse, magpies, chickadees, a few woodpeckers and great horned and snowy owls make up most of the winter bird population.

Grouse turn white in the winter, as do some

Invisible(?) "fool chicken"

members of the nonflying animal population. Summer or winter, grouse think their camouflage makes them totally invisible. As a result, it's often possible to walk up to within a few feet of one of these birds before it will attempt to fly — thus its nickname "fool chicken." Nothing can be more endearing than a "fool chicken" hen in early summer clucking over a family of 8 or 10 fluffball chicks.

The most effective camouflage expert is the killdeer, whose plaintive calls are familiar to all river fisherman in the SNRA. The mother killdeer doesn't camouflage herself — in fact, when her nest area on a gravel bar is approached, she goes into a very effective "broken wing" act to divert attention from eggs or chicks that so perfectly match the stones of the bar that the intruder may step on them before he sees them.

Fishermen are also privileged to observe water ouzels, or "dippers," in mountain streams. These cheerful little gray and brown caricatures of birds bob "hello" from midstream rocks, then walk under the water to hunt for aquatic insects. Their nests are perfectly woven baskets hidden in cracks of streamside cliffs or even under waterfalls.

A large number of ducks nest and raise their families along the lower riverbanks and lakeshores. Geese seldom nest here, but the haunting calls of migrating flocks are often heard on moonlit autumn nights.

Recommended Reading

Craighead, John J., Frank C. Craighead, Jr. and Ray J. Davis, *A Field Guide to Rocky Mountain Flowers.* Boston: Houghton Mifflin, 1963

d'Easom, Dick, *Sawtooth Tales.* Caldwell, Idaho: The Caxton Printers, Ltd., 1977.

Niehaus, Theodore F. and Charles L. Ripper, *A Field Guide to Pacific States Wildflowers.* Boston: Houghton Mifflin, 1976.

Peterson, Roger Tory, *A Field Guide to Western Birds.* Boston: Houghton Mifflin, 1961.

Ross, Clyde P., *Geology Along U.S. Highway 93 in Idaho.* Moscow, Idaho: Idaho Bureau of Mines and Geology, Pamphlet #130, 1963.

Yarber, Esther and Edna McGown, *Stanley-Sawtooth Country.* Salt Lake City: Esther Yarber, printed by Publishers Press, 1976.

Winter resident Canada jay fluffs its feathers to stay warm

Travel to the SNRA

In contrast to Yellowstone and Grand Teton National Parks on the other side of the Continental Divide, tour buses are uncommon in the Sawtooth National Recreation Area. Regrettably, public buses are even more scarce here — in fact, they are nonexistent, as are all other forms of public transportation. Private motor vehicles provide the only practical means of transportation within the SNRA, and only limited public transportation serves the gateway at Ketchum/Sun Valley.

Scheduled airlines, buses and trains serve Boise, Twin Falls and Salt Lake City. Check with your travel agent for local air service to Hailey Airport. Sun Valley Stages operates a bus service from Twin Falls to Sun Valley. However, they do not operate all the time—call or write ahead for a schedule. Sun Valley Taxi-Limo provides taxi and limousine service from the Hailey airport on demand.

Several air-taxi and charter services operate from the Hailey airport. Names, addresses and telephone numbers are in the directory. These services can land you at Stanley, Smiley Creek or Atlanta airstrips as well as Hailey, if you desire.

Automobile rentals are available in Hailey and Sun Valley as well as Boise, Salt Lake City and Twin Falls. Highway mileages to Ketchum from the three approach cities are: Boise, 153; Salt Lake City, 295; Twin Falls, 83. Mileages from other western cities are: Butte, 321; Cheyenne, 675; Idaho Falls, 155; Pocatello, 169; Portland, 580; Reno, 536; San Francisco, 759; Spokane, 510.

Accommodations and Services

The Sun Valley/Elkhorn complex, nine miles south of the SNRA headquarters, is a major, year-round resort community. A wide range of goods, services and amenities is available there or in nearby Ketchum and Hailey. One of the best sources of information on what is available and where to find it is a *Telephone Directory and Guide* for sale by Names 'N Numbers, Inc., P.O. Box 2728, Sun Valley, ID 83353, telephone (208) 726-5111. For example, 53 local restaurants and 17 motels are listed in the classified section. You can also find eight art galleries, one ballet studio and seven hot-tub suppliers.

Reservations for a number of motels and resorts in the area are available through Central Resort Reservations, P.O. Box 979, Sun Valley, ID 83353, telephone (800) 635-4156.

Farther north, in the SNRA and around its perimeter, facilities are not so plentiful. Groceries, camping supplies and sporting goods are available in Stanley and Obsidian and at Redfish Lake and Smiley Creek resorts. Stanley

Sun Valley Lodge during the summer season
SUN VALLEY NEWS BUREAU

21

and Lower Stanley also have a state liquor store, several motels, restaurants, gift shops and a hotel.

Public restaurants serving all meals during the summer season are at Smiley Creek Resort, Obsidian, Redfish Lodge, and Sawtooth Lodge at Grandjean. The Idaho Rocky Mountain Ranch serves dinners by reservation in its huge, rustic lodge north of Obsidian.

GUEST RANCHES AND RESORTS

Two guest ranches and three resorts operate within the SNRA during the summer season. Busterback Ranch is in the southern part of the Sawtooth Valley. Busterback has operated as a nordic ski resort since 1976, and has become quite famous for its accommodations and cuisine as well as for its excellent skiing. Extensive remodeling and additions to the ranch buildings, completed in 1986, have made it possible to open this operating cattle ranch to summer guests as well. A complete program of ranch and backcountry recreation is planned.

The Clark-Miller Guest Ranch, a rustic landmark in the Sawtooth Valley since the early 1930's, is no longer open to the public. Its former owner, Isabell Miller, probably the most widely known and loved resident of the valley, died in 1986. As of publication time, no one was sure what would become of the ranch.

Farther north in the valley, on the east side of Highway 75 two miles north of Obsidian, Idaho Rocky Mountain Ranch features decorative log architecture on a grand scale. The main lodge was built in 1929–30 to satisfy the fantasies of a New York millionaire industrialist about how a western ranch house should look. The lodge, the guest cabins and much of the furniture were hand-crafted from trees cut on the 1,000-acre ranch. Decorative wrought-iron hardware was forged on the site.

The ranch operated as a private club/dude ranch for many years; then, after extensive remodeling and modernizing, it reopened as a guest ranch in 1977. The property is now a working cattle ranch. No organized recreational activities were offered as of the summer of 1986. However, this may change in the future.

Meanwhile, the view of the Sawtooths from the veranda is still magnificent and the cabins and lodge rooms are very comfortable. Guests may use a hot-spring swimming pool and a

Redfish Lodge

private trout-fishing pond on the property. The spacious dining room serves breakfasts and dinners for resident guests and dinners for nonresident guests by reservation.

The largest and most comprehensive resort in the SNRA is Redfish Lake Lodge, at the north end of Redfish Lake. Accommodations are in the lodge, several cabins, two motel units and an RV park. Extensive waterfront activities include a swimming beach, fishing and sailboat rentals, scenic tours of the lake and ferry service to Redfish Inlet Transfer Camp. Trail rides and horse-pack trips are available from nearby Redfish Corral. A general store, restaurant, cocktail lounge, laundromat and showers are open to the public. Taxi service from the Stanley airstrip can be arranged.

Down at Grandjean, in the South Fork of Payette River canyon on the west side of the Sawtooth range, unpretentious Sawtooth Lodge offers the only resort facilities in the northwest quadrant of the SNRA. Guest facilities are rustic log cabins and an RV park. Simple, but tasty, meals are served in the lodge. Saddle and pack horses are available from the stables at this resort, and there is a hot-spring pool. The real attraction of Sawtooth Lodge, however, is its location beside a famous trout-fishing river at the base of a network of trails into the Sawtooth high country.

Another item of interest is the tiny hydro-electric power plant that produces all the electricity for the resort from a 2- or 3-inch penstock dropping 1,000 feet or more down the side of the canyon.

At Sawtooth City, in the upper (south) end of the Sawtooth Valley, Smiley Creek Resort offers limited lodging in the main building and cabins. A few RV spaces are also available. The lodge is the post office, grocery store, restaurant and filling station of Sawtooth City. Smiley Creek is the only resort in the SNRA to have its own airstrip—just on the other side of Highway 75 from the lodge.

TRAILER AND RV PARKS

Hansens' Trailer Park, on the east side of Highway 75 north of Obsidian, is the only commercial trailer and RV park within the SNRA. Hansens' very pleasant sites are on a wooded bench overlooking the lower Sawtooth Valley. Only a few overnight sites are available, however. Most of Hansen's guests are long term.

Above: Idaho Rocky Mountain Ranch
Below: hot spring pool at Sawtooth Lodge   23

Recreation and Scenic Areas

You don't have to go into the back-country of the SNRA to find scenic beauty and recreational opportunities. As a matter of fact, more than two-thirds of the SNRA's visitors are perfectly happy to go no farther than the paved roads and the five big lakes. Here are details of some of the things you can do and see within easy reach of your vehicle.

CAMPING

Around the lakes and along the rivers of the SNRA are 29 improved campgrounds with a total of almost 500 campsites. Most of these have piped water and all have garbage collection. A few even have flush toilets. The most heavily used camps are at Redfish, Little Redfish and Alturas lakes. On the other hand, sites

Day-float trip on the Salmon River below Sunbeam

Power Plant Campground near Atlanta

are almost always available in the campgrounds along Highway 21, northwest of Stanley. Locations and details about the improved campgrounds are on the map inside the back cover.

If you're willing to rough it a little, there are many primitive campsites along the secondary roads of the SNRA. Most are in very scenic places, and some have picnic tables and pit toilets. In addition, a large number of improved and unimproved campgrounds are in the National Forests adjoining the SNRA. Check the Sawtooth, Challis and Boise National Forest maps for locations.

FISHING

The SNRA and surrounding areas are justly famous for fishing. Good stream and lake fishing for trout, whitefish and kokanee salmon is still within easy walking or boating distance. Don't count on catching a big chinook salmon, however. The proliferating dams downstream on the Snake and Columbia rivers, along with other environmental hazards and overfishing, have drastically reduced the Salmon River salmon runs. The upper Salmon River has been closed to salmon fishing since 1979. The Sawtooth Fish Hatchery at the south end of Sawtooth Valley, completed in 1984, is a last-ditch effort to save the salmon run.

Steelhead-trout runs have also been affected, but only a few native fishermen and other fanatics seem to care, since the run usually reaches Stanley by the first of April, when most fishermen are far away.

Idaho state fishing regulations apply in the SNRA, and an Idaho license is required. The general trout limit is six fish. Be sure to check the regulations carefully — there are a number of summer-spawning-stream closures in the SNRA. Most likely to affect you are the closures of the Salmon River above Hell Roaring Creek, Alturas Lake Creek below the lake, Valley Creek from the Salmon River to its East Fork, and the East Fork Salmon River.

Natives of the area will tell you that trout fishing in the Big Wood River is nothing compared to what it used to be, and that may be true, but it's still pretty good. Five miles or so of the river below the SNRA headquarters are now "catch and release" water, and a few 16- to 18-inch fish are hooked there on flies each summer. Farther up the river, along Highway 75, the Idaho Department of Fish and Game plants catchable-size rainbow trout during the summers, and the fishing can be very good at times.

The Fish and Game Department also plants catchable-size rainbows in Alturas, Pettit, Redfish and Stanley lakes and at a number of locations along the Salmon River from the Highway 75 bridge at the north end of Sawtooth Valley down to Robinson Bar. In addition to the trout, resident populations of kokanee salmon are thriving in Alturas and Redfish lakes. In late August, spawning kokanee often cover the bottom of Fishhook Creek where it flows into Redfish Lake, turning the creek red. Redfish got

Some people work at fishing...

...while others relax

26

its name from the spawning sockeye salmon that came into the lake from the Salmon River in the old days. Only a few sockeyes are still able to make the trip.

The best trout fishing accessible by automobile is in the South Fork of Payette River near Grandjean. This is a big, magnificent flyfishing river with an excellent population of native trout. A walk or horseback ride of a few miles to fish the river in Big Meadow above Grandjean will be well rewarded.

That often heard statement, "Fishing ain't what it used to be," is not really true in the SNRA backcountry. Before the white man came here, none of the high lakes and few of the streams had fish in them at all. Now some of them are overstocked. By far the most successful introduced fish is the eastern brook trout, now abundant in most of the high lakes and streams of the Sawtooth Range. California golden trout and Montana grayling are supposed to be established in a few places in the Sawtooths, but they are not easy to find. Beautiful native cutthroat trout live primarily in the streams and lakes of the White Cloud Peaks. Here again, those gorgeous high lakes didn't have cutthroats in them until the fry were hauled in.

If you want to sample some of this backcountry fishing, many of the lakes and streams are within reach of a day hike or saddle trip.

Kokanee salmon ascend Fishhook Creek to spawn

MOUNTAIN CLIMBING

One look at all that vertical granite in the Sawtooth range will tell you that climbing is popular here. Surprisingly, the sport developed relatively recently in the Sawtooth area. The Grand Tetons, farther east, have been climbed extensively since the early 1900's, but many first ascents in the Sawtooths, Boulders and White Clouds date from the mid-1930's, and technical climbing didn't really get going here until the 40's and 50's.

Dave Williams, Sawtooth Valley homesteader, guide and outfitter, teamed with Robert and Miriam Underhill to make a number of the first ascents. Dave Williams' grandson, David Lee, was the first wilderness and backcountry zone manager of the SNRA.

Experienced mountaineers have no trouble climbing most of the peaks of the Sawtooths, White Clouds and Boulders without technical aid, following routes up steep ridges, talus slopes and snowfields. For vertical rock climbers, however, highly fractured and loose rock make high-angle technical climbing almost impossible in the White Clouds and Boulders, and limit the possibilities in the Sawtooths. Climbers who are new to the area should use guides or at least get as much information as possible before climbing. Good orienteering ability using topographic maps is essential for any unguided trips.

Good rock and easy access combine to concentrate the majority of the Sawtooth climbing in an area around the Grand Mogul and Mount Heyburn near the inlet of Redfish Lake. Other vertical faces with good rock are on and around Warbonnet Peak and the Finger of Fate, but fairly long approach trips and bivouacs are required to reach them.

Since access to much of the best climbing is by way of Redfish Lake, the Redfish Lake Lodge has become an information and support center for climbers. Jack See, the lodge manager, is a knowledgeable source of information about climbing. It's also a good idea to check in at the Stanley Ranger Station, and you should always sign the trail register on the way to a climb. Sawtooth Mountain Guides, Stanley, was the only climbing guide service operating in the SNRA in 1987.

In Ketchum/Sun Valley, Backwoods Mountain Sports, The Elephant's Perch and the Snug

Company are good sources of information about climbing, and they also sell and rent equipment.

BOATING AND SAILING

Once or twice each summer a spectacle of vivid color and unusual grace takes place on Alturas or Redfish Lake. As many as 50 sailboats from south Idaho and surrounding states gather to

compete in regattas on the big lakes. The contrast between brilliant sails, indigo water and solid green hillsides adds up to some wonderful photographic opportunities. Of course, you don't have to wait for a regatta to sail — most any summer day will do just fine. Capricious mountain winds offer a special challenge to wind surfers and catamaran sailors.

Power boating and water skiing are popular on Alutras, Pettit, Redfish and Stanley lakes. Public boat ramps are available at all but Pettit Lake. Redfish Lodge sells fuel and rents power boats, fishing skiffs, canoes and paddle boats. Mooring slips and ties are also available there.

Only nonmotorized boats are allowed on Perkins, Yellow Belly and Little Redfish lakes.

RIVER FLOATING AND WHITEWATER TRIPS

The Indians called the Salmon the "River of No Return" for good reason — few braves who embarked upon its foaming waters and disappeared from view between the dark stone walls were ever seen again. To return nowadays, you just climb into the van with the raft loaded on top, and drive back up Highway 75 beside the river. Not all of the Salmon River in the SNRA is all that rough, anyway. By late summer the stretch from Stanley to Basin Creek can be safely floated by almost anyone in anything from a 15-man raft to an inner tube. Below Basin Creek, however, the water gets whiter and the going gets rougher.

The easiest way to float the upper Salmon is with one of the commercial outfitters who conduct day trips out of Stanley. Names, addresses and telephone numbers of the outfitters, as of 1987, are in the directory.

No permits are required for private floats or white-water runs within the SNRA. However, state law requires you to wear a life preserver. You should also contact the Stanley Ranger Station to find out about up-to-date river conditions and to let the staff know of your plans. Keep in mind that the water is always cold and that high water can make the river extremely dangerous.

Above: between races at Alturas Lake

Below: loading up a Salmon River float trip

The Grand Mogul and other peaks above the inlet of Redfish Lake are popular rock climbing sites

Motor Trips

Literally hundreds of miles of main and secondary roads in the SNRA are open to motor travel during the summer. A remarkable amount of superb scenery can be observed from your vehicle, but some short walks from selected stopping places will pay surprising dividends.

The nine motor trips described here were planned to give you as much variety of scenery as possible, and to take you to a number of historic sites. All but two of the trips can be completed in a modern sedan, although some of the roads may be a bit rough and dusty. The upper part of Trip 4 requires a high-clearance vehicle to get into Germania Basin, and a four-wheel-drive to go into Washington Basin. Trip 6 is easier and safer in a high-clearance vehicle, and a four-wheel-drive may be needed to get up a steep, rocky pitch 2 miles from the end of the road. Trailbikes should be able to negotiate any of the roads with ease.

Mining relics at historic Custer townsite on the Yankee Fork road

31

1–Ketchum to Stanley Ranger Station

This 60-mile, south-to-north transect on Highway 75, the "Sawtooth Scenic Route," provides a very pleasant introduction to the SNRA. An informative tour-tape for this trip and a player that plugs into the cigarette lighter socket of your vehicle is available at the SNRA headquarters, 8 miles north of Ketchum. You turn in the tape and the machine at the Redfish Visitor Center or the Stanley Ranger Station if you make the trip from Ketchum to Stanley. North-to-south tapes are also available, in which case you pick up the machine at the Stanley Ranger Station or the Redfish Visitor Center and turn it in at the headquarters on the south end.

The tapes point out natural and historical points of interest keyed to the mileposts along the highway, and give some general information about what the SNRA is and what you can do there. Some ecological and environmental information is also narrated along with a little propaganda about the U.S. Forest Service. That propaganda isn't all unjustified — the SNRA is a showplace for what the Forest Service can do when its efforts are pointed in the right direction.

As you leave Ketchum headed north toward the SNRA headquarters, the Ketchum Cemetery, where Ernest Hemingway is buried, is on the east side of the highway. (A more pleasant and fitting memorial to Hemingway is near Trail Creek just east of Sun Valley.) The flat below the highway on the west side, now filled with very expensive housing, was once an expanse of sheep pens and loading chutes when Ketchum was the sheep capital of the United States.

Three and a half miles north of Ketchum, the Lake Creek parking area and footbridge across the Big Wood River give access to a network of foot and horse trails offering opportunities to explore the riparian life zone along the river as well as some excellent overlooks of Ketchum and the river valley. This is a popular cross-country ski area in the winter.

You are not yet in the SNRA — the boundary is just north of the bridge over the North Fork of the Big Wood River. The modern architecture of the SNRA headquarters and visitor center, at the junction of the North Fork road, is a little startling at first glance, but really fits very well into its surroundings. The visitor information and exhibit area inside the building is especially handsome and helpful. The exhibits are well-executed and informative, and the information desk has a good supply of interpretive folders, maps and other publications, as well as courteous and helpful personnel.

The tour-tape you pick up here will guide you very well on the rest of the trip north to Stanley. Plan on taking not less than a half day for the one-way trip, or a full day for the round trip — there are lots of places to stop and look, and a picnic at one of the big lakes will add to your pleasure. A winter version of the same trip is described in detail in the chapter on winter activities.

Public information area at the SNRA headquarters and visitor center

2–North Fork of Big Wood River Road

A beautiful mountain stream bordered by spruce, quaking aspen and lush meadows, and flowing between towering peaks, is the main feature of this short drive. The good, gravel-surfaced road follows the first 5 miles of the North Fork above its confluence with the Big Wood River. Along the way you may see a sheep wagon parked in one of the flowery meadows while its occupants (usually two Peruvian men these days) follow their flocks on the mountainsides far above. Sheepherders' camps almost invariably set a standard of cleanliness and order that recreational campers would do well to emulate.

In early summer, a ford through the East Fork of the North Fork, 3.4 miles from the beginning of the trip, may be too deep for a low-clearance vehicle. The stream won't be too difficult to

Fishing the North Fork of Big Wood River within sight of the SNRA headquarters

wade, however, and it's an easy and very scenic walk to the end of the road.

STARTING POINT

The North Fork road turns off Highway 75 beside the SNRA headquarters, 200 yards north of the North Fork bridge (see Motor Trip 1).

DESCRIPTION

Beyond the SNRA headquarters and its support buildings, the road runs directly north through a wide flat bordered by the aspen- and spruce-lined river on the east and a steep spur ridge on the west. You can find marvelous displays of wildflowers in the grass and sagebrush a few yards away from the dusty road in midsummer.

A little over 1 mile from the highway, the road turns to cross the first bridge over the North Fork. The stream is 10-15 feet wide here, rushing over a clean bed of boulders and gravel and occasionally slowing in a quiet, tree-shaded pool. It looks like a good trout stream, and it is. From this bridge downstream to the confluence with the Big Wood River is the best fishing on the North Fork.

A lush little meadow, through which Murdock Creek winds to join the river, is east of the bridge. The first of three public campgrounds along the North Fork is in a grove of lodgepole pines on the north side of the meadow.

Caribou campground is next, on the east side of the road beyond a side road leading west to Camp Sawtooth, a private organization camp. Beaver have dammed the stream in a flat just above Caribou, creating a number of pools and channels lined with willows. As the valley narrows and the road gets a little steeper, look for a number of avalanche trails running down the steep slopes across the river. Recurring slides keep the trees from growing, or tear them out, making these wide "trails" down the mountainsides.

We cross another bridge at Cougar campground, 3 miles from the starting point, below where the river has cut through some terminal moraines. The road climbs and twists over the moraines and drops down to cross a third bridge to the east bank at 3.5 miles. As you turn northwest now, you come to the ford through the East Fork. If you don't think you can get through the ford, there is room to turn around and park while you walk to the end of the road.

The valley opens up again above the East Fork, revealing marvelous vistas of the highest peaks of the Boulder Mountains on three sides. Just 4 air miles north, Ryan Peak, highest point in the SNRA, tops the ridge at 11,900 feet. You can see up the West Fork of the North Fork can-

yon from near the end of the road to the snow-capped ridge on the east side of Boulder Basin.

On the way back, try fishing in the gorge between the second and third bridges. Idaho Fish and Game often plants catchable-size rainbows below the third bridge.

3–Upper Salmon River

A 4-mile drive from Highway 75 will take you, not quite to the source of the Salmon River, but to where the river is so small that you can step across it. The upper end of the Sawtooth Valley is an expanse of beautiful meadows, set off by tree-clad mountains. Several beaver colonies do their utmost to slow down the flow of the newborn river.

STARTING POINT

The Upper Salmon River road turns south from Highway 75 a quarter mile east of the first bridge over the river north of Galena Summit, near milepost 164.

DESCRIPTION

The road leads southeast from the highway through sagebrush-covered, low hills toward the base of the high ridges leading up to Galena Summit. You pass a large complex of sheep pens and loading chutes on the right a little more than a mile from the highway. You may see a sheep wagon or two here with accompanying horses, dogs and herders.

Opposite the pens and before you cross little Camp Creek, a side road turns up the hill to the east. This is the old road over Galena Summit. The old road will probably be in good enough shape that you can drive up it a mile or so to get an idea of what it was like to drive over Galena Summit before the new highway was built. A spring and seep area in an aspen grove about .6 mile up the hill was covered with an astounding display of yellow and red monkey flowers in late July. Don't count on being able to drive all the way up the old road to the summit unless you're

riding a trailbike — slides often block the road near the top.

Back on the Upper Salmon River road, you turn south and then southwest to come out on a bank above the river where it runs through a series of beaver ponds in a meadow, 3 miles from the starting point. The road climbs slightly over another hump, then skirts the east edge of a large, flowery meadow where the little river flows in wide meanders. At the upper end of this meadow, a large grove of lodgepole pines shelters Chemeketan campground, available to groups by reservation. To get to the campground, you have to ford a stream that cascades down from the east to join the Salmon River below the trees. This tributary isn't any problem to ford, but it is bigger than the "river" it flows into.

A very large meadow covers the floor of the valley above Chemeketan. A sign at the edge of the campground warns "4-WHEEL DRIVE RECOMMENDED." This is a wet meadow with patches of willows and beaver dams in the middle. It's also a beautiful place for a short walk to admire the riot of moisture-loving wildflowers — shooting stars, buttercups, death camas, cinquefoil and marsh marigolds for starters. Be sure to jump or step across the Salmon River before you drive the 4 miles back to Highway 75, just so you can say you've done it.

4–Pole Creek Road to Germania and Washington Basins

The Pole Creek/Germania Basin road runs through the scenic gap between the White Cloud and Boulder mountains. This isn't exactly a low pass at 8,600 feet, but it is more than 2,000 feet lower than most of the peaks to the north and south.

The road ends in spectacular Washington Basin, 16.5 miles from Highway 75. Although not much is happening there now, picturesque relics and old log buildings testify that Washington Basin has been the site of extensive, if not too productive, mining activities for almost 100 years. You will need a four-wheel-drive vehicle, trailbike or reasonably good hiking legs to travel the final 3 miles from Germania Basin into Washington Basin, and a high-clearance vehicle may be necessary to climb the hill to Pole Creek Summit. Since this is the primary access to a number of trails into the White Clouds and Boulders, improvement of the road as far as Germania Basin would be a boon to backpackers and motor tourists alike.

STARTING POINT

The Pole Creek road turns east off Highway 75 a half mile south of the Smiley Creek Resort in Sawtooth City. The junction is signed for Valley road #194 and Pole Creek road #197. Pole Creek road turns east off Valley road 2.3 miles from the highway.

DESCRIPTION

After crossing the Salmon River not far from the highway, the road climbs and wanders eastward through sagebrush-covered hills before turning north and dipping down to a bridge over fast-flowing Pole Creek at the lower end of a large meadow, 2.2 miles from Highway 75. The Pole Creek road turns east at the top of the grade north of the creek. A sign at the intersection reads "GERMANIA BASIN - 11."

You drop down into the meadow near the creek for a short distance, then climb slightly over a low bench above the Pole Creek Guard Station before skirting the north edge of another large meadow. Both of these meadows are assembly points for bands of sheep in late summer, and pens and loading chutes are in the edge of the trees at the east end of the upper meadow.

Mature lodgepole-pine forest covers the flat floor of the valley for more than a mile above the meadows, except for some spruce and aspen along the creek. The good, gravel road wanders past excellent primitive campsites, but there are

Sheep in Pole Creek Meadow

no improved campgrounds. Fishing is fair for small rainbow trout. A trailhead for Champion Creek on the north side of the road is signed 1.2 miles from the Valley road junction.

The valley narrows to a canyon 4 miles from the Valley road junction, and the road narrows and deteriorates as it begins to climb more steeply up the north side of the canyon opposite avalanche-torn Grand Prize Gulch, joining from the south. The going gets very steep and rough after you cross Pole Creek 2 miles farther on, and low-clearance vehicles may have to turn back short of Pole Creek Summit.

Magnificent views open up at the summit, back down Pole Creek canyon and up to the White Cloud and Boulder peaks north and south. If you've made it this far, the next 3.5 miles to the lower end of Germania Basin are easy.

Germania Basin is an idyllic valley in the transition zone between montane forest and subalpine habitats. Germania Creek springs from marshy meadows at the head of the valley to meander through waist-high grasses and myriad wildflowers, picking up volume from icy springs bursting from the sidehills along the way. Lodgepole pines and subalpine firs line the sides of the meadows, giving way to scattered whitebark pines on the higher ramparts. A trailhead for Champion Basin is near the west end of Germania Basin.

Scars of past mining efforts show on the lower ridge in Washington Basin

At the lower, east end of Germania Basin, 13.3 miles from Highway 75, a narrow road turns north up the canyon of Three Cabins Creek. A sign at the turn warns "NARROW STEEP ROAD." The sign is accurate — only four-wheel-drive vehicles or trailbikes should attempt this road, and there is no place to turn around until you get down to Washington Creek on the north side of the ridge. It is a very pleasant, but vigorous, walk of 3 miles on the road to the upper part of Washington Basin.

The Washington Lake/Chamberlain Basin trailhead is just beyond the crossing of Washington Creek at the bottom of the hill north of the first ridge. The jeep road then turns west, crosses a tributary creek, and climbs up the ridge between the two creeks for a little over a mile to top out on the northeast rim of Washington Basin.

Directly across the steep-walled basin, a spur ridge, site of the Black Rock Mine, has been honeycombed with tunnels and shafts. On the south side of the basin, a 10,288-foot peak dominates the skyline and spills long slopes of talus into a narrow, turquoise-colored lake that is the source of Washington Creek. Unbelievably close to the top of this peak, several more tunnels have been driven at the juncture of limestone strata and a layer of reddish, mineralized rock.

As you follow the jeep road up past a number of old cabins and diggings, 10,519-foot Washington Peak, farther northwest, comes into view.

The "NO TRESPASSING" signs that you see here apply to the buildings and mine workings only. The claimant of a mining claim on public land does not own the land, and therefore, cannot deny access or travel across the claim. Man-made objects, including buildings, on the claim are presumed to be the property of the claimant. Abandoned mine tunnels and shafts are extremely dangerous and should never be entered.

One hopes that large-scale mining will never be resumed in this beautiful, subalpine basin. If it is, modern mining will not be picturesque, as previous effors now appear — it will be downright ugly. Inclusion of the basin in a designated White Clouds Wilderness would reduce the possibility of renewed mining.

5–Beaver Creek and Old Sawtooth City

This short excursion from Highway 75 doesn't lead to spectacular scenery, but it does give you a few clues as to what life was like in a mining boomtown a century ago.

STARTING POINT

Highway 75 crosses Beaver Creek 1.3 miles north of Smiley Creek Resort and 37 miles north of Ketchum. The Beaver Creek road turns west off the highway a tenth of a mile north of the Beaver Creek bridge. The intersection is signed.

DESCRIPTION

The sign at the turnoff gives a distance of 3 miles to Sawtooth City (Old Sawtooth City). The distance is really not more than 2.5 miles. Start off southwest on a fair gravel road for a quarter mile, then turn directly south for almost a mile across a wide meadow to come close to the creek as you enter open lodgepole forest.

Another .8 mile southwest brings you to a small clearing where a little-used road branches left. Remnants of the Old Sawtooth City cemetery are on the north side of the clearing.

In another meadow, .5 mile farther on, a sign and an old cabin on the right side of the road tell you that you are in Old Sawtooth City. Most of what is left of the town — 8 or 10 log buildings in various states of disrepair — is among scattered trees between the road and the creek.

In 1882 this quiet spot was a beehive of activity. At least 250 people lived here, and the town had a hotel, grocery, restaurant, laundry and at least three saloons. Four miles farther up the canyon, every man who could swing a pick was digging away toward the silver lode that would make them all rich. They never found the lode, and what ore they did find was almost impossible to smelt. By 1884 Sawtooth City was almost deserted.

You need a four-wheel-drive vehicle to go the rest of the way to the Beaver Creek mines. None of the mine buildings are still standing.

6–Fourth of July Creek

A rough, dirt road runs 11.5 miles east from Highway 75 to end at a clutter of old and new mine buildings and cabins under the towering north face of Blackman Peak. The heart of the White Cloud Mountains is only a few miles farther east, surmounted by 11,815-foot Castle Peak.

This is one of those roads that discriminates against drivers of modern sedans — you will need a high-clearance vehicle to get more than 5 miles from the highway and, depending on the condition of the road at the time, you may need four-wheel-drive to negotiate the last 2 to 3 miles of the road.

A trailbike will not only get you to the end of the road, but also up the trail beyond to Fourth of July and Washington lakes. In fact, trailbikes can make a round trip of about 35 miles up the Fourth of July Creek road, across on trails to Washington Basin, and back down the Pole Creek road to Highway 75.

STARTING POINT

Look for the Fourth of July Creek road sign on the east side of Highway 75, 48 miles north of Ketchum and one-tenth mile south of the bridge over Fourth of July Creek. A hundred feet north on the other side of the highway, the Hell Roaring Trailhead road leads west.

DESCRIPTION

The first mile of the road ascends very gradually through sagebrush on the alluvial bench south of the creek. Don't be in a hurry — barring the unlikely event of a road grader having traversed it, the road is rutted, chuckholed and liberally sprinkled with boulders. In a narrowing valley beyond a cattle guard, the second mile of road is on private land as it passes through meadows and groves of mixed conifers beside the creek. You cross another cattle guard at 2 miles, and at 2.2 miles, cross Fourth of July Creek on a narrow wooden bridge.

A half mile beyond the first bridge, the road climbs higher on the north side of a wider, lush valley, and at 4 miles from the highway, it traverses a beautiful grove of large aspens before turning to cross to the south side of the creek again on a relatively new bridge at 5.3 miles.

You cross to the north side of the creek again at 6.3 miles as the valley narrows to a rocky canyon. Talus slides and broken cliffs crowd the road against the creek for most of the next 2 miles. The road traverses a bulldozed area of 1 or 2 acres 8.2 miles from the highway. This clearing is the result of differing opinions among factions of Forest Service management about where the Fourth of July trailhead should be located. The road beyond the clearing was still open as of 1986, although it was signed "NOT MAINTAINED." It is unlikely that you will get much farther without four-wheel-drive.

A quarter mile beyond the clearing the road turns away from the creek and climbs a rough, steep pitch that will test almost any vehicle.

Beyond this pitch, the road is much better as it climbs gradually on the north side of a wide valley, and the main ridge of the White Clouds comes into view. The first mine dump and a couple of broken-down old cabins appear opposite the junction of a jeep road that climbs south 2 miles to a point near Phyllis Lake, nestled under the west flank of a 10,713-foot, pyramidal, black peak.

A quarter mile farther on, the road ends at a group of sometimes occupied cabins. Other buildings, some old and some fairly new, are scattered up the lower slopes of Blackman Peak among waste piles and tunnel portals. Blackman Peak is named for George Blackman, a black man who mined for many years in Washington Basin.

Varicolored peaks and ridges, showing violently contorted rock strata, rise above 10,000 feet to the north, east and south. Across Fourth of July Creek, an excellent trail, open to trailbikes, leads up to Fourth of July and Washington lakes. Both lakes have good trout populations.

Do not enter the mines or cabins, and park carefully to avoid blocking access.

Upper end of the Fourth of July Creek road in 1979

7–Nip and Tuck Road

As you drive north on Highway 75 between the Redfish Lake road and Stanley, you are looking directly at a range of hills beyond Stanley that appears to be a perfect vantage point overlooking the town and the northern part of the Sawtooth Range. There are indeed a number of excellent viewpoints up there, and you can get to them on a road with the marvelous name "Nip and Tuck." In spite of its name, it isn't a bad road, although it is dirt. You can enjoy a very pleasant 2–3 hour round trip, including stops to enjoy the view, returning to Stanley by way of Highway 21.

STARTING POINT

Nip and Tuck Creek, on its way to join the Salmon River, flows through the middle of Lower Stanley. What looks like a driveway just east of the highway crossing of the creek is really the Nip and Tuck road. A forest Service sign, including the number 633, is hidden in the willows by the creek, and is visible only if you're coming upriver from the east.

DESCRIPTION

After 1.6 miles of steady climbing through the lower, narrow canyon of Nip and Tuck Creek, the road turns west across the creek into a grassy basin that is reputed to be the original site of the town of Stanley. If Stanley did begin here, there is nothing left now to document the fact. It would be hard to find a more pleasant spot for a settlement, though. Open lodgepole-pine forest lines the hills to the west, and a tiny creek meanders across the floor of the basin.

The road climbs westward to a saddle, 3 miles from Lower Stanley, and then runs through a belt of trees to come out on the top of a ridge overlooking Stanley Basin and all of the northern Sawtooth peaks. A quarter mile farther on, a road turns left to drop down and contour back east around the brow of the ridge. Spectacular views along this deadend road are well worth the 1–2 mile detour, especially if you can wait for one of the dramatic Sawtooth sunsets.

Nip and Tuck road turns north from the intersection and drops down a wooded valley overlooking the large basin north of the ridge. Keep left at the next two intersections, and you will soon come to the oiled Anderson Creek road leading back to Highway 21 and Stanley.

Stanley Basin and the northern Sawtooths from the Nip and Tuck road

8–The Ponderosa Pine Scenic Route

Highway 21, making a wide loop from Stanley around the north end of the Sawtooth Range, then turning south and west down the canyon of the South Fork of Payette River, is the Ponderosa Pine Scenic Route. Ponderosa pines don't grow much above 5,000 feet in central Idaho, so they are seen at only a few places on the perimeter of the SNRA. One of these places is the canyon of the South Fork Payette River near Grandjean, and that is where the Ponderosa Pine Scenic Route gets its name.

Along the way, you drive through miles of lush meadows, dotted with grazing cattle. The northern ramparts of the Sawtooths, including Thompson and McGown peaks and Copper Mountain, rise in snow-capped splendor behind the verdant meadows. At the other end of the trip you parallel several miles of the rushing, gravel-bedded South Fork of Payette River, one of Idaho's premier trout streams.

Highway 21 is an excellent, paved highway. The 41 miles from Stanley to Lowman have been rebuilt since 1970. This is the main access road to the SNRA from Boise, 131 miles from Stanley.

STARTING POINT

The starting point is the junction of Highways 75 and 21 in Stanley.

DESCRIPTION

As you head west from Stanley and milepost 131 on Highway 21, Valley Creek meanders through lush meadows on your right. On your left, the gently rolling hills and benches of Stanley Basin lead up to a soaring wall of the highest Sawtooth peaks, including Horstman, Thompson and Williams. The highway turns northwest just before you pass the Iron Creek road.

Beyond the Stanley Lake intersection, 4.5 miles from Stanley, the road is almost flat, running through wide meadows and stands of lodgepole pine. The Park Creek rest area, on a low hill at 7.3 miles, offers a magnificent view across the meadows to Thompson and McGown

The venerable Sawtooth Hotel at Stanley

peaks. Lightly used but very pleasant Sheep Trail campground is at milepost 122, and 2 miles farther on the road runs through Trap Creek Narrows and out into immense Marsh Creek Meadow. As you drive through the next 7–8 miles of open grassland, you will appreciate the rustic beauty of the "snake," or "zigzag," rail fences on both sides of the highway. They add just the right foreground touch to wide vistas backed up by towering peaks on the horizon.

An unseen divide in these wide meadows, around milepost 126, separates the streams draining west and north into the Middle Fork of the Salmon River from those draining east into the main Salmon River. The Cape Horn Guard Station is a mile or two across the meadow from the highway on the old Cape Horn road. At milepost 113 we start the turn around the north end of the Sawtooths and, after crossing Cape Horn Creek, begin the climb south to Banner Summit, the divide between the Salmon River drainage and the South Fork Payette River. The roadsides are very lush and lined with flowers along this gradual ascent. Cape Horn Creek tumbles cheerily north on the east side of the road as groves of lodgepole pines, sheltering excellent campsites, alternate with verdant meadows.

The road to Dagger Falls on the Middle Fork Salmon River turns west along with Cape Horn Creek at milepost 109. The highway continues

"Ziggy" rail fence complements the northern Sawtooth peaks and meadows

south beside Banner Creek to the summit in thicker forest.

Banner Summit, at 7,056 feet, is not very high, but the south side does drop off quite steeply. The highway descends toward the South Fork Payette through the canyon of Canyon Creek, a foaming cascade most of the way, with only a few quiet flats lined with cottonwoods and aspens. A good population of feisty little native rainbow trout resides in Canyon Creek. If you have time, a stop at one of the inviting turnouts beside the creek can be quite rewarding.

Around milepost 97, the first ponderosa pines appear along the roadside, and Highway 21 turns away from Canyon Creek to descend

Roadside scenic route marker

southwest down the north side of the South Fork Payette canyon. Just before and right at milepost 95, turnouts offer good views up and down the canyon, and of the white-water riffles and deep blue-green pools in the river at the bottom. Beyond milepost 94, the Grandjean road turns back sharply to the left, beginning its 7-mile route back up the canyon to the Sawtooth resort and the Grandjean campground and trailhead.

As we continue to drop down the side of the canyon, the ponderosa pines get bigger and more abundant until, at the bottom of the canyon, a few giants reach 150 feet in height and 7–8 feet in diameter at the base — truly magnificent trees. Beyond milepost 93, the highway is beside the river and soon crosses it for the first time.

The bottom of the South Fork Payette canyon is up to a half mile wide at this point, floored with benches, bars and flats of gravel, through which the fast-flowing stream has cut a contorted channel. It's a big river, impossible to wade across even in low-water periods. It looks as if it should be good trout fishing, and it is. A lot of dredging and other mining activity has taken place here in the past, but not much is going on now, and the water is beautifully clear, flowing over an ideal gravel bed.

Below milepost 85, most of the river bottom is private land, and a mixed bag of summer homes, small homesteads and a few marginal resorts are scattered along the highway. The land up the sides of the canyon is all part of Boise National Forest, and several National Forest campgrounds are at scenic spots along the river. The Lowman Ranger Station is on the left between mileposts 73 and 74, and at milepost 72 you cross the river into the little hamlet of Lowman. Lowman has gasoline, beer, groceries, fishing tackle and a motel.

9–Stanley to Sunbeam and up the Yankee Fork

The Yankee Fork road was a very busy thoroughfare in the latter part of the 19th century — stagecoaches and wagons hauled miners, hangers-on, supplies and mining equipment up the canyon and, on the return trip, brought out gold as well as the lucky and the not-so-lucky on their way back to civilization. The road is still busy today, but most of the travelers are different. A few people are still looking for gold, but most of them are looking for good fishing, a place to camp, or a glimpse at history and where all that gold came from.

It's 13 miles down the twisting canyon of the Salmon River from Stanley to Sunbeam, and another 11 miles up the Yankee Fork to the historic townsite of Custer. All of the trip is on reasonably good road, and a lot of interesting things to see and do are along the way. If you're well-heeled and have planned in advance, you can cap a delightful day with a gourmet dinner at Robinson Bar, 4 miles down the Salmon River from Sunbeam.

STARTING POINT

You head east from Stanley, down the Salmon River on Highway 75, the Sawtooth Scenic Route.

DESCRIPTION

The Salmon River flows quietly, bordered by lush meadows, for 2 miles below Stanley. Then, as the canyon walls close in, the current quickens and the riffles begin to show a little white — just a hint of what is to come below Basin Creek, 9 miles down the road. Kayakers often practice here before tackling the big rapids downstream.

A little over a mile below Lower Stanley, a rough, dirt road turns up a canyon to the left, away from the river. This is Joe's Gulch, one of the few mining sites near Stanley that ever produced any substantial amount of gold. A lot of rock piles and the remains of a few old cabins are within a couple of miles of the highway, but the road is pretty rough.

Four large, developed campgrounds — Salmon River, Riverside, Mormon Bend and Basin Creek — are sited along the next 7 miles of the Salmon River. In the steep-walled canyon between Basin Creek and Sunbeam, only a few primitive sites are available, but there are a number of pleasant turnouts where you can picnic and watch the river for intrepid kayakers and the commercial day-float rafts from

Kayak lesson on the Salmon River at Lower Stanley

Stanley. Real whitewater roars around the rocks here, and the float trips can be pretty thrilling even from the bank. The rafts and rapids are a lot easier to photograph from the bank than they are from a raft or kayak.

On cool days, as you round a bend 12 miles from Stanley, you will see a cloud of steam hovering over the roadway ahead of you. This is Sunbeam Hot Springs, most accessible of the many hot springs in the SNRA. The springs flow from above the highway on the left. The hot, mineralized water then runs through pipes under the highway and down into a relatively quiet stretch of the river. A stone bathhouse, built in the 30's between the road and the river, has been vandalized and is now boarded up. Enterprising soakers have dug and piled rocks along the riverbank to form a series of pools with temperatures varying with the amount of river water circulating through the pool. The system is primitive, but it works pretty well. The water is between 150° and 200° where it flows from the ground, much too hot for bathing.

Another mile down Highway 75 brings you to historic Sunbeam and the junction of the Yankee Fork road. Sunbeam is of historic interest not only as the gateway to the fabulous Yankee Fork mining district during the 1880's and 90's, but also for an event that took place there in 1934. In 1910 Sunbeam was renamed in honor of the Sunbeam Dam, newly completed by the Sunbeam Mining Company in the gorge just above the confluence of the Yankee Fork. Previously, the settlement had been known by the more prosaic name of Junction Bar.

It didn't take long for fishermen and the fledging Idaho Fish and Game Department to realize that Sunbeam Dam effectively blocked the salmon and steelhead runs. The first fish ladder on the Salmon River was built about 1915 with the intent of getting the fish around the dam. It was 95% unsuccessful. The controversy continued through several ownerships of the dam and power plant, and it was not until 1934, many years after the dam had ceased to serve any useful purpose, that the Idaho Fish

The remaining part of the Sunbeam Dam still blocks much of the Salmon River channel

and Game Department succeeded in having it blown open.

As it turns out, the whole thing was something of a futile gesture, since the salmon and steelhead runs are now being killed off anyway by the Columbia and Snake river dams. It will be a long time before we see those dams removed. Nevertheless, it was an historic event, and you can see the remains of the dam from the wide parking area across from the junction of the Yankee Fork road.

The Yankee Fork roars down a narrow gorge beside the first 3 miles of the road. A few flat stretches offer opportunities for fishing, but except for salmon and steelhead in season, fishing isn't all that great. Three improved campgrounds — Blind Creek, Flat Rock and Polecamp Flat — offer camping and picnicking opportunities along the way.

Above Polecamp Flat, the canyon widens to a valley and the road wanders through and around 6 miles of man-made desert in the form of dredge piles. About the only good thing that can be said about the dredging now is that it did create a lot of ponds that are nesting and resting places for flocks of waterfowl. Of course, the herculean effort produced some gold, too. The Yankee Fork, now running clear through the dredge piles, looks fishable, and it is. However, the results are mostly whitefish. They rise well to dry flies and a one- or two- pounder will put up a good fight for a half minute or so, but most people don't think much of them as food.

Less than a mile above the second crossing of the Yankee Fork, you come to the almost ghost town of Bonanza. In 1881, booming Bonanza contested with Challis to be the county seat of newly created Custer County. Challis won and Bonanza began the long slide to oblivion. The only reasonably modern buildings in Bonanza today are the ones occupied by the Forest Service Guard Station. It's a beautiful site for a town, on a low ridge between the Yankee Fork and its West Fork. A few of the old log cabins are still occupied, and most of them are private property, so please don't trespass. An interesting "boot hill" cemetery is above the town to the west.

The Yankee Fork road is a wide, but rough, gravel thoroughfare from Highway 75 to Bonanza. Above Bonanza, it reverts to basic Forest Service gravel and dirt, narrow but passable.

A half mile above Bonanza, at the upper end of the dredge piles, sits the monster dredge that devastated the valley. The last operating owner of the dredge, J. R. Simplot, donated it to the Forest Service, and it is now a museum, maintained and interpreted by the Yankee Fork Gold Dredge Association.

Custer Historical Site is a little more than a mile up the valley from the dredge. Buildings in Custer are better preserved than those in Bonanza, and the McGown family and the Forest Service have established a mining museum that includes most of the old town. The museum buildings aren't always open, but even if they aren't, a stroll through the labeled relics outside is rewarding.

One and a half miles beyond Custer, the Custer campground is on a massive slide that at one time dammed the Yankee Fork and created a 2-3 mile long lake above the slide. The lake is gone now, and in its place is an idyllic subalpine basin surrounded by snow-capped peaks. The small stream wanders across the floor of the basin through flower-dotted meadows and groves of lodgepole pines and subalpine firs. A few native cutthroat trout can be induced to rise from the deeper pools by a discretely placed fly. Delightful primitive campsites are plentiful.

Abandoned dredge sits at the upper end of its dredge piles above Bonanza

The Backcountry

By 7:00 on July and August mornings there is apt to be a line of vehicles queued up on the Redfish Lake road and at other developed campgrounds, waiting for someone to leave so they can get a camping space. By contrast, at the same time of day, backpackers and wranglers in many of the back-country campsites will be eating a leisurely breakfast before packing up for the day's move without another party within sight or hearing.

For discussion here, "backcountry" is any place more than one mile from a road that can be traveled by a modern sedan or camper vehicle. The defini-tion covers more than two thirds of the almost 1,200 square miles of the Saw-tooth National Recreation Area. Trail-bikes and four-wheel-drive vehicles have access to narrow corridors in less than half of that 800-plus square miles of backcountry. That leaves a lot of square miles, including all of the Saw-tooth Wilderness and most of the high country of the Boulders and the White Clouds, that are accessible only on foot or horseback.

Trail ride on the Alpine Way overlooking Fishhook Valley—Heyburn Mountain and Horstman Peak on the skyline

47

THE TRIPS

There are trails in the SNRA for everyone; it's possible to do anything from an easy afternoon saunter along the shore of Pettit Lake to a mountaineering expedition along the crests of the White Clouds north of Castle Peak. The 22 trips described here fall between those extremes and are intended to invite you to see and experience, close-up, some of the biggest areas of spectacular, glacier-carved, unspoiled, mountain landscape left in the lower 48 states.

The trips are divided into three natural geographic sections: 1.) the Smoky and Boulder Mountains, 2.) the Sawtooth Wilderness and North SNRA, and 3.) the White Cloud Mountains. All three sections offer trips of varying lengths, from half-day hikes to trips of a week or more when layovers and side trips are included. All the trips go to places of unique beauty

The family pony substitutes as a pack horse on the way up Sand Mountain pass

with a multitude of photographic opportunities. All the trips pass through gardens of wildflowers and the descriptions tell you when these flowers are at their best. Most of the trips include fishing opportunities, and detail the locations, varieties of trout, and the best time to fish.

These 22 trips total three hundred and fifty-five miles of trail and are distributed over most of the geographical area of the SNRA. You can plan many more trips from the information presented here. Alternatives for both shorter and longer trips are suggested in the descriptions. Many of the longer trips are one-way or incomplete loops requiring car shuttles or pick-ups at the other end, because connections for complete loops just don't exist in many cases. But if you're forced to double back for lack of a pick-up or shuttle, you need not be disappointed. None of these mountains or lakes ever looks the same on two different days, or hours for that matter, and you'll be amazed at how much you see coming out that you didn't see going in. Besides, you'll get another chance at that giant trout that got away.

No attempt has been made to classify the trips by degree of difficulty. These are judgments that are best made at the time of planning your trip and should be based on who is in the party, what time of year it is, how much experience the leader has, careful reading of the description, and detailed checking of the topo maps for the area.

No extended off-trail, cross-country trips are included for several reasons: Off-trail travel in much of the backcountry is extremely difficult and, in some places, downright dangerous. In the event of an accident, rescue could take a long time and endanger the rescuers as well. There are plenty of very remote places to go without getting off the trails, and getting away from other people is not that much of a problem.

Some short off-trail excursions to lakes and other points of interest are included where they do not involve dangerous terrain. Opportunities for longer cross-country trips will be obvious to experienced hikers who make a careful analysis of the topo maps. Some are dangerous and some are relatively safe. Just keep in mind that loose rock in talus slopes and 20-foot cliffs don't show on the top maps.

Backpacking Cameras and Photographing the Backcountry

As I hope I've demonstrated in this book, the SNRA is a very photogenic place. Although my reasons for carrying cameras and using them may be different from yours, you might be interested in what I carry and how I use it.

Since I almost always shoot both color and black-and-white, I carry two 35mm SLR bodies. I use Nikon equipment, but that does not mean that I totally endorse Nikon products. I carry one camera on each shoulder except when it rains. If I meet a deer on the trail, it will never wait for me to take off my pack and get out a camera. A telephoto lens is mounted on one of the bodies. The other body has a normal or a wide-angle lens. I keep caps on the lenses, but do not carry the cameras in cases because of the extra weight and bother.

I normally carry four lenses: 50mm normal, 28mm wide-angle, 35–70mm macro-zoom and 135mm telephoto. The 50mm is included primarily because it is the fastest lens I own. I also carry a macro extension tube that fits any of the lenses for close-ups.

Other equipment items I carry are: a small hand-held light meter, a small non-automatic strobe light for fill lighting, yellow and orange filters for b/w film, lens brush, lens cleaning tissues and a short, lightweight tripod. I always try to carry more film than I think I will need, but I occasionally run short. I discard the boxes and instruction sheets before packing up, and write the film designation on the top of the plastic can with a waterproof marker. Exposed film goes back in the can for safer carrying.

When rain threatens, I may put one camera, wrapped in a plastic bag, in the top of my pack. The other one goes in a plastic bag, secured around the camera strap by a rubber band, and I carry it on my shoulder under my poncho. A helpful fellow traveler holds a poncho over my head and the camera when I take pictures in the rain. Plastic bags also help to keep nighttime condensation from the cameras.

With a good rest against a solid tree, log or rock I can usually manage exposures of up to ¼ second. For longer exposures, or if I'm feeling shaky, I set up the camera on the tripod, and trip the shutter with the self timer.

The little strobe light often saves pictures in bright sun situations when there is too much spread in exposure between light and shade. This is particularly true of backlit shots of people. It is also useful for shooting late evening pictures in camp that wouldn't otherwise be possible.

I use a yellow or orange filter to keep the sky from washing out in black-and-white scenic shots. The through-the-lens camera meters do not compensate entirely when reading through these filters, so I overexpose a little. For color shots I use UV and 81A filters to hold down the surplus of blue that is apt to show up at high altitudes and on cloudy days—for the same reason I try to avoid shooting color in the middle of the day. Early morning and late afternoon shots of large scenes are better for modeling and definition of natural features.

THE TRAILS

The trails, like the landscape, vary greatly from smooth and moderately level to rough and steep —even precipitous. In recent years the Forest Service has been handicapped by lack of funds and personnel to build, reroute and maintain trails. Some trails have been selectively abandoned and, with less use and little maintenance, will eventually disappear. Although backcountry use in the SNRA is constantly increasing, total trail mileage stays about the same. Bridges are needed in a number of places to replace very dangerous early season stream fords. Shortages of new trails and bridges reduce foot and horse access to some truly marvelous places and increase visitor pressure on existing high-use areas. Forest Service and national recreation priorities being what they are, the situation will only get worse unless we trail users get together and make enough noise to impress the bureaucracy.

The good news is that there are literally hundreds of miles of good trails in the SNRA and more hundreds of miles of passable trails. And, in comparison to trails such as the John Muir Trail in California's Sierra Nevada, even the most heavily used trails in the SNRA still have little traffic. Anyone who is willing to walk just a few miles can easily get away from the crowds.

Many of the backcountry trails were started in the 19th and early 20th centuries as pack trails for miners and sheep and cattle grazers. The routes were laid out for horse travel with as little clearing and digging as possible. These trails tended to run straight up the noses of ridges and to stay on high ground as much as possible. Horses could climb steep grades better than they could get through deadfalls, marshes and slides. There were fewer deadfalls to clear on high ground, and nobody cared much about erosion. If the rider wanted to get down to a lake or stream to catch a mess of trout for dinner, he bushwhacked or did without. A number of these old trails are still in use, mostly in the White Clouds. They're murder for modern-day backpackers who expect a lot of switchbacks. Some of them have also been badly torn up by recent trailbike use and many years of horse travel.

Later on, with the advent of tourists and dudes, the Forest Service built some new trails that were recreation oriented. These trails had more gradual grades, were blasted out of the sides of river canyons on occasion, and even had some switchbacks to make the ride easier. The destinations changed, too, to places where there was good camping, beautiful scenery and a lot of trout to catch, or deer and elk to hunt. These were still horse trails, though, not foot trails. During the 1930's and 40's Civilian Conseration Corps crews added some trails.

Some of the trails are a breeze...

...others get a little rough

Development of better, and lighter-weight, backpacking equipment and food during the 1950's and 60's increased the popularity of walking into backcountry everywhere. By the time the SNRA was established in 1972, hikers and backpackers outnumbered riders on the trails by a considerable margin and were no longer automatically labeled "hippie" or just plain crazy by old-time horse packers. During the middle 60's there were enough federal funds available to relocate and rebuild a number of trails, mostly in the Sawtooth Wilderness, to the Forest Service standards for new trails.

TRAIL SIGNS AND MARKS

Most of the backcountry trails are signed at trailheads and junctions. Some signs have not yet been updated to show the correct distances for relocated trails. These discrepancies are pointed out in the trip descriptions, but some may have been corrected since this book was written.

Some signs have been destroyed by vandals, both human and otherwise (porcupines), and occasionally you'll find one that has been turned 90° or 180° by some perverted humorist. Most of the lakes and some of the peaks are identified by signs along the trails that will help you establish your location if you're in doubt.

All trails are marked with blazes (peeled bark at eye level on trees) or, in treeless areas, with cairns (two or more rocks obviously stacked on top of one another).

GUIDED AND ASSISTED TRIPS

Today, foot blisters outnumber saddle sores among SNRA backcountry visitors by more than ten to one, but that doesn't mean that you can't find a horse to ride if you want one. The stable at Redfish Lake offers daily, half-day and full-day trail rides during the summer season, and so does the stable at the Sawtooth Lodge at Grandjean. Horse pack trips, in any degree of luxury you may desire, are also available. In Idaho, and throughout the Rockies for that matter, persons who provide these services are called outfitters. Names, addresses and telephone numbers of outfitters currently operating in the SNRA are available from SNRA headquarters or from:

Idaho Outfitters and Guides Association
P.O. Box 95
Boise, Idaho 83701
Telephone (208) 342-1438

Most outfitters will also make drop packs, pickups and supply drops for backpackers if arrangements are made in advance.

The majority of horse travel to the backcountry in recent years has been on privately owned stock. A free use permit is required by the

Top: Porcupine-gnawed location sign

Below: Rock cairn in Ants Basin

Wrangler loads a pack horse at Edna Lake

SNRA for any backcountry trip using pack or saddle stock. These permits may be acquired in advance from any SNRA office, the Boise Ranger District office in Boise, and Ketchum, Dutch Creek/Atlanta and Lowman Ranger Stations. Get a copy of the regulations for use of pack and saddle animals at the same time.

Backpacking guides are available in the SNRA, but who and how many they are varies greatly from year to year. Best sources of information about them are: SNRA headquarters, major resorts, and sporting-goods stores in Ketchum and Stanley. Most of the sporting-goods stores rent backpacking equipment.

CARE OF THE BACKCOUNTRY

I recently reread an old-time horror story. It was about 275 hikers, 16 wranglers and 80 pack mules in one group ravaging a swath through the high country of Kings Canyon and Sequoia National Parks. This group did not carry a single mineral-fueled stove. They built large wood cooking fires at every stop, a huge bonfire to gather around every evening, and innumerable smaller individual campfires. Who were these vandals? They were members of the Sierra Club High Trip of 1940 as recounted in the *Sierra Club Bulletin* of February 1941.

Times have certainly changed and, hopefully, we've come a long way in taking care of the backcountry in half a century. At least the Sierra Club has.

What the backcountry will look like 50 years, or even 10 years, from now depends on how we treat it today. In spite of a few horrible examples, most of the present visitors to the SNRA backcountry are treating it very well. If only past visitors had been a little more considerate, we wouldn't be seeing those few signs saying "OVERUSED CAMPSITE - PLEASE DO NOT CAMP HERE."

By comparison with more heavily used backcountry areas elsewhere, the SNRA backcountry is still pristine. There is still firewood available in much of the area, most of the lakes and streams are unpolluted, and campsites are generally clean. We can help to keep it that way by carrying cooking stoves, making small fires rather than big ones, never leaving fires unattended, packing out all our trash and other people's as well, washing dishes and ourselves in containers well away from streams and lakes, and removing all traces of our occupancy of campsites. Wilderness is one of the most precious things we can pass on to future generations.

Backpackers' camp at Ardeth Lake—note small fire and gasoline stove

One of the best sources of information on how to preserve wilderness, and have a pleasant and safe trip as well, is Thomas Winnett's *Backpacking Basics*, a good-humored distillation of knowledge gathered in more than 40 years of backpacking. This very informative little book is published by Wilderness Press. The two pages on stream crossing alone are worth the price of the book.

Backcountry Patrol - On any extended trip into the SNRA backcountry you may, if you're lucky, meet a cheerful and helpful person wearing a Forest Service sleeve patch. When you meet one, he or she will be carrying a radio, first-aid kit, axe, shovel, and one or two plastic garbage bags—empty or full depending on how many slobs have been in the area recently. Unfortunately, limited budgets and distorted Forest Service priorities have severely limited the number of backcountry rangers. In the summer of 1986, only one paid ranger and three volunteer rangers were available to patrol all of the wilderness and backcountry trails in the SNRA.

At the beginning of each five-day tour the ranger packs in to a base camp carrying 40–50 pounds of required equipment, food, camping gear and clothing. At the end of the tour he or she packs out with the same load minus the food, but plus one or two bags of trash. The load going out may total 60 pounds. After two days off, the cycle starts over again no matter what the weather is like.

Should an attractive young lady have to carry 60 pounds for 8–10 miles because you don't have the strength or decency to carry out what you carried in? The most surprising thing is that the rangers keep doing it summer after summer. It can't be just for the money.

Part of the wilderness rangers' duties is to inform people of, and enforce, backcountry regulations. They are authorized to write citations, but usually their role is to inform and help. You can help by picking up a copy of the regulations at a SNRA office or trail register and informing yourself.

One or two two-man trial maintenance crews are working somewhere in the backcountry throughout the summer. They carry radios and can help you if you are in trouble.

PREPARATIONS, PRECAUTIONS AND EQUIPMENT

There is not much to be afraid of in the SNRA backcountry provided you stay on the trails and plan ahead a little. For example, we have not seen a bear or rattlesnake in the SNRA. However, bears have been reported in the South Fork of the Payette canyon, at the south end of the Sawtooths around Atlanta and, in 1985–86, in the developed campgrounds at Redfish and Alturas lakes. It's still a good idea to hang your food at night, and when you're away from your campsite, to keep it away from raccoons, porcupines, squirrels and other small creatures.

Other things you *should* be concerned about for a safe and comfortable trip follow in their approximate order of importance:

Altitude Sickness - All the trailheads, with the exceptions of Grandjean and Atlanta, are between 6,000 and 7,000 feet above sea level and almost all the trips begin with a climb. This means that most flatlanders need at least a day to get used to the altitude before starting uphill with a full pack. The symptoms of altitude sick-

Wilderness ranger and friend talk to hikers at Baron Lakes

ness are violent headache, giddiness, shortness of breath and nausea. The cure is to stop and rest for several hours or, in exceptionally bad cases, return to lower altitude.

Drinking Water - Because of the high incidence of giardiasis, a bacterial intestinal disorder, all water in the SNRA outside of developed campgrounds should be treated before drinking. The best treatment is boiling for 4–5 minutes. Iodine-based treatment tablets are considered satisfactory.

Hypothermia - Sudden changes in the weather from hot sun to cold wind and rain, or even snow, can happen any time in this high country. These conditions can bring on hypothermia, even in temperatures above freezing, if hikers are inadequately clothed, overtired or wait too long to set up shelter. Symptoms are uncontrollable shivering, lack of coordination, incoherent speech and eventual lassitude.

Abandonment of a person suffering seriously from hypothermia means *death*. In bad weather every member of a party should watch all other members for signs of hypothermia. Treatment is simple, but not always easy. Get the victim out of the wind and wet and build a fire if possible. Strip all wet clothes from the victim and get him into a dry sleeping bag, then put another unaffected person, also stripped, in the bag

with the victim to transfer warmth. Warm drinks, if available, will help, but *no* alcohol.

Prevention is much better than cure. Avoid unnecessary exposure. Give up your goal for the day, turn back if it will help, find shelter and build a fire. Even if you are held up for several days, you won't starve, but you could die of hypothermia.

Lightning - Thunderstorms are quite common on summer afternoons and evenings over the Sawtooths, White Clouds and Boulders. Huge piles of cumulus build up and discharge occasionally heavy local rains and spectacular displays of lightning around the higher peaks and ridges. From a mile or two away the thunder and lightning are awe-inspiring, but they can be terrifying and dangerous if you're in the middle of the storm. There is danger in these unstable mountains not only from lightning itself, but also from rock falls and slides triggered by thunder and lightning.

The safest place to be during one of these minor cataclysms is in the center of a wide valley in an extensive stand of short timber, with your pack and any other metal objects at least 100 feet away from you. Next best would be under a *solid* rock overhang or a large block of fallen rock that is not a high terrain feature.

Stay away from tall isolated trees, high open areas, sheer rock faces and slide chutes. Other than that, there's not much you can do but sit back and enjoy the show. If it's any consolation, we didn't hear of anyone being hit by lightning during the time we spent in the SNRA.

Report all forest fires you see as soon as you can. Do not try to put out fires of any size without help. The Forest Service allows some fires to burn out on their own under the SNRA Fire Management policy.

Mosquitoes and Other Insects - Mosquitoes are numerous in much of the backcountry from the time snow starts to melt through most of the summer. They're irritating during the day and at night they can keep you from sleeping if you don't have a properly screened shelter. For this reason alone, a good backpack tent is worth its weight and expense. A good tent will also keep you reasonably dry and warm in the unlucky event of a two- or three-day storm. Tube tents and tarps just don't do it after a few hours. Insect repellent is a must for daytime hours unless

Be prepared for unexpected changes in the weather

you're completely immune to the little buggers.

Horse flies and deer flies are a nuisance below 8,000 feet during July and August. Insect repellent doesn't seem to have much effect on these pests after a few minutes. Long pants will usually protect your legs, but the flies sometimes bite right through shirts. They do go away when the sun goes down.

Ticks are normally a problem only in early summer, but it's a good idea to look your body over at least once a day. If the tick's head is not embedded, simply pull it off gently and destroy it. If the head is embedded, pinch the skin up tightly to apply pressure to the head and, when the legs begin to wiggle, pull gently but firmly on the tick's body. If you're so unfortunate as to break the tick's head off under the skin, disinfect it thoroughly and hope for the best. If serious infection develops around the bite, get medical attention as soon as possible.

Stream Crossings - There are a number of unbridged stream crossings in the SNRA backcountry that are dangerous during the high runoff period, usually in June and early July. Check the trip descriptions carefully if you're planning a trip then. Some streams on which the lower and more difficult fords should not be attempted during high water are: Warm Springs and Big Casino Creeks in the White Clouds; Elk Creek, Redfish Lake Creek and South Fork

Payette River in the northern Sawtooths; Pettit Lake Creek, Middle Fork Boise River, and Queens and Little Queens rivers in the southern Sawtooths.

For other difficult crossings it's a good idea in early season to carry 150 feet of climbing rope and follow the stream crossing procedures described in Winnett's *Backpacking Basics*.

You will have to wade some streams and bogs on most of the trips at any time of year. We carry cheap light-weight tennis shoes for this purpose so we don't soak our boots. The "tennies" are usually tied on the outside of our packs drying out. We also wade in them to flyfish and wear them in camp, if they're dry enough, as a relief from boots.

Sunburn - High altitude and clean air allow more ultraviolet rays to get through and increase the hazard of severe sunburn. Persons with particularly sensitive skin should use sunblock lotions rather than tanning preparations. Hats are a good idea, too, not only to minimize sunburn but also to help prevent sunstroke and heat prostration.

MAPS AND PROFILES

Forest Service Maps - With a scale of ½" = 1 mile and without contours, these are only marginally useful as trail maps. They are, however,

Safe, but chilly, crossing
of the South Fork of Payette River

A little protective ointment on the nose
need not hinder romance

very useful as road maps to get to the trailheads since they show the routes of all unpaved roads and they are updated more often than USGS topographic maps. They also show the Forest Service numbers of the roads, which can be a great help at a remote crossroad where the signs show only those numbers. The *Sawtooth National Forest* map, published in 1985, is especially useful. It is available at SNRA offices and Sawtooth Forest ranger stations. The *Boise National Forest* map, useful for trailheads on the west and south sides of the Sawtooth Wilderness, can be purchased from the Boise Ranger District office in Boise or from any ranger station in that forest.

Topographic Maps - Thirty one USGS 7.5 minute quadrangles are required to cover all of the Sawtooth National Recreation Area. These quadrangles have a scale of 1 : 24,000, or approximately 2½ inches to 1 mile. The applicable quadrangles are listed in the introduction to each backcountry trip. In addition, the SNRA *Backpacking* and *Horseback Riding* folders each have a map on the back with a grid showing the locations of the 31 quadrangles. A limited supply of all the quadrangle maps is for sale at the SNRA offices, or they can be obtained by writing:

> Western Mapping Division, USGS
> 345 Middlefield Road
> Menlo Park, CA 94025

Most of the Ketchum, Sun Valley and Stanley sporting goods stores also stock some of the maps.

Since the 31 quadrangles involved were issued between 1963 and 1972, a number of new and relocated trails do not appear on them. The trip descriptions note where the trails differ from the routes shown on the maps and give added detail in those areas.

The topographic maps are only of value, of course, if you know how to use them in conjunction with a compass. Again I recommend *Backpacking Basics*, published by Wilderness Press. If you plan to do any off-trail exploring, map-and-compass orienteering ability is absolutely essential.

Elevation Profiles - A profile is included in the introduction to each trip to give a quick picture of the ups and downs. These graphs are not cross sections of the terrain over which you will be traveling. They are graphs, with a greatly exaggerated vertical scale, of the relationship of distance to altitude gained or lost. Actual elevation changes can be quickly calculated from the numbers on the vertical scales.

DESCRIPTIVE TERMS

Trails - The trip descriptions give information on the composition and condition of the trail tread, whether or not the trail has been relocated from the route indicated on the topo maps, some comments on its origin and past use, and a running description of the rate of ascent or descent and the switchbacks involved. Steepness is defined by the following terms:

level	0 to 2% grade
gradual	2% to 5% grade
moderate	5% to 8% grade
moderately steep	8% to 12% grade
steep	12% to 20% grade
very steep	more than 20% grade

The amount of traffic you might expect on a particular section of trail is indicated, but actual use may vary greatly.

Camps - Availability of firewood and drinking water is noted in all campsite descriptions. Rating of campsites from poor to excellent is based on views, unique natural features, privacy, proximity to fishing and side trips, protection from the elements, and how badly the site has been used. Except for primitive toilets and horse tie-rails in a few heavily used sites, there are no developed campsites in the SNRA backcountry.

Fishing - Evaluation of fishing in the backcountry streams and lakes is based on my personal experience with some additional input from other fishermen I met on the trail. I fished only with flies, but that doesn't mean that you have to. If I caught or saw fish, at least you know there are fish there.

Travel Times - The number of days allowed for each trip is based primarily on how long it took our party to walk it. We seldom walked more than six or seven hours a day. On the other hand, no layovers are included in the alloted days. You can add those as you please. As a rule of thumb, the times between points are based on a rate of one hour for every two level miles plus one additional hour for every 1,000 feet of ascent or steep descent. This rate includes some resting time. Unless you're trying to prove something and aren't interested in enjoying the scenery, 10 miles a day is about maximum for this country.

Horseback riders should make their own conversions, but basically they should be able to travel at least twice as far as a hiker does in a day.

THE TRAILHEADS

Four trailheads in the Boulders and White Clouds are accessible only to four-wheel drive vehicles, and four more can be reached only by pickups or other high-clearance vehicles. A marvelous solution to this problem would be designation of all of the Boulders and White Clouds as official wilderness. This action would obligate closure of these intrusive roads to all vehicular traffic. Even without official wilderness designation and purchase of existing mining claims, the roads could be locked, limiting access to legitimate miners only. Unfortunately neither alternative is apt to happen in the near future and those of us without the right kind of vehicles will simply have to walk or ride a horse the extra miles. The trip descriptions tell you how far you can get with each type of vehicle.

Three trailheads for the Sawtooth Wilderness—Yellow Belly Lake, upper Alturas Lake Creek and an alternate route to Hell Roaring Creek (which may be closed by the time you read this), require four-wheel drive or high clearance. No more than 3 miles of extra effort is involved in walking to any of the three. The rest of the Sawtooth trailheads can be reached by a modern sedan. Some of them require a lot of driving, however. For example, the 135 miles from Ketchum to Atlanta is a six-hour drive, a good part of it on unpaved roads. You can fly to the Atlanta airstrip from Hailey in 15 minutes, but then you have the problem of getting from the airstrip to the trailheads.

TRAIL MANNERS

Consideration of your fellow hikers and riders dictates that you not cut across switchbacks, especially in the downhill direction. Besides the erosion damage brought on by cross-cutting, there is a definite danger of dislodging rocks to roll down on people below.

Hikers and backpackers should stand or sit quietly clear of the trail when meeting or being overtaken by horses. This is not to show deference to a higher social order—horses may shy when crowded or frightened by unexpected movements or noises. Hikers as well as riders may be injured.

Trailbike riders should stop their engines and pull their machines to the side of the trail when meeting hikers or equestrians—the SNRA regulations say so. Hikers being overtaken by trailbikes should step off the trail to allow the machines to pass. Horses should be turned off the trail at the earliest opportunity to allow trailbikes to overtake. Meanwhile, trailbikes should not follow closely behind horses.

Chewing gum wrappers are the most prevalent eye-sore along the trails. The old maxim, "If you can pack it in full, you can pack it out empty" certainly applies.

Backpacking couple step ashore from the Redfish Ferry at Redfish Inlet Transfer Camp

Trips in the
Boulder and Smoky Mountains

1–West Fork of North Fork, Big Wood River

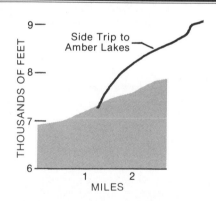

You can make this pleasant walk up a glacier-carved valley on the east side of the Boulders in half a day or extend it to a strenuous full day or overnight by climbing up to Amber Lakes. Elk have been sighted occasionally in the West Fork valley. Other animals, birds and wild flowers are plentiful. The valley was cut through a fairly representative part of the mixed-up geology of the Boulders, and it is an excellent place to observe the awesome effects of winter avalanches.

The very steep climb to alpine Amber Lakes shows the transition from Hudsonian to Arctic life zones in a hurry. There are no fish in the Amber Lakes, but the upper North Fork and its tributaries have small-to-medium brook trout.

Although this trip is near Ketchum and the SNRA headquarters, the trails are very lightly used. Trailbikes are not allowed.

Topo map is the *Amber Lakes* quadrangle.

Trail through the talus below the crest on the north side of Boulder Basin

STARTING POINT

Turn off Highway 75 at the SNRA head-quarters 8 miles north of Ketchum. The North Fork road runs straight ahead past the head-quarters parking lot and ends after 5 miles where the West Fork of North Fork joins the North Fork. Description of the drive is in Motor Trip 2. Just beyond a bridge over the North Fork at 3.4 miles, a ford crosses the East Fork of North Fork (on the topo map the road does not appear to cross this creek). If the water is high, you will not be able to get through this ford in a low-clearance vehicle. In that event, there is room to park on both sides of the North Fork bridge and you'll have an additional 1.5 miles to walk in each direction.

A trail sign and a register for the North Fork trail going on up the canyon are at the end of the road. The West Fork trail sign and register are in the trees west of the North Fork.

DESCRIPTION

Good campsites, with an adequate supply of firewood, are in the grove of spruce, fir and lodgepole in the flat between the two streams. Fishing for brook trout in either fork, or below their juncture, is good if the water isn't too high.

The trail is well-defined and reasonably well-maintained as it climbs moderately on the north side of the canyon away from the stream. In less than a mile of travel in mixed Douglas fir and lodgepole pine you will come to evidence of the tremendous avalanches that have run down the south wall of the canyon, across the stream, and up as far as the trail on the north side. At 1 mile

Butterfly in goldenrod

the trail drops down beside the stream near a dam of avalanche debris.

A branch of the trail crosses the stream here, and then recrosses to the north side within 200 yards. Along that piece of trail on the south side of the stream is the beginning of a trail up the east side of Amber Gulch, leading, after 2,000 feet of rough climb in less than 2 miles, to the two Amber Lakes. There is no trail sign, and the trail does not appear on the *Amber Lakes* quad-rangle. It is shown on both the Sawtooth National Forest map and the SNRA giveaway map as going past Amber Lakes, then over the 9,600-foot ridge to the south and down Konrad Creek to Highway 75 across from Wood River campground. We never found the trail, and the prospect of climbing slide-torn Amber Gulch from the north is very discouraging. We did talk to a couple who claimed to have done it and who raved about the scenery and the solitude. So there's a one- or two-day challenge if you're adventurous. If you do go, you won't meet very many other people.

West of Amber Gulch the West Fork Trail traverses more forest on the north side of the creek and then, at 1.5 miles, enters a willow-choked flat where a number of active beaver dams block the stream. Above the beaver dams the trail climbs moderately steeply over a volcanic outcrop north of a narrow defile through which the stream cascades. Clark's nutcrackers, grouse and pine squirrels abound in the lodgepole forest. You cross a small flat and climb moderately up another low ridge where tall, dark, metamorphic rock peaks come into view at the head of a wide U-shaped valley.

The open floor of this typical glacier-carved valley is a mass of wildflowers throughout the summer. Almost every variety of flower to be found in the SNRA, except for high alpine ones, can be found here in season. At the upper end of the valley two forks of the stream join above a low dike of limestone before falling through a slot and wandering down the valley floor. The valley is rimmed by thick subalpine fir.

The trail disappears in the valley 2.5 miles from the trailhead, although the topo map shows it continuing northwest for another mile. Rest for a while by the waterfall, catalog the many varieties of flowers, look for birds and butterflies and, just maybe, you'll see an elk before you return the way you came.

2–Boulder Basin to Pole Creek

A magnificent panorama of the highest peaks in the Boulder Mountains is the high point (literally) of this three-or four-day hike. The distance is 18 to 23 miles, depending on the starting point. More than a dozen peaks topping 10,000 feet, plus two immense mountain basins, can be seen from the 10,500-foot northwest rim of Boulder Basin. Forty or fifty off-road vehicles and trailbikes may be in Boulder Basin on a midsummer weekend, but over the rim to the north you might not see another person for a week.

Elk are fairly common in the high basin at the head of the South Fork of the East Fork of the Salmon, and mountain goats may be seen occasionally on the high peaks and ridges.

Smaller animals, including pikas and birds, are abundant.

Don't depend on eating fish on this trip. There don't seem to be any in the Boulder Basin lakes or in the upper reaches of the South Fork of the East Fork. The main stem of the East Fork is closed to all fishing until early September because it is a salmon spawning stream. We couldn't find any trout in the West Fork either, and the stream in Grand Prize Gulch is too small to fish. The scenery more than makes up for the lack of fish, however.

This is a one-way trip requiring a pick-up on the other end or a car shuttle. Of course you can do part or all of it as a round trip if you like. You can also shorten the trip a little, and the car

Canyon of the South Fork of the East Fork of the Salmon River

shuttle even more, by coming out on Gladiator Creek above Galena Lodge instead of Pole Creek. New signs and blazes have been placed at the Gladiator Creek Trail junction with ·the West Fork Trail since we were there.

Topo map quadrangles you will need for this trip are *Easley Hot Springs, Galena Peak* and *Horton Peak*.

STARTING POINT

Boulder Basin is the starting point but, without a four-wheel drive to get there, you will probably have to start 3 miles and almost 2,000 feet below the basin. This fragile, and breathtakingly beautiful, high-altitude basin cries out for protection as wilderness, but patented mining claims have so far precluded that action. Barring the fortunate circumstance of the entire miserable road sliding off the side of the mountain, a few misguided, barbaric individuals will continue to cut tracks into pristine alpine meadows which will not heal for a hundred years.

The Boulder Creek road begins on the north side of Highway 75 just east of milepost 141 at the top of Phantom Hill. Take the right fork at the first **Y** to cross the creek within a half mile of the highway. The road continues up the east side of Boulder Creek in open sagebrush-covered hills, then enters a parklike stand of Douglas fir at a little less than 2 miles from the highway. A quarter of a mile into the woods there is a trail register beside the road. There is no register higher up in the basin.

About a half mile beyond the register there are some old mine workings and an abandoned cabin on either side of the road. This is probably as far as you should go with a passenger vehicle. A pickup may be able to go another half mile, then it's all four-wheel-drive the rest of the way.

At 3 miles the road recrosses to the west side of the creek and makes a very rough traverse across a talus slope. Beyond this talus the road climbs less steeply in Douglas fir and lodgepole pine before coming out on a huge talus slope just past more miners' diggings and well up from the creek. The next half mile up the side of the talus is a rough, steep climb if you're walk-

ing and a spine-jarring, nerve-wracking ride if you're not. There are compensating views across and up and down the canyon.

Beyond the talus slope two small waterfalls tumble down the rocks on the left before the road forks in a small flat. The forks come together again above. On each fork the road is very steep and has been torn up by previous traffic. Even some four-wheel-drives can't make it up this pitch. On a single road again, you cross the creek and climb, first very steeply, and then moderately, past stunted subalpine firs to where the road turns west into the first meadow at the lower side of Boulder Basin. You are now at 9,100 feet elevation. The ridge behind you to the east is over 10,000 feet and some of the peaks ahead, surrounding the basin, tower to more than 11,000 feet.

Except for the scar of the road and some

Walking up the Boulder Basin road

branching tracks, the meadow around August 1 is a bright green carpet dusted liberally with flowers. To name just a few, there are shooting stars, marsh marigolds, Indian paintbrush, lupine and alpine buttercups. West of a small hump and sparse forest at the upper end of the first meadow, the road forks again. The left fork leads west, crossing a branch of Boulder Creek in another meadow below where the creek has cut a slot through a rock shelf. Less than a half mile from the fork, and beyond a screen of taller firs, this branch of the road ends in what is left of Boulder City.

Boulder City consists of a number of cabins in various states of disrepair, tilted this way and that around a small basin where a fork of Boulder Creek originates in a number of springs. On the southwest side of the "town," tumbledown remains of a large mill building

stagger up a solid rock slope. Boulder City had its heyday around the turn of the century, but a few people lived here off and on until much later.

Having seen Boulder City, go back to the road fork and follow the right fork northwest in a moderate climb around a shoulder of rock before turning west and crossing two more small meadows beside a tributary of Boulder Creek. At 5.6 miles from Highway 75, after climbing another shelf, the road forks again at the base of a large talus slide from Peak 11041. The right fork leads north to a small, higher basin under the northwest rim of Boulder Basin. The left fork climbs a ridge of rock to end beside the largest of the Boulder Basin lakes. This road fork is the starting point for the trip to the East Fork of the Salmon and, eventually, Pole Creek.

Cabin at Boulder City

Boulder Basin lake

DESCRIPTION
Boulder Basin to East Fork of Salmon River

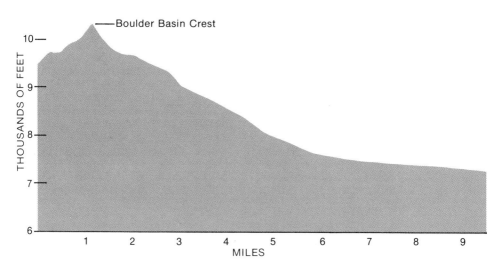

There are a few fair campsites along the little creek below the final road fork in Boulder basin, and two or three good sites beside the largest lake. These would be excellent sites if they weren't so littered and worn. This round, roughly 12-acre lake is in a solid rock basin with Boulder Peak and an almost 11,000-foot ridge as backdrop to the south and west. Remnants of two miners' cabins sit on the low ridge on the north side above the outlet stream, and a number of prospect holes have been drilled into the cliffs to the west. It's a marvelous place to watch a sunset reflecting from rugged Boulder Peak.

Start the trip with a steep climb on the north fork of the road across the talus slope at the base of Peak 11041. After a quarter mile, level out in a delightful garden hanging under the northwest rim of the basin. Some trailbikes and four-wheel-drives do get this high, but don't appear to have done a lot of damage. A number of springs burst forth from the base of the talus on the west side of the flat, and little streams meander through the grass between ponds lined with shooting stars and marsh marigolds. Struggling whitebark pines outline the lower side of the flat and a few cling to the nearer slopes, but the higher ridges are all above timberline.

The road continues along the southwest side

of the flat and ends on a rock knob. As you enter the flat, look for the trace of a trail angling up the talus of the north wall and strike out across the flat, aiming for where the lower end of the trail should be. You're not apt to find the trail at the bottom of the slope, but you can pick it up a little higher up in the scree. Be sure to get some water from one of the tiny streams or tarns in the meadows. It's a long, dry climb over the 10,500-foot north rim unless you find some remnant snow banks. A multitude of wildflowers bloom in the flat during the short summer—including alpine heathers (both white and pink), elephant's heads, bistorts, tiny blue violets and short, yellow alpine daisies. A fine stand of alpine sunflowers grows on the drier slope just below the talus.

Once you've found the faint trail in the scree, follow it on a steep climb for slightly more than a quarter mile northwest to a solid ledge which may still hold a snow bank in midsummer. The trail above this ledge is even less distinct, and appears to go up almost directly north from the center of the ledge. What trace there is soon turns northwest again and goes past some old prospect diggings at the northwest side of the talus before disappearing completely. Now climb very steeply north over ledges and broken rock toward the lowest notch on the skyline. An occasional stop to admire the alpine flowers springing from each tiny pocket of soil will make the climb easier.

Another quarter mile will bring you to the top of the rim and just about the most magnificent view in the Boulders. All of Boulder Basin spreads out at your feet. Boulder Peak dominates the skyline, although the 11,041-foot peak to the west is higher. Far off to the southeast the entire ridge of the Pioneer Mountains, including the Devil's Bedstead, is in view. The geology of the nearby mountains is very diverse. There are light gray and pink to dark brown granites with small crystals, slates, shales, sandstones and some limestone, but no volcanic rock. Finely broken scree forms long slides down the mountainsides, and quartz and dark red mineralization show in fractures of the distorted strata.

North of the rim lies a virtually treeless basin of gray, brown and pink rock, larger than Boulder Basin, tipped to drain northeast into a tributary of the South Fork of the East Fork of the Salmon River. Directly west is a small lake in a cirque on the high side of the basin, still frozen in the first week of August 1978. This basin is a favorite helicopter ski area in the late winter and it's easy to see why—there must be miles of pristine open snow slopes then.

Just beyond a notch in the jagged rim, the trail is well-defined for a short distance, headed down almost southwest across a dark brown scree slope. Then it switches back into larger talus and is lost. Work down the steep slope northwest to avoid even steeper slopes and cliffs directly below to the north. With luck you can pick up the trail again below where it crosses a light-colored talus slope still going northwest.

When the trail disappears, descend on the best traverse you can find and look for a faint track above the east bank of the small stream threading the bottom of the basin. As the basin narrows to a valley draining north, willows appear in wet areas and grassy meadows lie between the stream and the talus slopes on the sides.

As we were eating lunch beside the trail here, three cow elk came up the valley toward us. On seeing us, two of the elk retreated while the leader stood and barked (yes, elk do bark) at us from 100 yards for almost 10 minutes.

At 1.5 miles below the crest between the basins, climb over a volcanic outcrop opposite a tributary tumbling in a series of falls down a rock face on the west side of the valley. The valley narrows to a canyon below and turns northwest. Beginning at the outcrop, thin patches of whitebark pine and subalpine fir are

Almost treeless basin north of Boulder Basin

interspersed with open, sagebrush-covered slopes.

The trail is very hard to find below on the steep sagebrush-covered slopes, but stay on the northeast side of the canyon. Within a mile there are reassuring blazes on an isolated whitebark and the trail reappears beyond it for a steep drop of a quarter mile into the first grove of Douglas fir. There is an occasional blazed tree in the grove, but not much sign of a trail among the deadfalls. Continue to bushwhack across an avalanche path and through more trees and sagebrush until, at 4.5 miles, the creek you have been following joins the South Fork of the East Fork as it flows out of a canyon from the south.

Beyond the confluence of the two streams you should be able to find the trail again, fairly close to the stream on the east side as the wider canyon turns north. In .3 mile come to a log drift fence, built across the canyon by the Forest Service to keep cattle out of the upper reaches. There may not be any cattle, but if you open the gate, please close it behind you. The trail is much easier to follow below the fence, and some of the deadfalls have been removed. The descent is moderately steep through Douglas fir and lodgepole pine forest, an avalanche path and a few small meadows for 1 mile to the crossing of a good-sized tributary from the east side of the canyon. You could camp not too far from this stream, if necessary, but there are no obvious campsites.

The canyon widens now into a flat-floored valley and the trail descends gradually, well away from the South Fork on the east side. About 2.7 miles from the first drift fence is another fence. Three quarters of a mile in open grass and sagebrush below the second fence, the trail turns west and crosses the East Fork of the Salmon just below where the South Fork and West Fork join. Don't try to cross to the west side any farther south, the South Fork runs through a series of beaver dams and spruce bogs above its confluence with the West Fork.

A trail register is on the east side of the river crossing, 9 miles from the starting point in Boulder Basin. Until 1978 a trailhead here was reached by 33 miles of gravel and dirt road from the East Fork junction 4 miles below Clayton on the Salmon River. Then a rancher puts gates across the road and stopped all traffic 15 miles north, above Little Boulder Creek. It's possible the road may be open when you read this, but don't count on it.

The East Fork of the Salmon flows northeast from this trail and stream junction in a wide, shallow valley among rolling sagebrush hills. Spawning salmon made wide **V**'s in the shallows as we crossed in early August. Since it is a spawning stream, the river is closed to all fishing except during September, October and November.

A number of excellent campsites are in aspen groves in the flat north of where the West Fork joins the South Fork.

Waterfall into the South Fork of the East Fork of the Salmon River

East Fork of Salmon River to Pole Creek

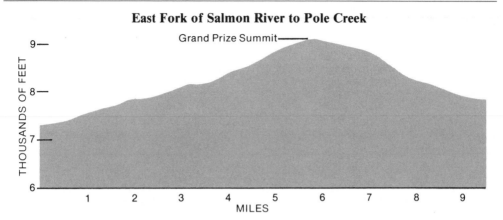

Pick up the West Fork of the East Fork of the Salmon trail on a jeep track as it makes a short, steep climb from the flat to a bench 200 yards north of the campsites by the West Fork. The trail from here to Pole Creek is open to trailbikes but does not have heavy trailbike use. There is no trail register on this side of the river.

The jeep track climbs moderately west for .5 mile through open sagebrush, then turns north up the hill and ends. Our well-defined and maintained foot trail continues west, climbing moderately, well above the creek through aspen, Douglas fir and open sagebrush slopes. One and a half miles from the East Fork you will find the first drinking water on the trail, a tiny stream on a bench shaded by aspen, spruce and fir.

In another .5 mile the trail comes close to the north bank of the West Fork in a stand of big trees where pools in the stream invite a try for trout. Maybe you'll have better luck than we had.

Between 2.5 and 3 miles from the river, cross a large open area where avalanches have run down both sides of the canyon. Then you re-enter heavy forest, walking on duff, to come out into the open at 3.5 miles opposite a tributary plunging down another avalanche path.

In the next strip of forest upstream from the tributary, we disturbed a pair of nesting golden eagles.

Next you ascend a moderately steep slope in open forest, where an occasional subalpine fir now shows up, well above the creek on the north side. At 4 miles there is a quarter mile of steep climb on narrow tread, north of a narrow defile and 100 yards above the brawling stream. Halfway up the climb a cascading, flower-lined creeklet in a side gully offers a resting spot. The valley widens above this steep pitch and the trail climbs moderately to come out on a small ridge overlooking a meadow of about 50 acres with two ice-cold springs on the north side. Small stream channels meander through the flower-carpeted flat to the creek on its south side. High peaks of the north end of the Boulder crest form a backdrop above the head of the valley. There is no obvious evidence that anyone has camped here, but there are good sites east of the meadow.

The trail across the meadow is indistinct. Stay on the north side and look for blazed trees where you re-enter the forest well away from the creek. Then you begin to climb to the head of the West Fork valley and the top of the divide between the East Fork of the Salmon and Pole Creek, which runs into the main Salmon in Sawtooth Valley. A moderate climb, with some steep pitches, through open forest, rock ledges and small meadows levels out at 5 miles near a spring that is shown above the Galena Gulch trail on the Horton Peak quadrangle. The West Fork trail has been relocated north of the route shown on the topo map. In the basin ahead of you the trail from Gladiator Creek, over the high ridge to the south, joins this trail for a few hundred yards and then takes off over the north ridge to eventually run down Galena Gulch to Pole Creek. New signs have been erected to help you find the Gladiator Creek trail if you want it. We could not find it.

Our trail turns south across the alpine basin, then turns west again beside the little stream that tumbles from the south ridge and runs east to become the West Fork of the East Fork of the Salmon. There are a number of excellent campsites among the whitebark pines and flowers on both sides of the stream. Wide mats of sandwort, with its tiny, white, five-petaled blossoms, spread over the gravelly soil in dry sunny areas. Shady and more moist spots are filled with alpine heathers, both pink and white flowering.

The top of the divide is about two hundred yards northwest of where the trail leaves the creek. Start down through mounds of glacial debris, lodgepole forest and small grassy meadows for a quarter mile, turning more north, then drop steeply northwest down a gully to a wide flat that has been swept clean by a large avalanche from the peak to the east. Cross this flat going northwest and pick up the trail again as it snakes steeply down another gully to a lush meadow with a stream meandering through it. Cross once at the head of the meadow and two more times at the lower end to come out on the north side of the stream where it begins its plunge into Grand Prize Gulch. The trail turns away north up the side of the ridge and, in less than a quarter mile, meets a jeep road that climbs out of the gulch to a mining prospect on the ridge above. A new sign here says "TRAIL" and points back the way you came.

The jeep road descends moderately north-west through a tongue of trees and across a sloping meadow, then more steeply through a heavy forest of subalpine fir, lodgepole pine and spruce. Out of the trees again, you begin a series of five steep switchbacks west down a bare slope to the bottom of Grand Prize Gulch at 7.5 miles from the East Fork of the Salmon.

Across the canyon from the jeep road a tremendous avalanche has cleared the entire side of the mountain and run down the floor of Grand Prize Gulch for more than a quarter mile. Trees up to 2 feet in diameter were carried down and piled like jackstraws at the bottom, completely covering the creek in places. The road crosses the creek in the middle of the avalanche area and drops moderately down the southwest side of the gulch, entering heavy timber again above the little creek.

Within .5 mile below the creek crossing, the road turns southwest out of Grand Prize Gulch and onto the side of Pole Creek canyon. After .8 mile of moderate descent through an old burn, where the new growth of lodgepole pines is now 10–15 feet tall, the road doubles back to cross Pole Creek on a bridge that was broken through when we were there. Just beyond the bridge is a campground and the Pole Creek road. The campground is 9 miles from the East Fork of the Salmon and 18 miles from the starting point in Boulder Basin. If the Pole Creek bridge has been repaired, you can drive almost any vehicle up into Grand Prize Gulch and cut a mile and a half off the distance.

Avalanche debris at the bottom of Grand Prize Gulch

3-Prairie Creek to Prairie Lakes

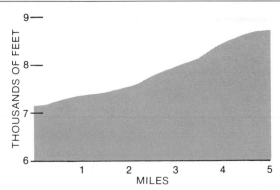

The round trip day hike to Prairie lakes is reasonably close to civilization at Ketchum/Sun Valley and is a good warm-up for more serious hiking in the higher mountains of the SNRA. It is 5 miles uphill going in and another 5 miles downhill coming out, with a fairly even grade all of the way. The high point, at Prairie Lakes, is 8,700 feet, which is not very high compared to points on many of the other trips.

There is beautiful scenery, but not as spectacular as in the higher mountains. Wildflowers abound, and you will probably see deer, porcupines and other smaller wildlife. There are some small rainbow trout in the lower reaches of Prairie Creek and a few larger ones in the biggest Prairie Lake. The smaller lakes are too shallow to support a trout population. The trail is open to trailbikes, but not many use it. In fact all traffic is light.

There are excellent campsites at the lakes, along upper Prairie Creek, and at Miner Lake, 1.5 miles up Miner Canyon. An easy two- or three-day trip could be planned to include the Miner Canyon side trip.

Topo Map is the *Galena* quadrangle.

STARTING POINT

Prairie Creek road junction is 18 miles north of Ketchum on the west side of Highway 75 between mileposts 146 and 147. The trailhead is at the West Fork of Prairie Creek, a little more than 2.5 miles from the highway. The Prairie Creek road is rough, but not steep, and is passable to most vehicles.

Turn right at the fork near the first car-camp up Prairie Creek and stay uphill away from the creek until you reach the crossing of the West Fork. The ford may be passable, but there's not much point in crossing, since the track on the other side peters out within .3 mile.

DESCRIPTION

Although all of this trip, except for the first 1.5 miles of the Prairie Creek road, is actually outside the boundary of the SNRA, the area as far as the crest of the Smoky Mountains is administered by the SNRA and, for all intents and purposes, is a part of it.

Start the trip by fording the West Fork of Prairie Creek to the south side. The crossing should be no problem unless the water is unusually high. There are no trail signs at the ford. Do not follow the trail up the north side of the West Fork. After crossing, follow the jeep track south for .3 miles and look for a trail register at the end of the track.

Southwest of the register the well-maintained trail runs close to Prairie Creek for a short distance where the creek cuts through some jumbled terminal moraines. It then turns away from the creek to come out, at .5 mile from the register, in an open meadow with scattered groves of lodgepole pine and spruce. There are beautiful displays of arnica, cinquefoil, Indian paintbrush and red penstemon in the moraines and the meadow. Much of the meadow is wet in early summer, so the trail runs above it on the northwest side. Halfway up the meadow you cross a tiny creeklet in a slide area. The entire slide is filled with moisture-loving flowers including cow parsnip, yellow and red monkey flowers, death camas and several varieties of mint.

The trail continues southwest through a belt of trees and another meadow to come close to the creek again at 2 miles from the trailhead. Then you climb gradually for another .3 mile to the Miner Canyon Trail junction. A sign here gives a distance of 6 miles to Norton Creek. Miner Lake, not on the sign, is a little more than 1.5 miles, and a climb of 1,100 feet, up the canyon. Norton Lakes and Norton Creek are farther south over a 9,800-foot ridge.

There is no sign for Prairie Lakes at the junc-tion, but the trail fork is very clear, climbing moderately southwest away from the creek in spruce and Douglas fir. It levels off somewhat through intermittent forest, grass and sagebrush slopes and, at 3 miles, makes a short, moderately steep climb to come out above the creek where it has cut through another terminal moraine. In this area porcupines have girdled lodgepole pines 5–6 feet above the ground, indicating the snow level at the time the porcupines were hungriest.

Whitebark pines begin to show up in the forest at about 8,000 feet and, at 3.5 miles, there is easy access to the creek beside a poor campsite. Climb moderately through more moraines to top out beside a small, atrophied lake on the left, notable for its chorus of frogs. Above this lake, cross Prairie Creek, a single step at this point, and climb over a few more moraine ridges to reach the east shore of the largest of the Prairie Lakes at 5 miles from the trailhead.

The five Prairie Lakes are in a large, verdant basin surrounded by Smoky Mountain peaks and ridges reaching almost 10,000 feet. Three small lakes nestle under the steep ridge east of the larger butterfly-shaped lake beside the trail; another small lake is buried in heavy forest on the northeast side of the basin. Tall spires of subalpine fir reach for the sky along the shores of the lakes and above them, on the high rocks, weather-beaten whitebark pines stand guard at timberline.

A number of excellent campsites are in the firs south of the large lake. It's a beautiful place to spend the night, or to have lunch. The lake is shallow enough that it warms to almost comfortable swimming temperature by late August.

The trail continues south over the rim of the Prairie Lakes basin and down the backbone of the Smoky Mountains to Baker Lake and the Baker Creek road, but that's well out of the SNRA area. Back the way you came, it's all downhill unless you take the side trip up to Miner Lake.

Short sections of this trail have been relocated and rebuilt since the Galena quadrangle was printed, but generally the route is close to that shown on the map.

Penstemon and asters

4–Mill Creek and Mill Lake

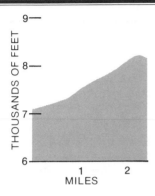

This half-day, 4 mile round trip is of interest primarily for the mixed-up geology of the Mill Creek canyon and lake basin. There are good campsites at the lake, but the water is not very palatable and there are no fish. It's a steep climb, good training for longer trips in more remote areas.

Topo map for the trip is the *Galena* quadrangle.

STARTING POINT

A little over 2 miles up the Prairie Creek road (see Backcountry Trip 3) a small sign points to Mill Lake, no mileage is given. A dirt track leads south down to a campsite, with a picnic table, near Prairie Creek. This is the starting point.

DESCRIPTION

Cross Prairie Creek on foot logs near the campsite and pick up a jeep trail leading south on a bench above the creek. Two hundred yards up this road is a trail register. Take time to sign in. A third of a mile south of Prairie Creek the trail turns west and crosses Mill Creek near the remains of a log bridge. On the west bank, well above the creek, look for the foot trail climbing up the steep canyon.

Climb moderately steeply for less than .5 mile in fairly heavy timber, then drop down to cross the creek and climb a very steep, open slope on the east side. Many flowers decorate this slope in July, and the creek below is quite beautiful, running over logs and among mossy rocks.

The canyon above you is completely filled with broken rock and other glacial debris plowed down this far by a relatively recent glacier. The trail climbs steeply south along the open east slope and soon passes above where the creek springs from under the debris blocking the canyon. You next traverse west above the beginning of the creek, then climb steeply south again over mounds of moraine material. Make another traverse east through sparse forest and begin another very steep climb south over broken rock that has not yet acquired any vegetation. Stop at a belt of trees and look back down the canyon, up the West Fork of Prairie Creek canyon, and to the south end of the Sawtooths far to the north.

Now you turn east around the shoulder of a large moraine and dip down southwest into a bowl with Mill Lake at the bottom. The trail ends in a forest of subalpine fir and whitebark pine east of the lake. You can, however, walk on up the wide, glaciated valley south of the lake for 1–2 miles.

A glacier once ran down this far from the higher ridge to the south, pushing a huge volume of debris torn from the valley above. When the climate changed, the glacier stopped here and melted, leaving the piles of debris to form a porous dam across the canyon, Water now drains at a fairly constant rate through the middle level of the debris and comes out to form the creek in the lower, unglaciated canyon. The level of the lake fluctuates 10–15 feet depending on the inflow of water from the valley above. A band of very weathered and ancient driftwood extends all around the lake at the high-water mark, since there is no place for it to go.

There are excellent campsites in the open forest east of the lake and plenty of firewood in the driftwood ring. However, the lake and the inlet stream are highly colored with glacial milk and are disagreeable, although probably safe to drink. There are no fish in Mill Lake, evidently because of the rock dust in the water.

Enjoy the stark scenery, which includes 10,336-foot Norton Peak on the southwest horizon, marvel at how much rock a short glacier can move, and return the way you came.

Trips in the
Sawtooth Wilderness and
Northern SNRA

5–Alpine Creek Lakes

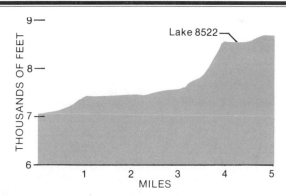

Just beyond the often crowded campgrounds around Alturas Lake lies a verdant valley leading to a series of little-visited lakes set like jewels in the rough matrix of the southern Sawtooth peaks. It's a moderately strenuous one-day round trip to one of these lakes,

and a genuinely strenuous hike of several days to some of the others. The upper end of the trip is off-trail.

Trailbikes are not allowed on this trail, since most of it is in the Sawtooth Wilderness.

Topo map is the *Snowyside Peak* quadrangle.

**Rugged peak and ribbon falls
southwest of Goat Creek crossing
on the Alpine Way**

STARTING POINT

Drive all the way around the north side of Alturas Lake on the paved road past the campgrounds. This road turns west off Highway 75 near milepost 169, 40 miles north of Ketchum. The pavement ends just beyond the Alturas Inlet campground. Continue on the gravel road another 1.6 miles to Alpine Creek. Parking for the Alpine Creek trail is east of the ford, which is deep and has stalled a number of automobiles in the past. The trail is on the east side of the creek, not across the footbridge.

DESCRIPTION

Not far beyond the trail register, the well-maintained trail turns northwest and climbs gradually away from the creek in mature timber. Walk quietly on the duff-covered path through lodgepole and Douglas fir to see a variety of wildlife—pine squirrels, chipmunks, grouse, Clark's nutcrackers and several different woodpeckers. At a little less than 1 mile, cross an open grassy slope and climb moderately around the north side of a gray granite knob. The saddle beside the knob provides a good view of the wide, U-shaped valley ahead and the crest of the main Sawtooth ridge beyond. Note that the ridge directly ahead is gray Idaho granite, while the peaks a little farther north are typical pink and brown Sawtooth granite. You are almost on the dividing line between the Idaho and Sawtooth batholiths.

Beyond the knob, the trail goes through another belt of trees, turning west, then drops gradually down open sagebrush and grass slopes covered with wildflowers in season. At 1.7 miles the trail is near the creek again in the middle of the wide valley where a large avalanche has run down the north side, across the creek and up the south side, breaking off large trees 5–6 feet above the ground, snow level at the time. Just west of the avalanche path, in the edge of a lodgepole pine forest, is an excellent campsite.

We climb moderately again through alternating timber and open slopes on the north side of the valley. The trail is not always clearly defined as it crosses open slopes, but it does stay up on the north slope to avoid bogs on the valley floor until it reaches the head of the valley.

The official end of the trail is 2.5 miles from the trailhead, where you have dropped down beside the creek again in a heavily forested, boggy flat. The largest of the Alpine Creek lakes is a little over a half mile directly west and more than 900 feet higher at 8,522 feet elevation. Beyond Lake 8522 there are at least a dozen smaller lakes set in cirques on the east side of the main Sawtooth ridge. A west fork of Alpine Creek drains this basin and joins the main creek above a short, steep canyon beyond the end of the trail.

The main stem of Alpine Creek drains a larger basin to the north, where there are another six or seven lakes. A very steep, poorly defined use trail climbs north through heavy forest on the east side of the canyon for .5 mile before entering a wider basin surrounded by sawtoothed crests. Another mile of more moderate climbing brings you to the first of the north Alpine Creek lakes. Other lakes can be reached by cross-country travel carefully directed by map and compass. Plan on a two- or three-day trip to see these lakes.

A faint trail continues west to more often visited Lake 8522 and the lakes beyond. Cross several channels of the creek where the trail first approaches it in the flat, and look for traces of a trail climbing west through mounds of glacial till. You should soon come out on a solid rock

Campsite at Lake 8522

74

shoulder south of the fork in the creek. Continue to climb steeply west on the south side of the west fork. Above a series of waterfalls and cascades you can cross to the north side or continue up the south side of the creek. There isn't much choice; both sides are very steep and there's not much of a trail.

After a little more than a half mile of very strenuous climbing, which will probably take an hour, you will top out on a low rim at the east end of Lake 8522. The lake is hourglass-shaped, about a half mile long and a quarter mile wide at the widest point. Two granite islands, topped with whitebark pines, jut from the crystal clear water near the outlet. Steep, bare granite and talus border the north side of the lake. Shelves of the same gray granite with pockets of trees border the rest of the shoreline. Some excellent campsites are nestled in lodgepole pines and subalpine firs not far from the outlet.

The sawtooth ridge outlining the horizon on the west side of the basin is all pink Sawtooth granite. Huge talus slides reach to the crest of the ridge in some places. Faint tracks lead around both sides of Lake 8522, giving access to the other lakes higher up.

Lake 8727, a moderately steep quarter mile southwest of Lake 8522, is the easiest of the other lakes to reach. Walk around the south side of Lake 8522 and begin climbing west just beyond a small talus slide. When you come within sight of an outlet creek from the lake above, turn south and climb east of the creek into the bowl containing Lake 8727. This cirque lake is on the dividing line between Idaho and Sawtooth granites; the open, outlet side of the cirque is gray Idaho granite contrasting with pink and brown cliffs of Sawtooth granite on the other sides. The water is slightly colored by glacier milk from snowfields on the Sawtooth crest. A number of excellent campsites are situated in groves of subalpine fir south of the outlet and well away from the shoreline.

The other lakes in the basin are mostly in bare rock northwest of the first two lakes. To reach them, take compass bearings and climb the rocks to the lakes you want to see.

Several days can be spent exploring the two basins, or you can have lunch beside one of the lower lakes and return to civilization before dinnertime. There are brook trout in some of the lakes, but fishing is only fair.

A tiny granite island seems to float on the deep, quiet waters of Lake 8522

6–Alturas Lake Through the Heart of the Sawtooths to Yellow Belly Lake

Cross the southern Sawtooth crest, hike down into the Middle Fork Boise River canyon, climb back up to the heart of the Sawtooth Wilderness at Spangle Lakes, continue through Tenlake Basin, pass Vernon and Edna lakes, climb Sand Mountain Pass and drop down past Farley Lake to Yellow Belly or Pettit lakes. That's a quick itinerary of this four- to six-day backpack trip that offers a good sampling of varied Sawtooth Wilderness terrain. The trip is close to being a loop, but does require a car-shuttle or hitchhike between Alturas and Yellow Belly or Pettit lake.

Spectacular scenery is everywhere along the 36 miles of trail, and almost all of the streams and lakes have fish in them. Parts of the trail down Mattingly Creek are just about the worst there is in the Sawtooth Wilderness, but traffic is light. On the other hand, the trail from Edith Lake junction to Yellow Belly is one of the most heavily traveled sections, so you get a little bit of everything.

Crossings of the Middle Fork Boise River may be dangerous or impossible during high run-off and there may be snow on the Tenlake Basin divide and Sand Mountain Pass in early season. The first 4.5 miles of trail from Alpine Creek to Johnson Creek junction are outside the SNRA and are open to trailbikes. There is fairly heavy trailbike and horse traffic on this section of trail.

Topo maps for the trip are *Snowyside Peak* and *Mount Everly* quadrangles. However, the route does dip south onto *Marshall Peak* and *Atlanta East* quadrangles for short distances.

Above: canyon of the Middle Fork of Boise River

Opposite: Fishing the evening rise at Farley Lake

Starting point is the Alpine Creek trailhead. Directions for getting there are in Backcountry Trip 5. Unless you plan to hitchhike back to Alpine Creek, you need to arrange for a pick-up or leave a vehicle at Yellow Belly trailhead or Tin Cup Transfer Camp. Directions for Tin Cup are in Backcountry Trip 7.

To drive to Yellow Belly Lake, turn right off the Pettit Lake road immediately after crossing the outlet creek. There is a sign at the junction for the horse transfer camp, but none for Yellow Belly. Keep right at the next road fork unless you have horses with you; the left fork goes to the horse transfer camp. The dirt road continues east over hills covered with sagebrush and clumps of timber, then north around the huge moraine separating Pettit and Yellow Belly lakes. You will encounter a steep, torn-up pitch after the road turns west, 2 miles from the junction at Pettit Lake Creek. A four-wheel-drive vehicle will be able to get over this pitch and go 2 more miles to the end of the road and the trailhead at the upper end of Yellow Belly Lake. If you don't have a four-wheel drive, you will have to walk out to this point at the end of the trip, or over the moraine to Tin Cup Transfer Camp, if you've left your car there.

DESCRIPTION
Alpine Creek to Middle Fork Boise River

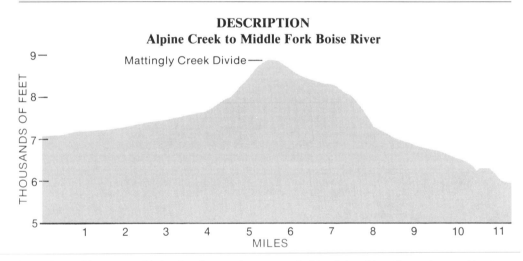

From the parking area at Alpine Creek cross the footbridge above the ford and head west on the jeep road on the other side. If you have a vehicle that can get through the deep ford, you will probably be able to drive another 2 miles. Don't try the ford in a modern passenger car—you're not apt to make it.

The road follows the north side of the flat upper valley of Alturas Lake Creek through lodgepole pine, spruce and grassy meadows. At 2 miles both the road and the creek fork. The left fork of the road goes south across the creek and up Jake's Gulch. The right fork turns west, uphill, and within a quarter mile there is a trail register to sign.

Continue west up the old road trace on the north side of the wide valley. After a half mile of moderate climb, the road turns north up an alluvial fan and the trail continues as a footpath climbing gradually southwest through a grove of lodgepole pine and then on an open slope. A number of springs pour out above this alluvial slope, but all the water disappears into the gravel before it gets down to the trail. In fact, Alturas Lake Creek also disappears at times in its gravelly bed below.

A little more than a mile from the trail register, the valley turns south and narrows as the trail crosses a flat meadow west of the creek. Within another mile you cross the creek near an excellent campsite in a grove of spruce and then climb moderately up the other side. As the trail climbs higher on the south side, the valley turns west and becomes a steep-sided canyon. Cross three small tributary creeks and zig-zag steeply up to Johnson Creek trail junction 4.5 miles from Alpine Creek trailhead. A fairly new junction sign gives a distance of 7 miles to "MIDDLE FK. BOISE R. TR."

The trail is not as well-maintained above the Johnson Creek junction, but is still clear as it climbs steeply northwest in heavy timber across feeder streams of Alturas Lake Creek. It next climbs north with rudimentary switchbacks up a steep, gravelly slope to a beautiful meadow atop Mattingly Divide. An elaborately carved sign beside the trail marks the wilderness boundary. An older sign on a subalpine fir west of the trail gives a distance of 10 miles back to Alturas Lake. That must be to the outlet end of the lake; it's not more than 7 miles to the Inlet campground. The same sign says 6 miles to Middle Fork Boise, which is probably correct.

A profusion of alpine asters and brilliant blue gentians bloom in the divide meadow the first week of August. The trail is not very distinct beyond the boundary sign, but with a little care it can be followed north into the basin at the head of Mattingly Creek. Cross the basin and come out on a gravelly, sparsely forested slope above and east of the small creek. One mile from the wilderness boundary, drop down and cross the creek as it turns northwest. Continue on the southwest side of a wet meadow and willow thicket for a half mile on poor but level trail with rough rock or mud tread. At the bottom of the meadow a small talus slide squeezes the trail beside the creek, and it soon crosses to the north bank. Climb over the toe of another talus slide as the creek turns west, dropping into a deep, steep-sided canyon.

The next mile of trail, to where the canyon turns southwest, is the roughest and steepest of the entire trip. There are points where the faint track almost disappears in the rocks and brush, or seems to cross the creek, which it doesn't. Below a narrow gap, where the creek tumbles in a series of falls and cascades lined with yellow monkey flowers, the trail stays up on open slopes beneath the canyon wall. As the trail turns southwest there are excellent views down to and across the Middle Fork Boise canyon. Take it easy climbing down and take time to look for dwarf fireweed. It is unique here—it's

normal range is much farther north.

Two and a half miles below the first creek crossing, level off across a pleasant meadow before crossing and recrossing the creek in a grove of large spruce. Good campsites are located in the trees near the crossings. The trail is much better as it continues southwest down the canyon intermittently in heavy forest and on rocky and brushy slopes. About 4 miles from the wilderness boundary on Mattingly Divide, the trail becomes wider as it follows an old wagon road that once connected Atlanta to diggings up Mattingly Canyon. After another mile of moderate descent, the old track doubles back and drops steeply to cross Mattingly Creek and angle even more steeply up the southeast side of the canyon. These grades must have been very hard on horses and wagons. For that matter, they're pretty tough on backpackers after a long day.

We contour almost level on what is more obviously the remains of a road as the creek falls away precipitously on its way to the Middle Boise. Next, round a rocky shoulder and descend steeply on the east side of the Middle Fork Boise River canyon for a quarter mile to a wide bench and a **Y** in the trail. Both forks lead to the Middle Boise trail. Take the right fork north to a junction just south of Mattingly Creek, where a sign gives a distance of 12 miles back to Alturas Lake. That leaves 10.4 miles from the trailhead at Alpine Creek. None of this trail has been rebuilt or moved significantly from the route on the topo maps.

There are excellent campsites under large Douglas firs on both sides of Mattingly Creek and in a flat closer to the river. Water, firewood and fishing all rate "excellent" at this very pleasant stopover. Trout in the river grow to 9–10 inches. Although they are all rainbows, they are surprisingly variegated. Some are light-colored with brilliant markings; others a few yards away are very dark with hardly any markings. All are uniformly delicious when fried.

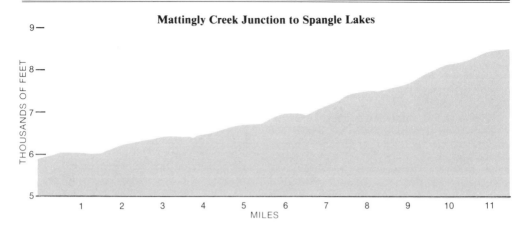

The first 3.5 miles north to Rock Creek is a pleasant stroll on good trail never more than moderately steep. The trail stays 200–400 yards east of the river, running through open Douglas fir forest, occasional meadows and patches of alders where seeps and spring issue from the side of the canyon. The trail has been rebuilt recently, with the addition of a switchback or two in steeper spots, but has not been relocated significantly. Two miles north of Mattingly Creek a sign points west across the river to Misfire Creek falling down the steep west wall. There is no trail up Misfire Creek.

At a little over 3 miles, you come to a lovely meadow that was once a lake before the river cut through the rock slide at its lower end. Excellent campsites are between the trail and the river in the forest at the north end of the meadow and just south of the first crossing of Middle Fork Boise River. The river ford crosses two channels in a rocky outwash 100 yards or more above where Rock Creek flows in from the northwest, By late summer someone may have placed footlogs across the rushing channels and made the crossing relatively easy, but in early summer it is dangerous, and should be attempted only with the extra security of proper roping techniques.

Rock Creek Trail junction is in the flat north of the crossing. If you want some extra mileage and solitude, the Rock Creek Trail climbs 1,400 feet in 3.5 miles to Timpa Lake. Another 10 or 12 lakes lie in a trailless alpine basin north of Timpa Lake and just south of a major east-west crest in the center of the Sawtooths. It is possible to cross this crest north of Low Pass Lake to

reach a trail near Lake Ingeborg, but there is no trail over the crest and there are permanent snowfields on the north side, so those who are not experienced mountaineers will want to return to the Rock Creek junction.

The Middle Boise canyon turns directly east from Rock Creek, narrows and becomes more rugged. The trail climbs moderately north from the junction on two rebuilt switchbacks before turning east on the north side of the canyon, well above the river. We continue climbing moderately east on the dry, mostly open slope for another mile before dropping down to the next river crossing. The stream is smaller here, and the crossing is on a perfectly safe large footlog 50 feet above the ford.

On the south bank of the river is a lush, cool forest of giant spruce and Douglas fir with an understory of elderberries, currants, alders, grasses and wildflowers including 3–4 foot delphiniums. Seeps and springs make the tread muddy in places. In less than a half mile, cross the river to the north side on a log jam 75 feet below the trail ford. Then you make a moderate climb with one switchback up the north slope and continue northeast for a half mile to the next river crossing in a spruce bog. There are two channels this time, both crossed by substantial footlogs.

Beyond this crossing the canyon turns north again, and after a quarter mile in heavy forest you climb moderately steeply over a half-mile-wide avalanche trail running down the east side. Numerous small streams fall from the canyon walls above and flow down across the trail. The well-watered slope is covered with wildflowers in August: 5-foot-tall delphinium spikes and brilliant magenta monkey flowers bloom along the stream courses. It's a beautiful place for a rest stop, and a look back to the south where a jumbled mass of granite peaks and ridges, including Mattingly Peak at 9,921 feet, fill the horizon above the canyon.

From this stop, continue climbing moderately through bands of forest, in which subalpine firs begin to appear, then over more slide areas for another mile to a wider part of the canyon floored with flat meadows. The river—a small stream at this point—wanders quietly through the grass and willows, widening into a small lake before dropping into the narrower canyon below. At the lower end of the meadows are several campsites, heavily used by horse packers.

The trail skirts the east side of the meadows and crosses the stream where it spreads out in three or four channels below a grove of trees. It is a wet, boggy crossing and backpackers may prefer to go up into the trees to cross. The

Equestrians approaching Little Spangle Lake

Flytrip trail junction is in the grove, as are a number of good campsites. You have come 4.5 miles from Rock Creek and it is 2.5 miles and a 1,000-foot climb on rebuilt trail to Spangle Lake. Someone has commented on that climb by carving a "1" in front of the "2" on the sign to read "12".

The trail up Flytrip Creek ends at Heart Lake, 2 miles east and 1,000 feet higher, in a large, lake-studded basin below Snowyside Peak. It's a very beautiful side trip if you have time to do it.

The next mile and a half of the Middle Boise trail north of Flytrip junction has been rebuilt and relocated from the route on the *Mount Everly* quadrangle. A lot of longer switchbacks have been added and only small parts of the climb are more than moderately steep. The new trail has 11 switchbacks to the top of the first ridge, and 10 more to the marshy meadow below Little Spangle Lake. Along the way you will have recrossed the small Middle Fork Boise River and several small tributaries. Outstanding views down the rugged canyon help ease the strain of the climb.

You cross west over the now tiny river at the bottom of the marshy meadow and climb gradually northwest to two more switchbacks up a low, timbered ridge. Turn north and step across the Middle Boise for the last time, make two more switchbacks west, turn northwest again through a gap, and come out by the northeast shore of Little Spangle Lake. Spangle Lake and a major trail junction are 200 yards north through a draw.

Spangle Lake is vaguely heart-shaped, more than a quarter mile across, obviously deep, and steep-sided except on the south side where it is separated from Little Spangle Lake by a low, rock ridge only a few yards wide. Lodgepole pines, whitebark pines and subalpine firs line the shoreline wherever they can gain a foothold. Little Spangle Lake is in a shallow basin just south of the larger lake. It is shallow, with a contorted and boggy shoreline and many islands. People have camped in poor sites between the two lakes, but the only good campsites are up a small valley on the northeast side of the big lake.

Small brook trout abound in both lakes, but Spangle Lake is hard to fly-fish because of steep banks and trees down to the waterline.

Spangle Lakes to Sand Mountain Pass

THOUSANDS OF FEET

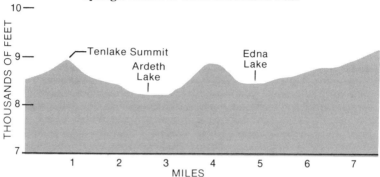

Tenlake Summit
Ardeth Lake
Edna Lake

MILES

The trail from Spangle Lakes junction to Tenlake Basin and Ardeth Lake climbs moderately northeast up the side of the ridge east of Spangle Lake. This is a well-maintained trail, recently rebuilt and heavily used by both foot and horse travelers. In a quarter mile you can look down into a little meadow beside the lake at the bottom of a small valley leading northeast. The only good campsites in the area are in the trees at the upper end of the meadow.

At less than a half mile you turn north across a small creek, double back, and contour around to recross the stream and make a longer leg back south to the nose of a higher ridge on the east side. Now climb moderately steeply northeast, then turn west to a rock shelf where this new trail crosses the trace of the old one running straight up the valley. Take off your pack for a few minutes and walk out to the edge of the shelf to admire the views south down Middle Boise Canyon, west across Spangle Lake to the snow-covered escarpments above Lake Ingeborg and east to Glens Peak. Two hundred yards of gradual climb northwest brings you to the thin line of gaunt, ancient whitebark pines at the ridgecrest. The crest is slightly less than a mile from Spangle junction.

From the top of the ridge west of Glens Peak you can see at least six of the many lakes in Tenlake Basin. The largest one is Ardeth Lake, about an airmile away and slightly east of north.

The north side of the ridge is talus except for a few granite knobs sticking through the broken rock. Eight new switchbacks descend moderately steeply through the talus to the first pond in the basin. In some years snow hangs on this north slope all summer, and you will have to stomp through it or glissade down across the switchbacks. However you get there, the trail passes the west side of the first small pond.

From the marshy pond the trail leads almost directly north, soon crossing two small creeks and then descending moderately down the west side of a valley running north to Ardeth Lake. After almost a mile in lodgepole pine and subalpine fir forest, you overlook a flat bordered by a beautiful beach on the southwest side of Ardeth Lake. Farther down, a side trail leads back to this camping area, but you may find it pretty crowded; horse packers maintain semipermanent camps here throughout the summer.

Hikers start down the north side of the Tenlake Divide

A quarter mile farther, at the outlet end of the lake, are a number of good campsites that would be rated excellent except for heavy use and shortage of firewood.

Spectacular sunsets seem to be staged at half mile-wide Ardeth Lake for the benefit of campers at the outlet camps; the setting sun flames the cliffs across the lake and the permanent snowfields on Glens Peak above—all reflected in almost perfect inverted image in the still waters below.

For the more mundane, fishing off the log jam at the outlet may produce fat brook trout to 12 inches.

Just west of the outlet creek is a junction with a trail that goes down the valley northwest to connect with the South Fork of Payette Trail. It's 17 miles downhill to Grandjean trailhead. Our trail skirts the north shore of Ardeth Lake, then climbs over a ridge to Edna Lake 2.5 miles east. The climb southeast up the ridge has 14 steep switchbacks not shown on the *Mount Everly* quadrangle, although it is an old trail. The tread is rocky and dusty through sparse timber, but there are compensating views across the lake and down northwest toward the South Fork of Payette.

Level off temporarily around a granite shoulder at the top of the switchbacks, then climb steeply again east to a gap in the ridge-crest. Just east of the gap a small, contorted lake, dotted with islands, lies in a shallow basin. Brook trout to 10–12 inches cruise lazily near the shore.

The trail skirts the north side of the lake and then, a quarter mile east, overlooks the basin containing Vernon, Edna and Virginia Lakes. From the trail, you can see only Vernon Lake and a small unnamed lake to the south under an almost 10,000-foot bare granite peak. Across the basin, 10,211-foot Payette Peak caps the vertical ridge north of Sand Mountain Pass.

The badly-worn trail on the east side of the ridge descends in nine switchbacks, varying from moderate to steep, over granite ledges with pockets of lodgepole and whitebark pines and subalpine firs. Turn north and east around Vernon Lake and across its outlet, then walk through a draw to come out above the east shore of Edna Lake. Vernon Lake is about 100 acres, Edna probably 200. Both are very pretty lakes with excellent campsites in the forest around gently sloping shorelines. Plenty of medium-sized brook trout challenge the fisherman.

As the trail climbs gradually northeast away from Edna Lake, there is a junction 2.5 miles from Ardeth Lake. The left fork follows the South Fork Payette River, which has its source

Backpacker and horse packers at Edna Lake

here, northwest to Grandjean. The right fork goes east over Sand Mountain Pass. On the right fork, we contour another quarter mile northwest, then climb four moderately steep switchbacks northeast up the side of a ridge. From here to Sand Mountain Pass the trail has been rebuilt and relocated from the route shown on the Snowyside Peak quadrangle.

Above the first switchback, circle east partway around a small valley. At the head of the valley, climb moderately around the shoulder of a ridge, cross the toe of a talus slope and make two switchbacks southeast beside the talus. You may see pikas busily storing hay in the broken rock. Continue east along the edge of more talus, then dip down slightly north to cross the lower end of a long, open valley. Climb moderately steeply to the top of a large moraine on the north side and continue climbing moderately east, then north, to come within

300 yards of shallow Lake 8861 in a grassy cup, a beautiful place for a rest stop before the final mile to the pass. By late August the water may even be warm enough to swim.

Between a quarter and a half mile east of Lake 8861, we start the first of eight new moderate switchbacks up the sandy slope of Sand Mountain. Many other ridges in the Sawtooths are talus all the way to the top, but this is the only one with slopes of sand and gravel all the way to the top on both sides. Apparently the surface granite has disintegrated completely and slid down the steep slopes east and west. This crest, like many others in the SNRA, has its row of contorted whitebark pines enduring in the most exposed and inhospitable location possible. About half of the lineup is dead snags, but it's a miracle that any of them survive at all, let alone grow to 30–40 feet, as many do before giving up.

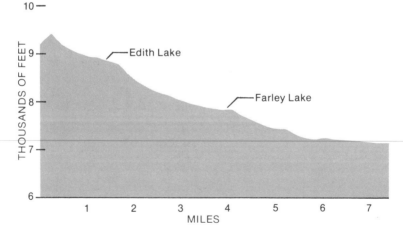

Sand Mountain Pass to Yellow Belly or Pettit Lake

Sand Mountain Pass tops out at a three-way junction on a narrow crest of sand and gravel between two peaks to the north and south. The west trail comes up from Edna Lake. The south trail contours around the east side of the south peak and drops down to Toxaway Lake at 2.1 miles. Our north trail starts climbing immediately around the west side of the north peak and eventually leads down past Edith and Farley lakes to Yellow Belly and Pettit lakes.

Make two long switchbacks up the west slope of the peak north of the pass, then contour north below the crest of the ridge to another saddle where the trail crosses over to the east side. As you go around the north face of the peak you've just passed, you have fine views down the canyon to Yellow Belly Lake and across Sawtooth Valley to the White Clouds and Castle Peak. Gnarled trunks of live and dead whitebark pines in the foreground frame the view.

Five new moderately steep switchbacks lead down north over rock ledges and talus to a small, wet meadow, then to another trail junction beside a tiny pond surrounded on three sides by talus slopes. You've come 1 mile from Sand Mountain Pass. Ahead to the north a trail snakes up a giant talus slope in at least a dozen switchbacks on its way to Imogene Lake on the north side of an east-west ridge. You could go out that way to Hell Roaring trailhead, but the shorter way is east past Edith Lake, a half mile below.

The upper part of Edith Lake trail is old, rough and badly worn. It starts down beside a creeklet flowing east from the pond by the junction, then skirts the bottom of a talus slide, under which the creeklet disappears. When the stream reappears below the talus, the trail crosses, recrosses and finally combines with it for a way.

A quarter mile from the junction the trail turns away from the stream on a shelf and descends moderately steeply down the north wall of the Edith Lake bowl. This part of the trail has been rebuilt, is easier to walk, and offers a good overview of jewel-like Edith Lake. The 25-acre, deep-blue lake lies in a cirque, open side east, with a small meadow and patch of subalpine fir below the cliffs on the west side. Excellent campsites are on both sides of the outlet near the trail crossing and at the edge of the trees on the west end. Fishing is excellent, but the brook trout are not very big.

One mile of semi-improved trail, not relocated much from the route on the *Snowyside Peak* quadrangle, descends from Edith Lake to a junction on the heavily traveled trail between Farley and Toxaway lakes. After crossing the outlet, you drop down the canyon east of Edith Lake at a moderate rate, crossing the creek twice in the first half mile. Below the second

Looking down at Edith and Farley lakes from the trail north of Sand Mountain Pass

crossing the trail turns south away from the creek and descends more steeply with a few switchbacks through sparse lodgepole pine and subalpine fir forest to the junction.

It is 4.5 miles from the Edith Lake Trail junction to Yellow Belly trailhead. There is no good place to camp between the junction and the trailhead. If your timing is such that you need to camp for another night, you would be well advised to stay at Edith Lake or find a campsite between the Edith Lake Trail junction and Toxaway Lake.

Northeast toward Farley Lake, you will be on one of the most heavily traveled trails in the SNRA, part of the Alice/Twin Lakes/Toxaway loop, Backcountry Trip 7. Heavy traffic has taken its toll: the tread is deeply rutted and rough, with exposed roots and rocks.

A quarter mile below the junction, drop down on two steep, short switchbacks to cross the outlet creek from Edith Lake. This is the last good drinking water on the trail above Farley Lake. For the next 2 miles the trail is well up on the northwest side of the wide, glaciated canyon. At 1 mile you overlook Farley Lake, filling the bottom of the canyon. The creek on the canyon floor falls over a granite dike into the lake and over another dike a short distance below the lake.

There are essentially no campsites at or near Farley Lake. Attempts at camping have been made in the thick spruce forest on the east side of the outlet. The unfortunate results have been a number of small forest fires.

Farley Lake has plenty of brook trout in it, a few to 12 inches, but it is very difficult to flyfish because of steep banks, trees to the water's edge and a consistent, strong down-canyon wind on summer afternoons and evenings. Much better fishing for good-sized brooks is available in ponds in the creek above the lake.

The trail runs along a boggy shelf crossed by many small steams and thick with Labrador tea bushes, 200–300 yards above the lake. The tread is on boardwalk and corduroy for some distance. A quarter mile below Farley Lake two steep switchbacks descend close to a waterfall. A moderately steep descent continues beside the creek for almost a half mile to an open flat studded with glacial erratic boulders and carpeted with wildflowers. Three new, moderate switchbacks take you down another dike at the lower end of the flat. After wandering through some piles of glacial debris, you arrive at the only crossing of the creek. The crossing was on two good, solid footlogs when we were there.

East of the creek, climb over a few low lateral moraines, then level out through spindly lodgepole pines to the Pettit Lake junction 1 mile from the crossing. From this junction it is a half mile straight ahead to the Yellow Belly trailhead and 1.8 miles south over the big moraine to Tin Cup Transfer Camp beside Pettit Lake.

Tin Cup Transfer Camp

7–Alice/Twin/Toxaway Lakes Loop

This delightful and very popular three- or four-day loop takes you through some of the most spectacular scenery on the east side of the Sawtooth range. The 20-mile trip can be extended 2.5 miles by adding Sand Mountain Pass and Edith Lake to the north side of the loop. This addition, plus a layover day somewhere and a little off-trail exploration, could easily extend the trip to a very pleasant week.

Although campsites at Alice and Toxaway lakes are heavily used, they are still in reasonably good condition and are rarely so overcrowded that you will feel uncomfortable. Other locations, some a short distance off-trail, offer more isolation and a better supply of firewood.

Unless you are very unlucky, you can count on fresh brook trout to supplement your diet; fishing is good in all the larger lakes, and even better in small ponds and lakelets in the connecting streams.

Stream crossings should not be a major problem, even in early summer, but you may find some remnant snow drifts on the north side of Snowyside Pass through July.

One **topo map**, *Snowyside Peak* quadrangle, covers the entire trip.

STARTING POINT

This trip begins and ends at Tin Cup Transfer Camp beside Pettit Lake. To get there, turn west from Highway 75 onto the Pettit Lake road 43 miles north of Ketchum. At a crossroad 1.7 miles from the highway, turn right across the outlet creek from the lake, then left beyond the bridge to continue a half mile beside the lake to a large parking area. This is Tin Cup Transfer Camp. The trail register is at the trailhead west of the parking lot.

Death camas and asters bloom just below Alice Lake—subalpine firs in the background

87

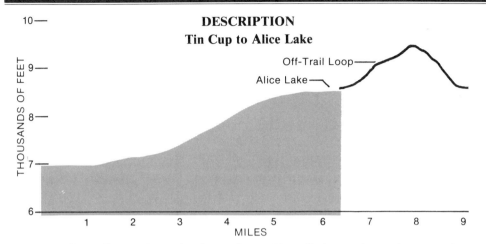

DESCRIPTION
Tin Cup to Alice Lake

THOUSANDS OF FEET

10—
9—
8—
7—
6—

Off-Trail Loop—

Alice Lake—

MILES
1 2 3 4 5 6 7 8 9

A quarter-mile-stroll west above the shore of Pettit Lake brings you to a junction with a trail north over the giant moraine between Pettit and Yellow Belly. You will come back that way.

Continue west on the excellent trail 100–200 feet from the lake. There may be families of mallard ducks along the shoreline and, until late August, the open, south-facing slope will be covered with wildflowers. Trout rising in the deep blue water just offshore may be a temptation to stop for a while, but you've just started.

At the upper end of Pettit Lake, 1.3 miles from the trailhead, the trail turns southwest through thick Douglas fir and lodgepole pine. The tread can be pretty mucky here early in the summer or after heavy rains. Tall monkshood blooms in the few openings. After a half mile in the woods, climb gradually on a glacial debris slope to the first crossing of Pettit Lake Creek, 2.3 miles from the trailhead. Cross on a log jam beside the ford. This crossing could be difficult during high runoff.

Climb moderately for a half mile in open forest southeast of the creek to a second crossing at the foot of a talus slide. A not-too-shaky footlog upstream from the ford will keep your feet dry if it's still there. Beyond a small moraine, start up a series of four new switchbacks built since the *Snowyside Peak* quadrangle was drawn. At the top of the moderate climb there are good views of 10,068-foot McDonald Peak, south across the valley, and down the valley across to the White Cloud Mountains on the eastern horizon. Below, a small beaver-dammed lake is barely visible through the trees.

You climb mostly south across the rocky slope, moderately for a quarter mile, then more steeply up a set of switchbacks and across a talus slope where pikas whistle constant alarms. Four more new switchbacks in talus bring you to another creek crossing and a pleasant walk up a wider stretch of valley, knee-deep in wildflowers—shooting stars, penstemons, sneezeweeds, sulfur flowers, Indian paintbrushes, yarrows, asters and sego lilies. As the valley steepens, cross the creek again to the northwest side and climb six new switchbacks to a cascade in a cleft of solid granite. Above the cleft you cross the creek on a genuine footbridge. A quarter mile or more above the bridge, an excellent campsite is on the side of the trail away from the creek.

The glacier-carved valley is wider now, studded with knobs of granite and lightly forested with subalpine fir. Cross the creek again (no bridge this time) and skirt the northwest sides of two small lakes. A heavily used campsite is in a lush meadow much too close to the second lake.

Just beyond the two small lakes and 5.9 miles from Tin Cup Transfer Camp, the trail approaches the north shore of Alice Lake, almost three quarters of a mile long and an average quarter mile wide. This beautiful alpine lake is set in a sculptured Sawtooth granite bowl and is surrounded by a thin line of subalpine fir and whitebark and lodgepole pines, except for the northwest side, where thicker forest steps back from the shoreline on a series of benches. As the trail turns west and starts to climb toward Twin Lakes, look for a side trail leading down to good campsites on the benches and an excellent site near a small inlet stream at the upper end of the lake. Firewood is getting scarce close to the campsites, so conserve as much as possible by using your stove. Fishing for brook trout in Alice Lake is very good, but you're not apt to catch any trophy-size fish.

Off-Trail Side Trip From Alice Lake

An extra day or two can be profitably spent exploring the large basin south of Alice Lake. A half dozen small lakes and a number of tiny streams provide water for innumerable isolated campsites. The scenery more than makes up for the lack of fish in the upper lakes.

Easiest way into the upper basin is to walk around the upper end of Alice Lake and pick your way up by the best route you can find east of the inlet creek coming in to Alice Lake from the south. Pockets of grass and heather, liberally sprinkled with alpine flowers, brighten the rocky route to an especially beautiful horseshoe-shaped lake .8 mile south and a little east. In a cirque farther southwest, permanent ice, half-covered with falling debris, lines one shore of the highest lake.

The terrain is steep, but not dangerous unless you try to climb the main ridge. It's a good opportunity to observe glaciation and alpine flora closeup and get away from other people on the trail for a while.

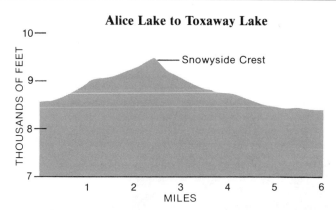

From the trail sign at Alice Lake, the trail slopes up gradually southwest through sparse timber until it comes close to a small creek. Beginning with two switchbacks here, the trail has been relocated to go north away from the creek and then west through a saddle to come out at 1 mile directly above the narrow band of rock separating the two Twin Lakes.

Twin Lakes basin is one of the more spectacular places in the Sawtooths. The unbelievably blue lakes fill the bottom of a large rose-and-russet-tinted cirque on the east side of the Sawtooth crest. Good campsites are in the relatively flat, sparsely forested area on both sides of the outlet stream from the lower lake. Fishing is good for brook trout to 10 or 12 inches.

The old trail ran along the northeast shore of the upper lake, then angled very steeply up the west wall of the cirque. Our new trail climbs moderately around the north side of the cirque, first looping around a side valley, then making two switchbacks up a talus slope. From the talus, climb moderately steeply west for more than a quarter mile to two more short switchbacks over a shoulder of rock. Before it passes through a narrow slot on the crest, the next quarter mile of trail is cut into the side of a very steep wall. The view down the side of the cirque gives the impression of looking between your toes at upper Twin Lake.

Snowyside Peak dominates the horizon southwest of this pass of the same name. It is a typical Sawtooth peak, formed of upthrust blocks of fractured pink and brown granite, surrounded by talus slopes. A permanent snowfield in a north-side cirque gives the peak its name. Northwest of the knife-edged crest two small lakes are visible in the rugged valley leading to Toxaway Lake. Just over the crest a network of tiny streams waters gardens of alpine flowers.

Fifteen new switchbacks between a tinkling stream and a massive, bare talus slide take you down the northwest side of Snowyside Pass at a moderately steep rate. Then traverses and switchbacks lead around the northeast sides of three small lakes in the bottom of the narrow valley. The second lake is light chalky blue due to glacial milk brought down by a snowmelt stream from Snowyside Peak. Below the third small lake and more switchbacks, Toxaway Lake comes into view as the trail makes a long traverse north away from the creek on a forested shoulder. More switchbacks and a couple of longer traverses complete the moderate descent to a crossing of the small creek where it slides and cascades over a series of granite shelves.

Detour around a wet meadow at the upper end of Toxaway Lake and begin climbing gradually around the northwest shore. A little over four miles from Twin Lakes you come to a junction with a trail leading north to Sand Mountain Pass. Virtually all of the trail from Twin Lakes to Toxaway Lake has been relocated and rebuilt since the *Snowyside Peak* quadrangle was published.

Toxaway is one of the largest glacial lakes in the interior of the Sawtooth range, almost a mile long and an average quarter mile wide. The lake fills the upper end of a wide valley that drains northeast to Yellow Belly Lake. A spectacular vista of high peaks, including Snowyside and another pyramidal peak of more than 10,000 feet, rises above the upper end of the lake. Abundant, fat brook trout to 12 or 13 inches await your fly or lure. Many good campsites are in subalpine fir groves on the benches between the trail and the northwest shore of the lake. A designated horse packers' camp and tie area is directly below the trail junction.

Permanent snowfield on the northwest side of Snowyside Peak

Toxaway to Pettit Lake

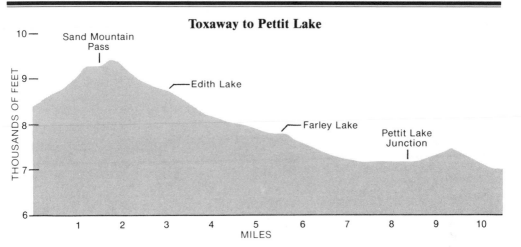

You have a choice of two routes from the trail junction on the northwest side of Toxaway Lake: straight down the valley or a 4-mile scenic detour by way of Sand Mountain and Edith Lake.

The trail leading 2.1 miles northwest to Sand Mountain Pass climbs moderately steeply up a long series of rebuilt traverses and switchbacks before contouring around the near side of buff-colored Sand Mountain to the pass itself. From the pass follow the route described in Backcountry Trip 6 to Edith Lake and back down to the trail junction between Toxaway and Farley Lakes.

From the Toxaway junction the trail down the valley contours, descending gradually, past the outlet end of the big lake and two small lakes along the creek to meet the trail from Edith Lake at 1.5 miles. The route from this junction past Farley Lake to the Pettit Lake junction is described in Backcountry Trip 6.

From the Pettit Lake junction, a half mile west of Yellow Belly Lake, a moderate climb of .9 mile on recently rebuilt trail brings you to the top of the moraine north of Pettit Lake. From the top it's an easy coast diagonally down the south side to the Pettit Lake trail and thence to a cold drink from the ice-box in your car at Tin Cup Transfer Camp.

Weathered remains of a whitebark pine in a talus slide

A thin, ragged line of whitebark pines stands at the top of Sand Mountain Pass

8–Hell Roaring and Imogene Lakes

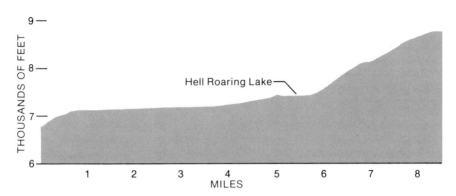

Watch the rising sun touch first the crooked granite tor called "The Finger of Fate" across Hell Roaring Lake from your campsite. Soon the serrated ridge behind the "Finger" shares the rosy glow. As a layer of mist rises from the still surface of the lake, a perfect inverted image appears, interrupted here and there by trout rises. Wisps of blue wood smoke drift overhead through pointed spires of subalpine fir and last evening's catch will soon be sizzling in the pan.

That's only the beginning of a three- or four-day, 18.5-mile round trip on excellent trails through magnificent scenery to some of the best lake fishing in the Sawtooths at Imogene Lake. Experienced (and preferably guided) rock climbers may want to test their skills on the "Finger" and other peaks along the ridge.

A semiloop trip of about the same length is possible by climbing over the ridge south of Imogene Lake and coming out at Yellow Belly or Pettit Lake, provided you can arrange a car-shuttle or pick-up at the other end.

There are no dangerous stream crossings and, except for the ridge south of Imogene Lake, snow should be off the trails by early July.

Topo maps are *Obsidian, Mt. Cramer and Snowyside Peak* quadrangles.

Starting Point

The road to Hell Roaring Lake trailhead turns west off Highway 75 almost directly opposite Fourth of July Creek road, 4 miles south of Obsidian and near milepost 174. As of 1986, the road was not signed on Highway 75. A half mile of dirt road leads directly west to a bridge across the Salmon River and the trailhead west of a **T** at the Decker Flat road.

A four-wheel-drive road that ran 3 miles up into Hell Roaring Valley below the lake may be closed when you read this.

DESCRIPTION

A sign at the trailhead just west of the Salmon River bridge gives distances of 5.2 miles to Hell Roaring Lake and 9.3 miles to Imogene Lake. Climb moderately steeply northwest for the first .3 mile on a poor tread, badly worn into glacial deposits interspersed with large boulders. The trail improves as it levels off on a bench, then climbs again, turning west around jumbled mounds of moraine material. One mile from the trailhead continue past a sign for Roaring Ridge trail. This trail doesn't appear on any maps and doesn't look as it if has been used.

Another .5 mile of short ups and downs through more piles of glacial debris forested with spindly lodgepole pines brings you into a wide, flat valley where Hell Roaring Creek belies its name by meandering quietly in contorted oxbows. The floor of the valley is sparsely wooded with small lodgepole pines and occasional groves of spruce and aspen. Grass, willows, Labrador tea and bush cinquefoil blend in a lush understory.

An excellent campsite is a few yards beyond where the trail approaches the creek. Small, spooky rainbow trout can be stalked in the crystal-clear sandy-bottomed stream but are hardly worth the trouble unless you are camping here and need them for breakfast.

Proceed on mostly level, good trail up the north side of the valley for another 2 miles, then climb gradually up the north side of the valley for 1.4 miles to the last moderately steep quarter mile over a terminal moraine damming the lower end of Hell Roaring Lake. Just over the hump, in big subalpine firs, is a junction signed "IMOGENE LAKE – 4.1" to the left and "REDFISH LAKE – 10.0" to the right. The Redfish trail, starting steeply north up the ridge, is little used.

A good campsite, with a troughed spring, is between the junction and Hell Roaring Lake. The Imogene trail to the left crosses Hell Roaring Creek on a bridge just below the outlet and 50 yards from the trail junction. As the trail turns southwest along the shoreline there are a number of good campsites on higher ground to the left.

Most of half-mile-long Hell Roaring Lake has a marshy shoreline, backed by heavy forest of subalpine fir and lodgepole pine. West, across the lake, crooked "Finger of Fate" rises in front of an extremely rugged Sawtooth ridge. Farther southwest the tip of Mt. Cramer is barely visible above a crenelated mesa closer to the lake. A log jam of several acres fills the outlet end of the lake providing cover for small brook trout that will rise avidly to flies morning and evening.

White-flowering parrot's beak borders the trail in marshy areas along the southeast shore of Hell Roaring Lake. Near the upper end of the lake a branch trail goes west to more good campsites under magnificent tall subalpine firs. Our trail continues southwest and soon begins climbing moderately up switchbacks on the east side of a large moraine ridge. More than a mile of trail has been relocated and rebuilt here, snaking back and forth across the brow of the ridge and the trace of the old trail which went straight up the ridge without any switchbacks. None of the new trail is more than moderately steep.

Level, but sometimes boggy, trail along the south shore of Hell Roaring Lake

You level out on a glacier-littered flat for .3 mile, then climb moderately on new switchbacks again to the west side of a low north-south ridge. A half mile of gradual climb up a valley brings you to a pond half-covered with water lilies and then a small grassy-shored lake. The upper end of the lake offers a good view of Mt. Cramer filling the western sky. Cross the small inlet creek and proceed south in a shallow

Ancient whitebark pine snag among the crags above Imogene Lake

canyon with solid granite on your right and rough moraine on your left. Beyond another pond in the creek .3 mile from the lake, climb two switchbacks on the west side of the canyon. As the trail turns south again, a waterfall is below on your left. The trail crosses the stream between the top of the falls and a cascade. Now climb gradually another .3 mile south over a low ridge to an overlook above the north end of Imogene Lake.

Imogene Lake, slightly larger than Hell Roaring, is kidney-shaped, with three or four islands and almost-islands. Much of the shoreline is steep, except for a marshy area around the inlet. Large brook and cutthroat trout cruise the deep water just offshore, rising for live and artificial flies even in the middle of the day. A 16-incher is not uncommon, and bigger ones have been landed.

Excellent campsites are on benches well above the north and northwest sides of the lake. A new, well-built trail follows the east shore. An old trail around the west side of the lake is still usable all the way to the inlet.

You have a choice now of returning the way you came or climbing the almost innumerable switchbacks 2.1 miles over the talus-both-sides ridge south of Imogene Lake to the Edith Lake junction and going on out to Yellow Belly Lake by way of Edith or Toxaway Lake (see description in Backcountry Trips 6 and 7). A little-used trail does connect the trailhead at Yellow Belly to a road at Mays Creek, 1.5 miles from the Hell Roaring trailhead, completing a loop.

Four small lakes lie in a basin west of the upper end of Imogene Lake, overlooked by 10,211-foot Payette Peak. They are well worth a day of off-trail exploration in relatively safe terrain. Fantastic scenery and a number of high cirque lakes are higher up around the north side of Mt. Cramer from Imogene Lake, but the off-trail approaches are tricky and dangerous and should be attempted only by experienced mountaineers.

9–Redfish Lake Creek and Cramer Lakes

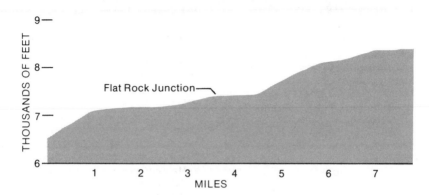

With the help of the Redfish Lake ferry, a moderate day of hiking will put you on the shore of Middle Cramer Lake in time to fish for good-sized brook trout while admiring a 20-foot waterfall plunging directly into the lake. Along the way you walk through a deep green canyon beside rushing Redfish Lake Creek. On both sides of the canyon are some of the best-known and most often climbed peaks in the Sawtooths. A day at alpine Cramer Lakes and a short day's walk back to Redfish Lake Inlet add up to a three-day trip. Distance is 7 miles each way.

If you want more solitude, you can climb the steep trail over the 9,500-foot ridge south of Upper Cramer and go on to aptly named Hidden Lake. Then, if you have more time and a lot of energy, you can continued on a rugged 36-mile loop to Edna Lake, Sand Mountain Pass, Imogene and Hell Roaring lakes, and back to Redfish Lake Inlet. Some of this route is described in Backcountry Trips 6 and 8. Don't try it in early summer—there will be a lot of snow in the higher elevations.

The first section of trail from Red-fish Lake Inlet to Flat Rock junction is heavily traveled. The creek ford at the junction can be dangerous.

The trip is on two **topo maps**, *Mt. Cramer* and *Warbonnet Peak* quadrangles.

STARTING POINT

Redfish Lake road junction, leading west from Highway 75, is 4.5 miles south of Stanley and .5 mile north of the Highway 75 bridge over the Salmon River, near milepost 185. Two miles up the Redfish Lake road, before you get to the visitor center, a sign on the right points to the backpackers' parking lot. Although you can go on around to Redfish Lodge to unload your packs, you must leave your vehicle here. Do not park in the campgrounds, in picnic areas or near the lodge.

From the parking lot or the lodge you can take the ferry or walk 5.5 miles over the Bench Trail to Redfish Lake Inlet Transfer Camp. Unless you are riding a horse or want to see Bench Lakes, the ferry is much the better choice. Make reservations for the ferry by calling Redfish Lodge. However, you can usually get on the next trip without a reservation by walking out on the dock with your pack. Be sure to arrange a time for a pick-up at the inlet when you want to come back. The operator is very good about meeting appointments, but he can't wait very long if you're not there at the appointed time.

The pleasant 15-minute ferry ride offers magnificent views of Heyburn Mountain and The Grand Mogul at the head of the lake.

DESCRIPTION

Redfish Lake Inlet Transfer Camp is a developed campground with a pit toilet, fire pits, picnic tables and a pole fence to keep horses from wandering through the grassy people-area. Boaters use it often for overnight camping and picnicking. Trails lead north, south and west from the camp. Our trail leads west up the creek. Sign in at the trail register 200 yards from the camp, then climb gradually in heavy timber beside the north bank of the creek for a half mile. Next you come out on an open slope at the foot of majestic Heyburn Mountain, and climb two moderate switchbacks to a junction with the Bench Trail. As you contour southwest around the base of Heyburn Mountain, there are innumerable opportunities for picture-taking.

Two miles from the lake along the good but heavily traveled trail, a number of house-sized boulders have fallen from the northwest wall of the canyon. Niches and caves under some of these provide shelter from storms for hikers and climbers. The granite on both sides of this canyon is solid, not shattered as it is in much of the Sawtooth range. Good rock and easy access combine to make it a popular place for rock climbing.

The rest of the way to Flat Rock junction is a moderate climb, mostly through heavy timber—lodgepole pine, subalpine fir and spruce—not far from the rushing creek and occasional waterfalls. Glimpses of magnificent domes and spires appear from time to time on both sides through breaks in the trees.

Just beyond a trail sign at Flat Rock junction, the Cramer Lakes Trail fords Redfish Lake Creek to the east side as the canyon turns south. The crossing for hikers is on a log jam 50 yards downstream. If the creek is high, you may want to wade above a granite shelf 200 yards upstream. Below the shelf on the west side of the creek an excellent campsite is sheltered in a grove of spruce.

The first .5 mile of the Cramer Lakes Trail is a delightful saunter, almost level, in open forest not far from the east bank of Redfish Lake Creek. The quiet creek slides over granite shelves and under overhanging spruce trees with hardly a murmur. Begin climbing up the east side of the valley and, 1 mile from Flat Rock junction, two new switchbacks not on the *Warbonnet Peak* quadrangle gain altitude moderately to the level of a hanging valley leading southeast. Continue almost level for another 1.3 miles around a shoulder and onto the northeast side of the valley, overlooking a small unnamed lake on the valley floor. Cross a small creek coming down from the east and climb moderately east of another creek for a quarter mile to the shore of Lower Cramer Lake.

The three beautiful, alpine Cramer Lakes are in granite cups, strung together within a half mile by a connecting creek. The lakes are progressively bigger from lower to upper. Upper Cramer Lake (about 75 acres) is directly under the rugged face of a towering 10,500-foot peak north of Mt. Cramer. A 20-foot waterfall, fed by the connecting creek from Upper Cramer, plunges directly into Middle Cramer. Large brook trout feed lazily in the deep water below the falls where it's very difficult to fish for them. Plenty of smaller trout cruise in more easily reached spots around the shorelines of all three lakes.

A number of good campsites are on the north side of the trail as it skirts the lower and middle lakes, and on the north end of the granite shelf between the middle and upper lakes. The trail turns south around Upper Cramer Lake and starts the climb over a high ridge to Hidden Lake and points beyond. Cramer Lakes are not usually overcrowded, but south of the ridge you will encounter hardly anyone until you get close to Virginia Lake, 5 miles south.

It's an easy half-day, all-downhill walk back to Redfish Inlet and the ferry.

Returning backpackers board the ferry at Redfish Lake inlet

The falls into Middle Cramer Lake

10–Alpine Way Trail—Stanley Ranger Station to Iron Creek

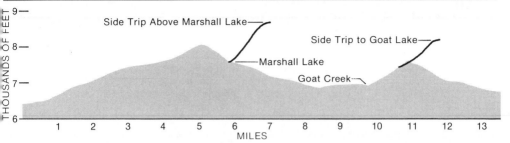

Alpine Way Trail snakes along the east side of the northern Sawtooths from Stanley Ranger Station north to Stanley Lake. It is an excellent early-season trip, giving you a chance to get close to the highest peaks without having to wade through a lot of snow. Wildflowers should be at their best between 7,000 and 8,000 feet during the first two weeks of July. Crossings of Goat and Iron creeks may be chilly and uncomfortable, but shouldn't be dangerous.

You will need a car-shuttle or pickup for this two- or three-day trip covering 13.5 miles—approximately the south half—of the Alpine Way.

The **topo maps**, *Stanley* and *Stanley Lake* quadrangles, can be deceiving. The trail appears to contour most of the way, but actually has a lot of ups and downs, some of them steep. Only Marshall Lake and Goat Lake (off-trail) have fish. The few streams are too small to fish.

This is one of the few places in the SNRA where you will need to carry water. The first 5 miles from the trailhead have no water at all and it's a long way between drinks on other parts of the trail. It is a nonvehicular trail. Foot

traffic is normally light, but day rides from the Redfish Corral go as far as Marshall Lake. They don't stay long, though.

STARTING POINT
Less than a half mile south of the Stanley Ranger Station, a dirt road turns west off Highway 75. Across the sheep driveway paralleling the highway, the road deteriorates to a jeep track and you will see a sign for the Alpine Way Trail. Park where you can find room among the lodgepole pines

Directions to Iron Creek Trailhead, for your pick-up or shuttle, are in Backcountry Trip 11.

DESCRIPTION
The jeep track becomes a foot trail after .3 mile of level walking southward. After another mostly level .3 mile amid glacial debris and sparse lodgepole pines, the trail turns southwest and starts climbing moderately up the brow of a moraine ridge. About 1 mile from the trailhead, where the trail turns more west across an open grassy area on top of the ridge, you come to a junction with a trail coming up the south side of the ridge from the Redfish Corral. There was no sign at this junction when we were there and the trail is not on the *Stanley* quadrangle. The heavily used horse trail appears to cross the Alpine Way, but actually it only makes a small loop and rejoins the trail a little farther up.

Continue almost level for .5 mile west across a jumbled moraine area, then start climbing moderately again just below the north side of the crest of the long, steep-sided moraine north of Fishhook Valley. Another trail junction with a trail from Fishhook Valley, and a trail register, are 2.7 miles from the trailhead. This trail is not on the topo map either, but there is a

Heyburn Mountain dominates the skyline south of Fishhook Valley

sign this time, pointing 1 mile to Fishhook Creek and 2 miles to Redfish Lake.

Your trail continues to climb moderately west in the edge of timber north of the ridgecrest. Take time to detour slightly along the open top of the ridge to see the spectacular view of the head of Fishhook Valley and The Grand Mogul, Heyburn Mountain (very different from this side), Thompson Peak and Williams Peak on the skyline. In early June there is also a profuse display of wildflowers—wyethia, sego lilies, lupine, blue penstemon, scarlet gilia, groundsel, bitterbrush, fleabane, alpine daisies and false dandelion.

A mile above the Fishhook junction, the top of the moraine ridge widens out into a parklike bench—open lodgepole forest with a grass floor. Next turn a little more north and climb moderately steeply over moraine ridges for a half mile, then turn sharply north and contour around an east buttress of Williams Peak. The pleasant walk passes through lush fir forest and open fields of flowers on a smooth tread cut into the steep east-facing slope. The open slope offers beautiful views across to the White Clouds and the north face of Heyburn to the south. At the north end of the half-mile, level contour you drop over the top of an east-leading moraine and diagonal west down its steep north side into a basin containing Marshall Lake. Splashing waterfalls on the west side of the basin are a most welcome sight and sound after 5 miles of dry trail.

Deep, blue-green Marshall Lake lies below on the north side of the quarter-mile-wide basin. A smaller hourglass-shaped, light turquoise pond nestles under the basin's south wall. Willows and a few beaver ponds fill the rest of the swampy floor of the basin, except for a tongue of trees along the lake's south shore. The trail descends in two switchbacks down the east edge of the bowl to the outlet creek, where excellent campsites are near the trail in mature Douglas fir forest. Additional excellent campsites, with a breeze and fewer mosquitoes, are in the lodgepole pines around the lake's north side. You'll also be closer to superb evening flyfishing for brook trout to 12 inches. Trees and willows along the shore may force you to wade a little, but it's worth it.

It's also worth the effort and the two or three hours required to climb a half mile and 1,000 feet higher over the wall by the waterfalls to an unnamed lake set in a bare granite cirque under the north face of Williams Peak. There is no trail to the lake, which is about the same size as Marshall, but it's fairly easy to pick your way up over granite ledges north of the falls. Once over the top, follow the outlet stream to the pristine lake rimmed with whitebark pines. Cliffs rise above the south side. In early July, 15-inch trout cruised the edge of the just-melting ice looking for something to eat. We had left our rods at Marshall Lake.

From Marshall Lake, start out north, then east down the valley of the outlet creek. Good trail, not as dusty from horse traffic now, descends moderately through heavy lodgepole and fir forest, coming close to the creek for a short distance before turning north out of the valley to curve around the shoulder of a mountain. The trail is not as well defined or maintained here and, in an area where pine beetles have killed a lot of lodgepole pines, many deadfalls

Dinner cooking at Marshall Lake

are across the tread. Continue around the mountain, descending gradually west, and then northwest to the Meadow Creek trail junction 3 miles (although the sign at the junction says 2 miles) from Marshall Lake. The Meadow Creek Trail goes east 1 mile to a road that returns to the Stanley Ranger Station.

From the Meadow Creek junction you climb moderately steeply west up a ridge, then turn north on the crest for 200–300 yards before crossing over to descend diagonally down the northwest side. As you top the ridge you will see and hear Goat Creek falls through the trees. Drop down to a shelf above Goat Creek canyon, then down again through a small gully and out onto a mound offering a good view of the falls. We then switchback northwest and descend to cross Goat Creek below what used to

The lake on the bench above Marshall Lake— still partially frozen in early July

be a lake, now a boggy flat with willow thickets and clumps of tall firs.

Crossing Goat Creek is not dangerous, but you do have to wade and the water is icy cold. There are excellent campsites in the edge of the forest below a wide avalanche path on the north side of the creek. Plenty of firewood has been brought down by the avalanche, which ran across the creek from the south ridge.

For a closer look at Goat Creek falls, follow the trail north to a shelf, then parallel Goat Creek upstream a quarter mile, cross the creek in a shallow canyon and climb back up southwest beside a tributary where you look almost straight up at the falls.

Having viewed the falls, you pick up the trail again where it diagonals southwest up the side of a steep ridge before making two long switchbacks (not shown on the *Stanley Lake* quadrangle) to cross over the ridgetop. Look for some giant Douglas firs along the way with snowbends at their bases. At the first switchback, you look across the basin to a high ribbon fall south of Goat Creek Falls. Williams and Thompson peaks loom up farther south on the skyline. It's possible to climb on around the basin from here (first on the old trail, then cross-country) past a granite knob and up beside the creek to Goat Lake, .8 mile southwest. It's spectacular scenery, but a very tough climb.

Back on the Alpine Way, you pass through a gap in the ridgetop and descend northwest along an east slope in sparse lodgepole pine. Then turn west around a point 1.8 miles from Goat Creek and drop down steeply into a ravine running north to Iron Creek. The trail goes down the bottom of the ravine for .3 mile, crisscrossing a tiny creek in disintegrated granite sand. At the bottom of the ravine, you turn west on the south side of the wide Iron Creek valley for .4 mile before going north to cross Iron Creek. An old footbridge has washed out, but may be replaced by the time you arrive. We crossed on a log jam 150 yards downstream.

On the north side of Iron Creek, Alpine Way meets the Sawtooth Lake Trail and combines with it for .6 mile going west, then north. Our trail turns east at the junction and descends at a gradual rate for 1 mile to the Iron Creek trailhead and transfer camp. A description of the smooth, wide, heavily traveled Iron Creek-to-Sawtooth Lake trail is in Backcountry Trip 11.

11–Iron Creek to Sawtooth and Stanley Lakes

Sawtooth Lake and Mount Regan must be the most photographed scene in the SNRA, and with good reason. They present a truly beautiful combination that is relatively easy to reach on a day hike of 9.8 miles, round-trip, on a well maintained trail. On the way you pass Alpine Lake, hanging in a pocket below 9,861-foot Alpine Peak.

The three- to four-day, one-way backpack trip starts with Alpine and Sawtooth lakes, goes west over the ridge north of Regan Mountain, doubles back to good fishing at delightful Trail Creek Lakes and ends up north at Stanley Lake for a total of 17 miles. To avoid having to arrange for a pick-up or car shuttle, or simply to see

Sawtooth Lake and Mount Regan with a skiff of September snow

more country, you can make a 23.5 mile loop by returning from Stanley Lake to Iron Creek on the Alpine Way Trail. Without the sidetrip to Trail Creek Lakes, the loop is 20 miles. A 2-mile, steep sidetrip to Hanson Lakes can be added and there are two other possible final destinations for one-way trips: Grandjean and Elk Creek.

The trail as far as Sawtooth Lake is heavily used and, because of over-use of the few campsites, you can no longer camp east of the main ridge. West of the ridge, traffic is relatively light and there are plenty of campsites, although firewood is getting scarce at a few of them.

One **topo map**, The *Stanley Lake*

quadrangle, covers the trip to Stanley Lake and the loop back to Iron Creek. If you want to go out to Elk Creek or Grandjean, you will need the *Elk Meadow* or *Grandjean* quadrangles.

STARTING POINT

Iron Creek road junction is 2.5 miles west of Stanley on Highway 21, just beyond where the highway curves northwest. The good gravel road ends with a loop at Iron Creek Transfer Camp, 3 miles from the highway. The parking lot is on the outside of the loop. A large signboard marks the trailhead at the upper end of the parking lot, and includes a trail map and distances to various points.

To get to Stanley Lake at the end of the one-way trip, turn west off Highway 21 at the Stanley Lake sign 5 miles northwest of Stanley. The trailhead is at the Inlet campground, 3.2 miles from the highway on a good gravel road. Please do not leave your car in a campsite; there are other places to park.

DESCRIPTION
Iron Creek to Trail Creek Junction

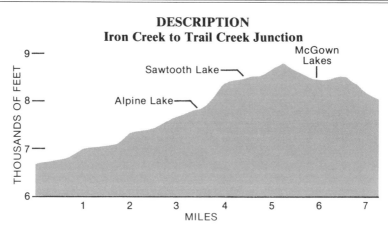

Starting from the Iron Creek trailhead on an excellent, wide trail, you climb very gradually southwest in a lodgepole pine flat for .3 mile before coming close to the creek for a short way. A trail register is in the middle of the flat. From the register you climb moderately over jumbled moraine material north of the creek, and come to the wilderness boundary at 1 mile. Two hundred yards from the boundary, in a wide, grassy valley, is a junction with the Alpine Way Trail leading south. (see Backcountry Trip 10).

After skirting the north side of a large meadow, you climb moderately over a small moraine, then turn north around a boggy flat to the north junction with the Alpine Way, .6 mile from the south junction. You will return to this junction from Stanley Lake if you decide to do the loop trip.

Our trail turns southwest, angling up a slope past large Douglas firs bent at the base of their trunks by the downhill pressure of the snow when the trees were little. Next, climb moderately up four short switchbacks, much as indicated on the *Stanley Lake* quadrangle, and continue climbing gradually west on the north side of Iron Creek valley. As you progress around the head of the valley, note the change from Idaho to Sawtooth granite in the peaks above you and in the deteriorated granite gravel of the trail tread.

Turn south and cross small Iron Creek 3.3 miles from the trailhead. South of the creek you climb a series of 15 new switchbacks to the top of a steep ridge, where you can look south through the trees down to beautiful little Alpine Lake. A steep side trail drops 200 yards through a thick stand of subalpine firs to the north shore. Thanks to a ban on camping after years of abuse, Alpine Lake is beginning to look pristine again, but fishing still isn't much.

Sixteen more rebuilt switchbacks climb west back and forth across the nose of the ridge above Alpine Lake. At the top of the ridge there are magnificent views of the peaks north and south and down the valley east to Stanley. None of the rebuilt trail from Iron Creek to the ridgetop is more than moderately steep.

A short traverse west leads to more short switchbacks up a wall and through a slot into the lower end of an alpine valley. Pass the south side of a small tarn and climb up slightly into the basin of Sawtooth Lake. This deep, oval lake is the largest lake in the Sawtooth Wilderness—.9 mile long and .4 mile wide—filling the bottom of a solid granite bowl where only a few trees cling to the rocky shoreline. Regan Mountain towers on the southwest skyline, directly opposite where the trail comes in. This basin was once a cirque from which a very large glacier flowed south and cut the wide, **U**-shaped valley that now holds the headwaters of the North Fork Baron Creek. Oddly, the lake now drains through a gap in the northeast wall of the cirque down into Iron Creek rather than south into Baron Creek.

Just south of a trail junction beside the outlet, a granite knob sticks up from the shoreline, offering a good vantage point to view the lake. An unusual feature of this knob is a number of completely flattened Douglas firs growing from cracks in the top of the rock. How they got here, where only subalpine firs normally grow, is a mystery. A trail to Baron Creek, and eventually Grandjean, runs along the east shore of the lake and south through the glacier-cut gap. Our trail

starts north with two switchbacks in talus, then turns west to climb in a long traverse across the north wall of the basin.

All along this moderate .5-mile climb are magnificent views of Sawtooth Lake and Regan Mountain. Two more new, moderately steep switchbacks complete the climb to the top of the ridge on the northwest side of the bowl, and then the trail descends, zigzagging west down a wide valley. A half mile from the crest, we pass north of the first and largest of the McGown Lakes in a shallow, inhospitable, bare rock basin. Two hundred yards farther west, the trail runs between two tiny lakes with a few trees and a couple of poor campsites, then turns southwest over a low hump to switchback down a steeper valley to a flat basin with large timber—subalpine fir, lodgepole and whitebark pine. A number of good campsites are in this basin, but the only water is a small, marshy lake at the north end.

From this basin you climb moderately steeply southwest over a ridge and descend 15 switchbacks down a rocky slope. At the bottom of the moderately steep descent, at the top of the divide between Stanley Lake Creek and Trail Creek, is a trail junction. Good campsites are among the large subalpine firs in the saddle, but you will have to go down at least a quarter mile in either direction to get water. West across the intersection, a trail leads up 1 mile to the top of 9,151-foot Observation Peak, aptly named since it overlooks most of the northern Sawtooth range and is topped by a fire lookout tower.

Side Trip to Trail Creek Lakes

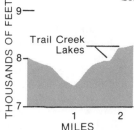

From the Sawtooth Lake junction, the trail down Trail Creek canyon contours down the east slope at a moderate rate as the deep canyon

drops away south. After crossing two small creeklets, where there are fair campsites, the trail levels off on a shelf where the main stem of Trail Creek cascades down from the east. The junction for Trail Creek Lakes is north of the creek in heavy timber, .7 mile from the junction on the divide. The trail down Trail Creek canyon drops down west beside the creek. The lakes trail goes straight ahead across the creek. A few good campsites are under big subalpine firs north of the creek.

Beyond the boggy crossing, our trail climbs moderately up the nose of a ridge to a rim overlooking precipitous Trail Creek canyon as it turns west toward Grandjean. Almost everything above this observation point has been heavily glaciated, whereas the canyon below shows the typical narrow **V** of unglaciated erosion. The Sawtooth glaciers were amazing and unique for the remarkable amount of rock they carved from the crests without ever going very far down the canyons.

From this viewpoint you turn east and climb steeply for a quarter mile, on a rough, eroded tread, to a good-sized bench bordered by a creek on the north and a steep talus slope on the south. Excellent campsites are here in a grove of subalpine firs. A large colony of pikas whistle and work in the talus.

One more steep pitch of 200 yards above the bench brings you to the first and largest of the Trail Creek Lakes. It's a gorgeous lake of about 15 acres with a high, pyramidal peak rising directly from the southeast shore. Big brook trout, at least 15 inches long, swim in the deep, crystal-clear water just off the rocky shoreline. The trail ends at several excellent campsites on a flat beside the outlet. More good campsites are in a small timbered valley on the east side that offers a route up to more lakes on a bench above.

If you can tear yourself away from this idyllic place (we were helped along by an early fall snowstorm), return 1.6 miles to the divide junction by the way you came.

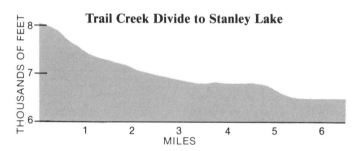

Trail Creek Divide to Stanley Lake

The Stanley Lake Creek Trail descends moderately north on the west side of a wide valley, coming close to the creek at .6 mile where it falls down a narrow canyon. Continue well up on the west slope for a short distance, then drop down steeply in open forest to the wilderness boundary .9 mile from the divide. What has been a good footpath now becomes a jeep track that once led to the Greenback Mine, high on the mountain to the west. The trail is now closed to motorized travel for another 2 miles north to the Hanson Lakes junction.

Below the wilderness boundary, you drop down some rudimentary switchbacks, level out and cross the creek to the east side. Then climb a little up the east slope and continue descending moderately above the tumbling creek. Less than a half mile from the crossing is an unsigned, and not very evident, junction with a trail that climbs up a side canyon and goes over the high ridge west to Elk Creek. It's a little-used trail and, if you want to go to Elk Meadow, you will have to find the trail in the side canyon on the other side of the creek.

Another 1.5 miles down the east side of the valley, over alluvial fans and avalanche paths, and through bands of lodgepole pine and Douglas fir, brings you to a junction for Bridal Veil Falls and Hanson Lakes. This trail is not shown on the *Stanley Lake* quadrangle, but it is there and you can see Bridal Veil Falls across the canyon. Hanson Lakes are 1 mile away, a very steep climb up the west wall.

On a definite jeep road now, open to motorized travel, descend gradually down the wider valley, where the creek meanders through willow thickets and meadows for 1.5 miles, and cross the creek to the west side. Detour away from the creek northwest over a bench and drop down a small valley northeast into dense forest of spruce, lodgepole and Douglas fir. The reason for the detour becomes apparent when you can hear, but not see, Lady Face Falls a quarter mile east.

You soon break out of the forest into a wide meadow with bands of lodgepole pines and willows. A half mile of level walking in the meadow beside a meandering creeklet brings you to a junction with the Alpine Way Trail going south. If you're making the complete loop to Iron Creek, this is the way back. Toward Stanley Lake, the trail continues much the same for a mile before tunneling through a final quarter mile of dense willow thicket to the trailhead by the inlet.

Surprise snow in September on the Trail Creek Divide

12–Elk Creek and Elizabeth Lake

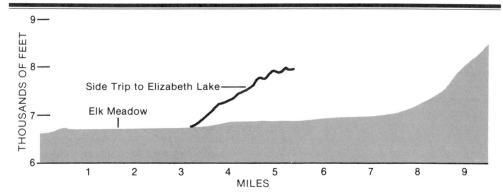

Where in the world can you wade, literally, through hundreds of acres of shooting stars, buttercups, marsh marigolds and dandelions while looking up to an unbelieveable backdrop of snow-covered peaks? Elk Meadow, that's where! The best time to see a sea of wildflowers is late June or early July. Farther up the canyon above the meadow, mushrooms pop out of the pine duff, whiter than the snowbanks beside them, and fat, light biscuit-colored puff-balls (safe to eat as long as the inside is firm and pure white) add a much-appreciated delicacy to the backpacker's diet.

You can go into the meadow in one day or, you can, in three days, continue to the head of the canyon and back, with a side trip to see the ice breaking up (and maybe catch a big trout) at Elizabeth Lake. If you wait until later in the year, you will be able to get over the ridge to come out at Grandjean or Stanley Lake and you won't have to wade so much water in the meadow, but you won't see all the flowers. The round trip, including Elizabeth Lake, is 20 miles.

Topo maps are *Elk Meadow, Grandjean* and *Banner Summit* quadrangles.

Marsh marigolds bloom as soon as the snow melts

STARTING POINT

At a crossroad on Highway 21, 8.5 miles northwest of Stanley and 3.5 miles beyond the Stanley Lake road, a sign, "ELK MEADOW 4" points southwest. Four miles reaches almost to the upper end of Elk Meadow and includes some trail. The trailhead is at a small meadow below Elk Meadow, 2.4 miles from the highway. The first 1.8 miles is good gravel road to a house beside Elk Creek. Beyond the house the road is basic dirt and rocks, and you may have trouble negotiating it in a modern sedan.

DESCRIPTION

The trail register and numerous excellent campsites are in a lodgepole pine grove on the north side of the small lower meadow. A jeep track continues southwest from the register and climbs moderately over a low hump through the trees for .7 mile to come out beside the lower end of Elk Meadow. The topo map shows a trail leading northwest from here a half mile to Lake 6805, but there is no sign and we never found the trail.

Elk Meadow is large, roughly 2.5 miles long and almost 1 mile wide at the widest point. Elk Creek meanders through it in a number of willow-lined channels, interrupted by beaver dams, ponds and access channels. A large part of the meadow is normally flooded throughout much of the summer and that nice straight trail you see running through the middle of the meadow on the *Elk Meadow* quadrangle just doesn't exist.

The trail appears to lead on through the trees beyond the end of the jeep track, but it becomes confused with crisscrossing cattle trails and soon gets lost in bogs, brush and deadfalls. The best course is to take off your boots, put on your "tennies" and slosh through the meadow, watching out for beaver channels and deep holes. The shallow water won't be too cold and wading will give you a chance to examine the myriad wildflowers close-up. Two miles of intermittent wading, not too far from the trees on the northwest side, should bring you to dry grassland near the upper end of the meadow.

Look for a tongue of meadow on the northwest side extending into the lodgepole forest at the upper end. The trail runs along the northwest side of that tongue of grass and into the trees for a quarter mile to a junction with the Elizabeth Lake Trail just before crossing Elk Creek for the first time.

Puffballs are safe to eat and delicious, but you must be certain that they are not "buttons" of other fungi.

Flower-filled Elk Meadow has a background of snow-capped peaks

Side Trip to Elizabeth Lake

Dark, mysterious Elizabeth Lake is a tough 2-mile climb on rough trail northwest from the upper end of Elk Meadow. You won't be bothered by very many people up there, and it's supposed to be good fishing. We didn't fish because it was still almost covered with ice the first day of July.

Start climbing gradually on an alluvial fan where you can hear a creek (out of sight to the south) tumbling down to meet Elk Creek. At the top of the fan you climb steeply west with a couple of zigzags, then traverse north along the hillside through large Douglas firs with snowbends at their bases. Next you turn back southwest and climb steeply again to turn west around a steep shoulder. At this point, .8 mile from the junction, magnificent views extend across to McGown Peak and other peaks in the northern Sawtooths, and to the White Clouds beyond.

You continue climbing steeply west on a south-facing, mostly open slope covered with fields of arnica, mountain goldenrod and wyethia. Walk back into forest again, up and down over two ridges and through two gullies, and then up a final steep pitch to a rim 50 yards above Elizabeth Lake.

The quarter-mile-long lake sits in a narrow cleft, surrounded by a thick forest of tall, dark subalpine firs. It was so quiet here on the first of July that we found ourselves talking in whispers. A few good campsites are in a small flat on the southeast side not too far from the outlet. The rest of the shoreline is very steep.

Three miles farther along this trail is Marten Lake and beyond that are trails down Trap, Swamp and Bench creeks to Highway 21. Of these three, only Trap Creek is in the SNRA. All these trails are open to trailbikes, but get little travel of any kind.

Upper Elk Creek

A few yards south of the Elizabeth Lake Trail junction, cross Elk Creek, flowing east at this point. This crossing can be dangerous if runoff is very high, but we didn't find it so high in the first week of July that we felt it necessary to rope across. The water was mighty cold, however.

South of the crossing, the trail stays on the east side of the valley, well away from the creek, and soon climbs moderately over the first of two lateral moraines. Just beyond the first moraine is a log drift fence, intended to keep cattle from wandering farther up the canyon from Elk Meadow. If there is a gate in place when you go through, please close it behind you.

After a short climb over the second moraine, you approach the creek again near a group of excellent campsites in open timber, 1 mile from the first crossing. Continue climbing very gradually on the east side of the canyon through open lodgepole, fir and spruce. Several small streams run down the east slope to water gardens of mosses and wildflowers and to refresh passing hikers. A second crossing of Elk Creek is 2.5 miles from the first crossing. Although both banks are lined with heavy timber, none of the trees has obliged by falling across the creek to provide a foot log, so you'll have to wade again. It's not so bad this time—the creek is much smaller.

Above the second crossing the trail is on the west side of a meadow littered with erratic boulders and huge trunks of fir trees swept down by avalanches that ran across the canyon from both sides. The spectacular headwall of the canyon looms above the upper end of the meadow, snow-choked during most summers until August. Less than a half mile from the second crossing the trail crosses the creek again, and it crosses three more times in the next mile as the canyon becomes narrower and steeper. Above some small falls the trail begins the serious climb up the headwall and east to connect with the Stanley Lake Creek Trail, 5 miles away over very rough terrain.

We were turned back in the first week of July by deep snow that bridged the creek and buried the trail, but not before seeing a multitude of marsh marigolds blooming in the icy runoff.

Mushrooms pop up as the snow melts back

110

13–Queens River to Grandjean

Five or six days of moderately strenuous hiking take you on a south-to-north transect through the heart of the Sawtooth Wilderness, from giant ponderosa pines in the flats along the lower Queens River to timberline at Lake Ingeborg and back down to the ponderosa zone again at Grandjean trailhead. The trail along beautiful upper Queens River and around three sides of Mount Everly is lightly used and may inspire you to plan some side trips and spend one or two extra days in that area.

Good fishing and majestic scenery may also tempt a layover at one of the high lakes just north of the central divide. There is apt to be more traffic around Everly, Rock Slide and Ingeborg lakes than in upper Queens River valley, but it still won't be overcrowded. You can bypass these lakes and shorten the 40-mile trip to 31 miles by going directly down Benedict Creek to the South Fork Payette, but you will have missed a unique and marvelous experience.

In addition to good lake fishing, this trip offers the best stream fishing in the Sawtooth Wilderness. Dark-colored, pan-sized rainbows rise avidly to flies in Queens River. The South Fork Payette River, where it meanders in wide meadows near Deadman's Cabin, is a flyfisherman's heaven—rainbow and brook trout to two and three pounds plus an occasional *big* fish.

Wildflowers are everywhere along the trail, birds and butterflies are plentiful, especially in the ponderosa pine zones, and we saw more deer on this

trip than on any other in the SNRA. Mountain goats have often been reported on the peaks and ridges above the high lakes, but not everyone is lucky enough to see them.

It's a long way around by road from the Queens River trailhead to Grandjean. In fact, setting up a car shuttle will take at least a half day on each end of the trip plus the long drive to either trailhead. We were lucky to have non-backpacking friends who wanted to see Atlanta. They dropped us off at the Queens River trailhead and came back

Giant Ponderosa pines in the flat
north of the Queens River trailhead

to pick us up at Grandjean six days later. Another possibility is to have your party flown in to the airstrip at Atlanta and take the Jo Dailey Trail 6 miles over the ridge to connect with the Queens River Trail. However, the closest landing strip to Grandjean, at the north end of the trip, is at the Warm Spring Ranger Station, 12 miles down the South Fork of Payette.

Backpackers should not attempt this trip before middle or late July. Crossings of the Queens River and the South Fork Payette River are dangerous or impossible during high runoff, and in early summer there is apt to be a lot of snow on the trails around Mount Everly and the high lakes.

Topo maps for the trip are *Atlanta West, Mount Everly, Warbonnet Peak, Edaho Mountain* and *Grandjean* quadrangles. The trail loops east on to the *Atlanta East* quadrangle for about 1 mile, but you won't really need the map.

STARTING POINT

Sixty-five miles of twisting, rough, dirt road lead from the end of pavement at Arrowrock Reservoir near Boise to the almost ghost town of Atlanta, on the Middle Fork of Boise River at the south boundary of the Sawtooth Wilderness. Five miles west of Atlanta, in the Middle Fork canyon, a dirt road runs 2 miles up the Queens River to a trailhead where the Little Queens River joins the Queens.

From Ketchum, two road routes lead to the Queens River trailhead:

1. Drive north to Stanley, west on Highway 21 and around the wilderness to Lowman (See Motor Trip 8), south on Highway 21 to Beaver Creek campground, east on forest road #384, which turns south to a junction, after 12 miles,

with forest road #327 in the canyon of the North Fork of Boise River. Next turn east onto #327, which goes over a ridge south to meet the Atlanta road, #268, in the bottom of the Middle Fork Boise River canyon. Follow this road 10 miles east to the Queens River turnoff—only 38 miles of dirt road on this route.

2. Drive south of Ketchum to Highway 68, west to the Anderson Ranch Reservoir turnoff, north past the reservoir on gravel and some pavement to Featherville, then north 8 miles on forest road #156 to historic Rocky Bar. Next climb northeast on #126, little more than a jeep road, 13 miles over steep ridges to the Atlanta road #268, 2.5 miles east of the Queens River turnoff. If #126 is impassable, continue on #156 15 miles to the same junction where #237 joins the Atlanta road from the north. This route is slightly shorter overall and has about the same amount of dirt and gravel as the route through Lowman, but the roads are much better the other way.

The Boise National Forest map is necessary to follow any of these routes to the Queens River trailhead.

The road to Grandjean turns east from Highway 21 near milepost 94—36 miles from Stanley. From the Stanley direction, the road turns back left at an acute angle, making it difficult to turn onto it. Three miles from the highway on the gravel road, cross Camp Creek, which cascades down a steep-sided canyon from the north. Beyond Bear Creek, at 5 miles, a side road leads south across the South Fork Payette River to summer homes on Wapiti Creek. Venerable Sawtooth Lodge is on a right fork of the road at 6 miles. Stay on the left fork for another mile to the Grandjean campground and trailhead.

Street scene in Atlanta

Upper Queens River canyon and the
south face of Mount Everly

113

DESCRIPTION
Queens River to Benedict Creek

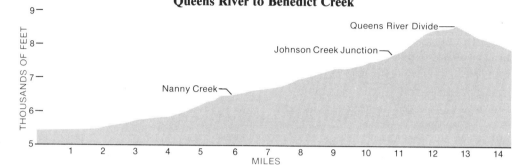

The Queens River road ends at a parking area and transfer camp on the south bank of Queens River just above that stream's confluence with the Little Queens River. Cross the river on a fine new footbridge. On the north bank are a trail register and signs for the Little Queens River Trail west and the Queens River Trail east. Start out level, turning northeast away from the river on an old jeep road across a wide flat in the **Y** between the two rivers. The trail crosses open meadows, with a few very large ponderosa pines here and there and many wildflowers not found at higher elevations—sego lilies, corn lilies, small white gentians, goldenrod, pink onion, yarrow, stonecrop and pussytoes.

Turn off the jeep road 1.5 miles from the trailhead at a sign reading "TRAIL" with an arrow pointing east. Shortly after leaving the road, the good footpath crosses a small creek, the first water since leaving the trailhead and a most welcome sight on a hot afternoon. The trees are closer together here and the pine-duff tread runs beneath some colossal ponderosas, 8–10 feet through at the bottom. A mile of very gradual climb, wandering about north and east among small mounds, brings you to a junction with the Jo Dailey trail, which climbs over a steep ridge and down to Atlanta, 6 miles south. This trail appears to be little-used.

You cross three delightful small creeks in .3 mile above the Jo Dailey trail, then come close to where the river flows out of a steep-walled, quarter-mile-wide canyon cut through solid granite. A half mile along the west bank brings you to the first unbridged crossing of Queens River. It is a good-sized stream and could be impossible to cross during high runoff. Look for

footlogs 100–150 yards upstream from the ford.

The dominant trees in the damper and thicker forest here are very large Douglas firs. Spruce and a few cottonwoods grow close to the river, and a lush understory includes thimbleberries, currants, stunted aspens, grasses, tall delphiniums and many other wildflowers.

Now we climb moderately up the east side of the canyon on rough and swampy tread to cross two overgrown avalanche paths above piles of rock and debris that have pushed the river against the west wall. Drop down into an open Douglas fir forest containing excellent campsites, and come to the next river crossing. There are several channels running swiftly between rocks, and no footlogs. High water could make it even more dangerous than the first crossing.

From the second ford 2 miles of moderate climbing on the open, sometimes brushy, west side of the canyon bring you to the base of a

Boy Scouts and leaders enjoy the excellent camping area at Nanny Creek

huge rock slide that at one time completely dammed the canyon. From the top of the slide, a steep, rough, quarter-mile climb, you can see that the river has cut a narrow channel back down to the canyon floor. Up ahead a tall, bare peak seems to fill the head of the canyon. Actually, Queens River runs around the west side of the 9,305-foot unnamed mountain, and a tributary, Nanny Creek, comes down a steep canyon from the east in front of it. The trail from the second crossing of Queens River to this point is in very poor condition and should be relocated and rebuilt.

Above the rock slide you go through a small pocket of fir, climb moderately again across a rocky slope, and then climb steeply over another rock slide. Cross more rocky slopes for a half mile before turning more steeply northwest to go around a heavily forested flat. A number of seeps and springs drain through this flat to the river, and the trail has been relocated from the bottom of the flat to the west slope. Some fair campsites are located in the drier areas along the old trail. At the upper end of the flat, the trail turns through a boggy area to cross to the east bank of the river above Nanny Creek. The ford is flat, wide and quite safe. Excellent campsites, 6 miles from the trailhead, are on the east side of the river between the trail and Nanny Creek.

Above Nanny Creek, Queens River flows gently down a wide, glacier-carved valley that is certainly one of the most beautiful places on earth in late July. Groves of subalpine fir alternate with meadows on the floor of the valley.

Two mule deer bucks in the upper
Queens River valley

Massive avalanches have kept many of the lower slopes clear, and these areas are a riot of wildflowers. Higher up the sides of the U-shaped valley are talus slides and craggy spires, typical of the Sawtooth granite from which the valley was carved. Higher still, snow-covered peaks accent the skyline above the valley walls.

We stood and watched two princely mule deer bucks, antlers in velvet, come down the trail toward us, then bolt in magnificent, effortless bounds when they finally saw us at 100 yards.

The river is a flyfisherman's delight, 20–30 feet wide, with a clean rock-and-gravel bottom and some deep pools below granite shelves. Low spirea bushes along otherwise open banks are loaded with fragrant blossoms shaded from pink to magenta. Carefully placed flies raise very dark-colored native rainbow trout to 10 or 11 inches. Landing these wild fish is another matter. Beaver dams offer a different kind of fishing for pan-sized brook trout in a few places where willow thickets line the stream.

After 1.5 miles of easy walking from Nanny Creek on good, lightly used trail on the east side of this idyllic valley, you climb moderately away from the river on a rocky slope, cross a meadow and hop a tributary creek in lodgepole pine forest. Then climb out onto another rocky slope and dip down into a wet meadow where old, rotting, log corduroy does little to keep your feet dry. The trail improves as it approaches the east bank of the cascading river. Marked by large rock cairns, it then turns to climb across the north end of the meadow and back into the forest before going north and leveling out again well above the river. A large, spired peak dominating the skyline slightly west of north could be mistaken for Mount Everly. Actually, it is an unnamed 9,472-foot peak, above the point where the Queens River valley turns northeast and begins to close in to become a canyon.

Around the turn, the solid granite bulk of 9,852-foot Mount Everly towers at the upper end of the canyon, and the trail heads directly toward it, crossing some small tributaries and coming closer to the river again as the canyon narrows. Four miles above Nanny Creek, just before the trail crosses the river from east to west, a sign points east up a little-used trail to "BLUE JAY LAKE." Neither the trail nor the lake is on the *Mount Everly* quadrangle and we didn't make the trip, but we'll always wonder what's up there.

There are no footlogs near this crossing, but the river is much smaller now and easy to wade. From the west bank, the trail follows a series of cairns northwest across a meadow, then goes straight up a hill a short distance before turning northeast through a grove of spruce and fir. You cross another rocky slope opposite two major tributaries falling down the other side of the canyon, and continue climbing moderately toward the base of Mount Everly. Southwest of the river, as it turns northwest in front of the mountain, the trail turns and climbs in the same direction on three steep switchbacks. Then you level out momentarily on a bench and turn north to cross cascading Queens River for the last time.

From the west Mount Everly begins to look more like a typical Sawtooth peak with broken blocks and spires above snowfields that cover the upper parts of massive talus slopes. The trail continues climbing moderately northwest toward the gap between Mount Everly and the peak to the west, then turns northeast to climb steeply on the side of a narrow canyon as a fork of the Queens River roars below. The other side of the canyon is a water-stained, vertical wall of vari-colored granite. After .3 mile you climb out of the canyon into a much wider valley, cross the creek and 200 yards farther on come to a junction. The trail heading northwest goes over a 9,250-foot ridge, past Arrowhead and Pats lakes, and eventually to a junction with the Johnson Creek Trail leading to the west boundary of the Sawtooth Wilderness. A trail down the *Little* Queens River back to the trailhead also connects with the Johnson Creek Trail, 7 miles west, so you can complete a 31-mile loop that way.

Our trail continues along the northwest base of Mount Everly, turning back across the little creek at the head of the valley and then climbing two moderately steep switchbacks beside a waterfall to a small basin directly north of the mountain. You cross this basin through a sea of marsh marigolds and alpine buttercups, and climb four short switchbacks to a saddle 12.7 miles from the Queens River trailhead. This is the divide between the drainages of the Queens River and the South Fork Payette River. Mount

Everly is an almost perfect pyramid from this side, most of its north face covered with permanent snow. To the southeast, Plummer Peak, 100 feet higher than Everly, tops a long ridge behind Everly and Plummer lakes.

From the saddle, the trail drops down, moderately at first, then more steeply on two new switchbacks, to a flat and a junction with a trail that leads back up south .8 mile to Everly Lake, and another .4 mile to Plummer Lake. Both beautiful alpine lakes are in a basin directly between the two high peaks with the same names. Unfortunately, the basin can be full of snow until mid-August.

Now walk through a carpet of heather across the sparsely forested flat to a crossing of the west fork of Benedict Creek, .5 mile northeast of Everly Lake junction. The trail continues down into a valley, then turns to curve around the nose of a ridge separating the east and west forks of Benedict Creek. Almost at the point of the ridge, .8 mile from the Everly Lake junction, you meet the Benedict Creek Trail coming up from its junction with the South Fork of Payette Trail near Smith Falls. That is the shortest way out to Grandjean. If you decide to go that way rather than making the loop around the high lakes, it will cut 9 miles off the trip, but you will miss some very special scenery.

Plummer Peak, east of and 100 feet higher than, Mount Everly

116

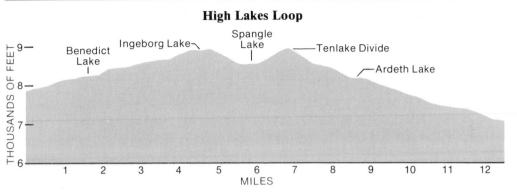

From the Queens River/Benedict Creek trail junction between the east and west forks of Benedict Creek, take the east fork to Benedict Lake. The Benedict Creek Trail, completely rebuilt in the '70's, is in much better condition than the Queens River Trail and is more heavily traveled. Around the east side of the ridge from the junction you get a first look at East Fork Benedict Creek as it slides over a glacier-polished sheet of granite and cascades into the canyon below.

You cross a couple of tributaries and swampy areas on real bridges and then, as the creek turns east, climb moderately on a series of new switchbacks to the point of another ridge just

Upper end of Benedict Lake

below Heather Lake (not named on the topo map). Heather is the first of three lakes in a wide glacial valley running almost north and south. Walk along the west shore of Heather Lake, and then climb very gradually past a second small, swampy lake to the outlet of Benedict Lake, 1 mile from the junction.

Quarter-mile-long Benedict Lake has a band of subalpine firs along its west shore. The other shores are marshy or steep rock. Halfway along the west shore, the trail makes two new switchbacks up a ridge. Beyond where the trail turns back, a couple of good campsites are on a shelf in the firs. Two sharp, 9,000-foot-plus peaks punctuate the snowy horizon at the south end of the valley. Benedict Lake has fair-sized cutthroat and brook trout, but we had difficulty catching any.

A new trail climbs gradually .4 mile from the switchbacks to cross the creek on a permanently placed, substantial footlog. Next, you walk up gradually on the east side of a cascade to a marshy meadow. Somewhere in this area, according to the map, a trail goes back across the creek and up to Three Island Lake in a higher basin .7 mile south. There is no sign and we did not see the trail. Our trail turns east and climbs five new switchbacks at a moderate rate past a waterfall falling toward a many-armed lake in the marshy basin below. More switchbacks cross the creek twice on bridges and top out by the north shore of Rock Slide Lake, 1.5 miles from Benedict Lake.

On the Sawtooth National Forest map Rock Slide Lake is named Robert Jackson Lake. The U.S. Geological Survey has a policy against naming natural features for living persons, and when the *Mount Everly* quadrangle was compiled it was discovered that Mr. Jackson, who had named the lake for himself, was still very much alive, so USGS arbitrarily changed the name to Rock Slide Lake. The basis for the name is very evident, a huge slide falling directly into the small, triangular lake from a mountain on the south side.

The trail contours south around the east slope of Rock Slide Lake basin, then climbs east in front of the rock slide to pass south of a boggy pond on a shelf above. One long switchback up a low ridge brings you to the north shore of .4-mile-long Lake Ingeborg.

Spectacular Lake Ingeborg is the highest lake of any size accessible by trail in the Sawtooth Wilderness. It sits in a shallow basin on an almost 9,000-foot plateau between the Benedict Creek and Middle Fork Boise River drainages. A high ridge towers above the west shore; the rest of the shoreline is low and open. The lake is very deep and is reputed to harbor trophy-size cutthroat trout as well as brooks. Many excellent campsites are among subalpine firs and limber pines around the shoreline, but on our visit deep snowdrifts lingered at the end of July and a howling afternoon wind made it anything but a hospitable place to camp.

The trail turns south to run halfway along the east side of the lake, then strikes out southeast across the plateau for .3 mile to a rim where Spangle Lake comes into view far below, backed by Glens Peak and the main Sawtooth ridge to the east. Two new, moderately steep switchbacks take you down a quarter mile to a jewellike little lake in a cirque nearly surrounded with vertical cliffs and a snowfield sloping right into the lake on the south side. We cross the outlet stream on the open north side of the cirque and descend seven moderately steep new switchbacks to Spangle Lake. Two hundred yards east of a log-jam crossing of the outlet stream, on the narrow rock ridge between Spangle and Little Spangle Lakes, is a junction with the Middle Fork Boise River Trail. From here you go north over the divide to Tenlake Basin.

The lakes and the 2.5 miles of trail from this junction to the junction near the outlet of Ardeth Lake are described in Backcountry Trip 6.

A sign at the trail junction by the camping area at the lower end of Ardeth Lake gives a distance of 1.5 miles down the steep canyon of Tenlake Creek to the junction with the South Fork Payette River trail. The trail has been

Spectacular Lake Ingeborg is reputed to harbor trophy-sized cutthroat trout

rebuilt since the sign was put up, and the distance is now more like 2 miles. Start out through the campsites, drop down to a small flat, turn east to the creek, and descend a series of moderate switchbacks and traverses, headed north on the west side of the canyon, then turn and cross Tenlake Creek just before it runs into the South Fork Payette. The crossing is on a footlog 50 yards upstream from the ford. The junction is in the **Y** between the two streams. The South Fork Payette Trail goes up to Edna Lake, 2 miles east—see Backcountry Trip 6.

In the down-river direction, the trail drops down to cross the river on a log jam just above a ford, then drops again moderately steeply northwest to a flat where the young river falls over a granite slab 5 or 6 feet high. Continue de-

scending moderately down the northeast side of the canyon for 2 miles, to where the trail turns west into a dismal swamp. The next 300 yards is mud, muck and stream channels as you cross both the South Fork Payette River and Benedict Creek in thick underbrush and spruce trees to reach the Benedict Creek Trail junction on the west bank. This entire crossing is flooded and utterly impassible, even on a horse, during high runoff. The Queens River Trail junction is 3.5 miles south up the Benedict Creek Trail.

Excellent campsites are on a flat down-river from the trail junction. The roar of Smith Falls, a few yards farther downstream, will help lull you to sleep. The now substantial river makes a spectacular drop of 50–60 feet in two steps into a vertical slot below.

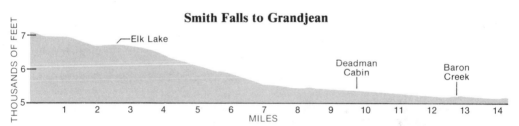

An excellent trail, rebuilt but not substantially relocated, leads down the west side of the South Fork Payette River canyon below Smith Falls. Beautiful stretches of river meander through tiny meadows and groves of large spruce in the wide canyon—flowing crystal-clear over bright beds of gravel and falling briefly over granite ledges to the next level. It's an ideal stream to fish, but unfortunately populated by only a few small brook trout.

One mile from the Benedict Creek Trail junction, the trail fords the river to the northeast side as the canyon and the river turn northwest. The river is 50 feet wide and 1½–2 feet deep at the ford, not difficult when the water is low, but potentially very dangerous when the water is high. There are no more crossings between here and Grandjean.

In the flat-floored, wide canyon below the crossing, the river is mostly hidden in spruce swamps, and the trail descends gradually through lush Douglas fir forest at the bottom of the northeast slope. Plenty of water flows in the

Roaring Smith Falls on the South Fork of Payette River

many small streams crossing the trail, and a verdant understory of grass, ferns, Labrador tea, currants, gooseberries, wild roses and many other wildflowers adds interest to the walk. Elk Lake is hidden in an extensive spruce swamp 1.7 miles below the last ford. The lake fills the depression left at the terminal end of the last glacier to move down the canyon. The river runs through the lake, and is rapidly filling the upper end with silt, which then becomes spruce swamp. Many good campsites are near the trail on the canyon's northeast side, but access to the lake is difficult. Fishing is reported to be good for both rainbows and brooks.

The canyon narrows below Elk Lake, and at .8 mile from the lake, the trail crosses a large rock slide through which the river has cut a channel. Just below the slide the river drops in a series of cataracts through a vertical-walled slot cut in solid granite. This is Fern Falls. New trail has been blasted through the canyon beside the cataracts for almost a quarter mile. Ferns, watered by the mist from the falls, line the walls of the canyon and explain the name. Below the falls a series of new switchbacks descend moderately to where the canyon opens up and levels out somewhat.

Very rank undergrowth of vine maple, ceanothus, mountain ash, currants and gooseberries almost chokes the trail in this lower canyon. New switchbacks have been added in the steeper places to hold the rate of descent to no more than moderate. It's very pleasant walking, but gets warmer, of course, as you go down the canyon. A recent, very large rock slide has come down the east side of the canyon 4 miles below Fern Falls, killing a large patch of Douglas fir. One tongue of the slide ran across the river, damming it temporarily and drowning more trees. Two more slides in the next half mile make the trail quite rough as the river cascades in a narrower canyon. The canyon widens to an open valley in the next mile, and the trail turns away from the river on a shelf where ponderosa pines appear again.

Now the very wide South Fork Payette River valley turns directly north, and the trail runs across alluvial slopes on the east side for 2 miles before coming in view of a large meadow on the valley floor. You soon drop down to meet an old jeep road where a wide bend of the river comes close to the east slope. Deadman Cabin

and the old settler's grave are within a quarter mile along the road. Excellent campsites are among the sparse lodgepole pines to the east.

The river runs swiftly but quietly through the meadow; 50-75 feet wide and 3-4 deep, with deeper holes in the turns of the wide meanders. Mossy boulders and logs on the otherwise clean gravel bottom provide cover for a remarkable population of rainbow trout, brook trout and whitefish. An evening rise on this stretch of the South Fork Payette is something to remember forever. The fish are not only numerous, they're big! A five-pounder may take your breath away—and your fly and leader as well. Springs and beaver channels make walking difficult in the meadow, but who cares.

You can walk on north on the road if you like, but the trail 50-100 yards east up the slope is drier and easier walking. Less than a mile from Deadman Cabin, a trail forks west across the valley to climb over the ridge and run down the North Fork Boise River to the west boundary of the Sawtooth Wilderness. Three quarters of a mile north of the junction, you cross fast-flowing Goat Creek on a bridge. Many excellent campsites are just north of the bridge, still within reach of fantastic fishing in the South Fork Payette River.

Continue well up on the east slope for a half mile, then descend past several very large erratic boulders that have rolled down from the higher slopes to a flat that is forested with lodgepole pine and occasional giant Douglas firs and ponderosa pines. You cross Baron Creek, 1.5 miles from Goat Creek, on another good footbridge. Both of these creeks would be difficult to ford. One hundred yards north of Baron Creek, come to a junction with the Baron Creek trail going east up the canyon to Baron and Sawtooth lakes.

North of Baron Creek the river curves close to the east side of the valley again and excellent campsites are on a flat below the trail. Another 1.5 miles of easy walking in parklike forest and then a slight climb over an alluvial fan bring you to the bridge over Trail Creek and the trailhead at Grandjean Campground.

Flyfisherman's paradise—the South Fork of Payette River near Deadman Cabin

14–Baron Creek and Baron Lakes to Redfish Lake

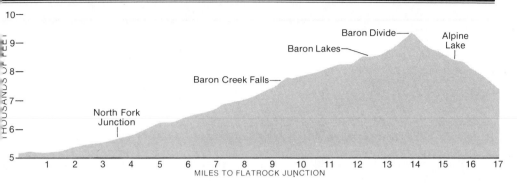

A west-to-east transect across the northern part of the Sawtooth Mountains takes you from the ponderosa belt at Grandjean up lightly traveled Baron Creek canyon, past spectacular Baron Lakes, almost to timberline on jagged Baron Divide, then down much visited but still beautiful Redfish Lake Creek to Redfish Lake Inlet Transfer Camp. The three-to-four-day, one-way trip of 19.5 miles can be extended by one day and 7.5 miles by making a side trip to Cramer Lakes (see Backcountry Trip 9).

If you want to make a full week of it, and avoid a car-shuttle or pick-up, a loop trip is possible by walking north from Redfish Lake to Iron Creek on the Alpine Way, up to Sawtooth Lake and down North Baron Creek or Trail Creek to the South Fork Payette trail and back to Grandjean. The loop will total close to 50 miles. Most of the northern part is described in Backcountry Trips 9 and 10.

Off-trail side trips are possible into the rugged high ridge country between Baron Creek and Goat Creek, but should be undertaken only by exper-ienced hikers familiar with orienteering in very rugged terrain. This area includes some of the most remote country and a number of the highest peaks in the Sawtooth range. Grandjean, Tohobit and Warbonnet peaks and Monte Verita (How did that Italian mountain get in there?) are the ones that have names.

Topo maps are *Grandjean, Stanley Lake, Warbonnet Peak* and *Mt. Cramer* quadrangles.

STARTING POINT

Start from Grandjean campground. Directions for reaching the campground are in Motor Trip 8 and Backcountry Trip 13.

DESCRIPTION

Start walking uphill from the trail sign on the east loop of the campground 150 yards to the bridge across Trail Creek in a grove of large aspen. The sign at the trailhead says 2 miles to the Baron Creek trail—at the Baron Creek trail junction a sign says 1 mile to Grandjean Campground. Split the difference and you'll be about right. Keep right at the Trail Creek Trail junction and follow good trail south across open slopes and through parklike forest, with a few giant ponderosa pines, .6 mile to a trail register at the Sawtooth Wilderness boundary. Continue almost level to the Baron Creek Trail junction 100 yards north of the Baron Creek footbridge. There are excellent campsites north of the junction on a flat between the trail and a

Tohobit Valley and Tohobit Peak
from the trail near Baron Creek Falls

123

curve of the South Fork Payette River.

The first 1.5 miles up Baron Creek canyon are a moderate climb on good trail well up on the mostly open north slope. Grass, chokecherry and spirea line the trail along with a few sparse groves of Douglas fir and aspen. Swarms of black-and-white-striped convict butterflies cover the spirea when it is in bloom. Next, you dip down slightly to a flat with large spruce and Douglas fir, then climb moderately steeply up an outwash fan to the crossing of the North Fork of Baron Creek. This could be a difficult crossing during high runoff.

Less than 100 yards beyond the creek crossing, and 2 miles from the South Fork Payette Trail junction, come to the North Fork Trail junction. Sawtooth Lake is 6 miles northeast up this trail. You may return on this trail if you decide to make a complete loop. Two excellent campsites, the first since starting up the canyon, are here on the east side of the North Fork.

Our lightly traveled but well-defined trail continues up Baron Creek as it turns southeast. Sections of the trail have been rebuilt, but it follows closely the route on the *Stanley Lake* quadrangle. The first mile above the North Fork climbs moderately steeply on a sparsely forested bench with good views of Grandjean Peak, southwest, and Tohobit Peak, slightly east of south and far up the canyon. Grandjean,

at 9,105 feet, is not one of the higher Sawtooth peaks, but its light gray Idaho granite has been spectacularly sculptured by glaciers.

You level off slightly among large Douglas firs, then make a short, steep climb into a very heavily forested area in the midst of which is Moolack Creek, 1.3 miles from the North Fork junction. Moolack Creek is bordered by sword-ferns and large cottonwood trees, unusual in the Sawtooths. One or two poor campsites are too close to the creek, but there are many better sites a short distance up the trail. Stroll through a delightful, parklike forest of big Douglas firs, with a grass floor, for 200–300 yards, skirt the edge of an impenetrable spruce bog, and then walk out into the open again, waist deep in pink-blooming spirea. A short half mile above Moolack Creek a beautiful campsite is behind a head-high boulder near a channel of Baron Creek, where it is spread out in another spruce flat.

The next 1.5 miles of wide, glaciated canyon is a beautiful garden, surrounded on three sides by snow-capped ridges and peaks. Small tributaries, dashing down to meet Baron Creek, are lined with alders, vine maples and tall quaking aspens. Widely spaced, giant Douglas firs, spruce and subalpine firs tower above gentle slopes covered with Indian paintbrush, fleabane, fireweed and mountain hollyhock. Ideal

Snow-bent Douglas fir beside the trail in Baron Creek Canyon

campsites are on a flat near the spruce-lined creek, .8 mile from the last campsite.

Two miles above Moolack Creek, the canyon narrows and the trail climbs on three new switchbacks to a vantage point opposite Tohobit Falls plunging down the southwest wall. Above a sign pointing to the falls, you begin another series of new switchbacks in thick subalpine fir forest. Next comes a .6-mile moderate climb across an open, rocky slope a little south of east, directly toward the headwall of the canyon. Then you enter another strip of forest and begin another series of switchbacks. On the sixth traverse, as the trees thin, you get a first glimpse of Baron Creek Falls, directly east at the head of the canyon. The next switchback goes back a long way northwest, to an excellent spot for photographs. Directly across the canyon Warbonnet Creek, not named on the topo map, falls from its hanging valley. Warbonnet Peak tops the jagged, snow-capped skyline to the south, and a multispired ridge rises above the head of the canyon to the east.

After traversing another steep, rocky slope and going through the next band of firs, you climb the final series of switchbacks, mostly in talus on a loose rock tread, to the top of the headwall. As you come out of the trees this time the top of Baron Creek Falls is directly ahead and you can see down into the hanging glacial

valley above Warbonnet Falls. At the top of the climb, the trail passes behind a granite knob northeast of the top of the falls. Drop your pack, take a break, and scramble to the top of the knob to admire and photograph the view back down the canyon and across to Tohobit Peak on the horizon.

Past the knob, the trail dips down beside Baron Creek above where the creek disappears into a slot in the rock and drops over the falls. An open meadow offers the first chance to fly-fish Baron Creek; it is lined with trees and brush in the canyon below. The stream is quite small, but does have plenty of pan-sized brook trout. You climb three moderately steep switchbacks to a glacier-smoothed granite shelf, cross a rocky slope to another piece of light-colored granite, and cross the creek on the first genuine bridge since Trail Creek at the trailhead, 9 miles back.

Continue climbing moderately south up the heavily glaciated valley, with some switchbacks, to cross the creek again on a footlog, a half mile from the first crossing. Good campsites are on the east side of the creek here. Two more sets of switchbacks, with a traverse between, bring you to a third crossing of the creek just below a small pond.

Little Baron Lake is off the trail about .3 mile west of the creek crossing. To get to the lake,

Switchbacking up the talus slope below Baron Creek Falls

Rebuilt trail above Baron Creek Falls

contour around the slope, keeping well below a solid granite knob, and climb over a low granite wall to drop into the lake basin. The 20-acre, oblong lake has a grassy shoreline backed by a phalanx of subalpine firs. On the west side of the basin, Sawtooth granite cliffs rise to a 9,837-foot unnamed spire. Excellent campsites, little used, are in the trees near the outlet. We didn't fish, but saw rises that were probably brook trout.

Back on the trail, continue up the side of the valley above the pond, then beside the creek again to a low shoulder of granite overlooking Baron Lake. This half-mile-long lake is in a steep-sided basin of rosy Sawtooth granite. Monte Verita's two 10,000-foot-plus ragged crests tower above the southwest rim. Several good campsites are in the subalpine firs on both side of the outlet. The rest of the shoreline is almost too steep to stand on, let alone camp on.

Two hundred yards around the east shore from the outlet, you start climbing seven moderate switchbacks east up the steep ridge between Baron and Upper Baron lakes. At the top of the switchbacks a quarter-mile traverse leads south along the ridge to a saddle overlooking the north end of Upper Baron Lake. The

one fair campsite at this lake is beside the trail as you drop down to the north shore. Upper Baron Lake, in another steep-sided basin, is about half the size of Baron Lake and has no outlet. There is no evidence of any great fluctuation in the water level, so it must drain through the rock dam at the north end. Both lakes contain pan-size brook trout, but fishing is nothing to brag about. Baron Lakes get a lot of traffic since they are only one full walking day from Redfish Lake Inlet Transfer Camp.

Halfway around the east shore of the lake, the good but heavily traveled trail starts a series of 29 moderately steep switchbacks that lead .6 mile east to the top of Baron Divide. On the way up, among scattered whitebark pines, you'll have plenty of opportunities to look and take pictures across the lakes to Monte Verita and an unnamed peak to the north.

From the top of the Baron Divide, you can see forever on a clear day—and that's most any day in summer. In addition to the already de-scribed view west, all of the eastern ridge of the Sawtooths, from the Grand Mogul south to Snowyside Peak, is in view east of the wide chasm of Redfish Lake Creek canyon. To the southeast a wide, U-shaped canyon, with

Whitebark pine snags above Baron Lakes

View down the Redfish Lake Creek Canyon

Cramer Lakes and 10,716-foot Mount Cramer at its head, hangs above the east wall of the larger canyon. Almost directly south, 10,582-foot Elk Peak rears above permanent snowfields that are the source of Redfish Lake Creek.

East of the divide, four moderately steep switchbacks descend to a small, stagnant pond. The trail then makes a wide loop north and back south in sparse whitebark pine forest to descend toward the middle of three lakes in a wide basin. Springs along the trail offer the first drinking water since Upper Baron Lake. Three new short switchbacks complete the descent to the middle lake, where the trail goes around the west shore and then crosses to the east side of the outlet stream. A steep drop of about 300 yards beside the stream leads to a crossing to the west bank and a short switchback up to the nose of a ridge. Alpine Lake soon comes into view in the basin below, and the trail makes three long, moderate switchbacks down to its north shore, 1.6 miles from Baron Divide.

A large camping area is on a flat between the trail and the north shore of the lake. Overuse and lack of firewood reduce these sites to a fair rating. There are a few better sites across the outlet on the east shore. Excellent sites are in the basin above, around the three little lakes.

There are two Alpine Lakes in the Sawtooth Wilderness (see Backcountry Trip 10). This one is teardrop-shaped, about a quarter-mile long, almost as wide, and surrounded by thick subalpine fir and lodgepole pine forest. Flyfishing is difficult because of the trees, but there are plenty of small to medium-sized brook trout if you can get to them.

From the camping area, descend moderately east a quarter mile, keeping north of Alpine Lake's outlet creek, to a light-gray granite ledge at the top of the west wall of Redfish Lake Creek canyon. There are magnificent views from here down the canyon and across to Mount Cramer. Descend gradually on a traverse north below the rim, then begin a series of switchbacks east down the side of the canyon. The upper switchbacks reach south almost to Alpine Lake's outlet creek as it tumbles down in falls and cascades. A surprising number of firs, lodgepole pines and spruce grow on this steep, almost solid granite slope. Below the switchbacks the trail descends northeast across a brushy slope, laced with springs and creeklets, to Flat Rock Junction, beside Redfish Lake Creek and 1.8 miles from Alpine Lake.

Descriptions of a side trip to Cramer Lakes and of the 3.6 miles down to Redfish Lake Inlet are in Backcountry Trip 9.

The flat rock that gives Flat Rock Junction its name

Trips in the

White Cloud Mountains

15–Champion Lakes

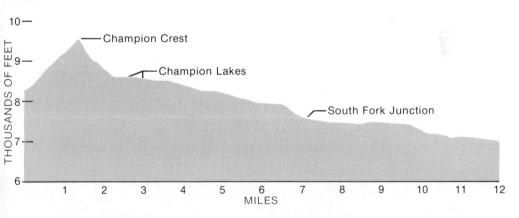

This one-way, three-day trip begins with a good sample of the steep, rough, sheepherders' and cattlemen's trails typical of much of the White Cloud Mountains. But there are also rewards.

Over the first ridge from Germania Basin is an absolutely beautiful mountain valley with three pristine lakes nestled in the trees on its floor. Fishing and camping are excellent, and it's all downhill from the top of the first ridge to the end of the trip.

Rock wall at the west end of
Red Ridge in the central White Clouds

If you don't have a vehicle that will negotiate the road over Pole Creek Summit, or can't arrange a car-shuttle or pick-up, you can still make a round trip from one end or the other. A round trip is easier from Champion Creek, but it's possible that you won't be welcome crossing private land at the beginning of the trip.

The one-way trip totals only 12 miles, but the first 2.5 miles to Upper Champion Lake may take the better part of half a day. All the trail is closed to trailbikes.

You will need three **topo map** quadrangles: *Horton Peak, Washington Peak* and *Obsidian*.

STARTING POINT

The trailhead is 10.3 miles from Highway 75 on the Pole Creek road (see Motor Trip No. 4) in the upper end of Germania Basin, 1 mile beyond Pole Creek summit. A trailhead sign, parking area and trail register are above the road on the north side. If the road has not been graded, low-clearance vehicles may have to stop 3.5 miles short of the trailhead, below the steep climb to Pole Creek Summit.

The pick-up point at the end of the trip is off the north end of the Valley road, which turns east from Highway 75 at a signed junction 2.5 miles north of the Pettit Lake road and .5 mile south of Fourth of July road. Turn left at a **Y** .6 mile from the highway and, unless there has been a recent change, you will soon come to a locked gate. Park your car off the road. You'll be coming down this road to the gate at the end of the trip.

DESCRIPTION

From the trail register in Germania Basin, start climbing steeply northwest in the bottom of a narrow ravine, crisscrossing the little creek on a rough and sometimes muddy tread. Grassy slopes facing south and west are dotted with large clumps of intensely blue mountain bluebells in mid-July. About .6 mile from the register, the trail turns north, first up a side gully, then directly up the ridge above. The ascent through scattered subalpine firs and lodgepole

Peruvian sheepherder at Pole Creek Meadow

130

and whitebark pines varies from steep to very steep on a well-defined but rough tread with only rudimentary switchbacks. Wind-blasted whitebarks, more dead than alive, guard a saddle at the top of the ridge, 1.2 miles from the trailhead.

Arctic plants grow at ground level on top of the ridge; moss campion, inch-high Townsendia, dwarf Indian paintbrush and alpine buttercups in the edges of remnant snowbanks. Tiny whitebark seedlings cling to crevices in the rocks where they can get a toehold.

Over the crest is incredibly beautiful Champion Valley: **U**-shaped, 3 miles long and more than a mile wide, containing three sky-blue lakes and a number of ponds set into the green carpet of forest at the bottom of the **U**. To the south, a long view extends across Germania Basin to the snow-capped crests of the Boulder Mountains. A trace of a trail going over the ridge east to Washington Basin can be seen in the long limestone talus slides east of the upper lake.

A quick look down the north side of the ridge you've just climbed will almost take your breath away. Below is a precipitous limestone talus slope. The trail, after making a short angle to the west, plunges directly down the slope. Dig in

your heels and get down the best way you can. It's very steep, rough and partly covered with snowbanks in mid-July. At the bottom of the talus, the trail goes east of a hump and down a gully into a cuplike meadow, probably a pond earlier in the year. You climb briefly over the north side of the cup and drop, very steeply again, to a meadow surrounding a small pond. A vivid display of globeflowers, shooting stars and elephants' heads fills the meadow in mid-July.

Circle the west shore of the pond and follow the outlet stream to Upper Champion Lake, which at about 100 acres is the largest of the three lakes. Subalpine fir and lodgepole pine forest extends around the low shoreline, except for an open space with grassy banks and weedy shallows on the northeast side. Excellent campsites are near the trail in the forest above the east shore. The trail to Washington Basin branches east half way around the lake.

Fishing for brook trout to 9-10 inches is very good in all three Champion Lakes. Some people even make the rugged 5-mile round-trip over the ridge from Germania Basin just to carry out a limit of trout.

From the upper lake you descend moderately north on good trail, winding through mounds

View south into the Boulder Mountains
from the crest above Champion Lakes

Excellent fishing for brook trout
in Upper Champion Lake
rewards the climb over the crest

131

of glacial debris. Small Middle Champion Lake is out of sight to the west. Open lodgepole forest allows occasional views of 10,519-foot Washington Peak, highest point on the ridge to the east. Beginning at .7 mile from Upper Champion Lake, the trail circles the east and north shores of Lower Champion Lake. Smaller than Upper Champion but otherwise similar, this lake also has excellent campsites in the trees back from the shoreline.

Beyond Lower Champion Lake, a large granite knob fills the lower end of the valley. Champion Creek drops down a steep canyon west of the knob and turns west, but our trail goes north through a meadow, past a pond and down a tributary stream. It circles around the north side of the knob, drops down to cross the tributary and continues west above the north bank of Champion Creek. There are excellent campsites here along Champion Creek, and at another tributary .7 mile farther west.

As the canyon widens, the trail stays on the north side, away from the creek, to avoid some wet meadows and spruce tangles. At 7 miles from the trailhead, a rough, nonvehicular trail leads up South Fork Champion Creek, over a 9,000-foot ridge, and down Twin Creek to Pole Creek road. It's possible to make a loop trip this way, but you would have to walk 6 miles back up the Pole Creek road to Germania Basin if you left your car there.

Our trail descends moderately west in a thick stand of lodgepole pine, drops off a bench, squeezes between the creek and an old talus slide, and levels out on the floor of a wide valley. Grass and sagebrush are interspersed with groves of lodgepole pine, Douglas fir and aspen where there are many excellent campsites. Another narrow stretch of trail between the creek and a slide leads to a long meadow with a huge beaver-pond area at its lower end. More beaver dams and willow flats downstream keep the trail up on the north slope in Douglas fir forest.

Beyond an open, sagebrush-covered slope, descend moderately through an aspen grove to a wide sagebrush flat and look for a line of trees marking an irrigation ditch. The trail follows the north side of the ditch to the end of the trees, then turns south and crosses two ditches. South of the second ditch, a sign reading "TRAIL" points to an old ranch road leading west. The road comes close to the north bank of Champion Creek opposite some old, log ranch buildings, passes more, newer buildings on the north side, and turns south to cross another irrigation ditch and the creek. Beyond the creek crossing, the road turns west again and descends moderately 1 mile to the locked gate where your car or ride is waiting.

By the time you read this, the last 2 miles or so of this trail may be relocated to bypass private land to a better trailhead.

Champion Lakes Basin—highest point at right is Washington Peak

16-Chamberlain Basin Loop

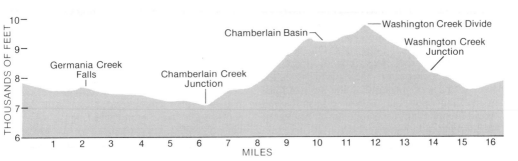

In Chamberlain Basin, tall stalks of rare green gentian dot the meadows around a small alpine lake at the base of Castle Peak, tallest in the White Clouds. Castle's almost 12,000-foot crenelated mass dwarfs a number of 10,000-foot-plus peaks around the west and north sides of the basin. Three more lakes, turquoise from snowmelt, are in cirques at the upper end of the basin.

This is the high point of a 16-mile, three-day loop trip through mountain grandeur at the south end of the White Cloud range. Quite a few people make the steep, 5-mile climb to Chamberlain Basin from the road below Washington Basin, but very few make the loop through scenic Germania Creek and Chamberlain Creek canyons. Many groves of quaking aspen make this an especially beautiful autumn trip, if you don't mind the chance of a little early snow.

Unlike most of the White Cloud trips, this one doesn't offer much fishing. There are a few small rainbow trout in Germania Creek and there are supposed to be trout in the Chamberlain Lakes. We weren't able to fish the lakes, so we can't say for sure.

Two **topo maps**, *Galena Peak* and *Boulder Chain Lakes* quadrangles, cover all but the very beginning of the trip. The trailhead and the first half mile of trail are on the *Horton Peak* quadrangle.

STARTING POINT

The trailhead, with a sign "THREE CABINS TRAIL TO BOWERY," is at the lower end of Germania Basin, just beyond where the road turns north to go over the ridge to Washington Basin. This is 2 miles east of the trailhead for Backcountry Trip 15. Unfortunately, it's also 5.5 miles beyond where you may be able to drive with a modern sedan, depending on road conditions. The 12.5-mile drive up Pole Creek road from Highway 75 is described in Motor Trip 4.

DESCRIPTION

East of the wide, lush meadows of Germania Basin, Germania Creek starts down a shallow canyon. You pass a register 300 yards from the road, then descend moderately north of the creek. As the canyon gets narrower and steeper, the good trail climbs around several outcrops and then, 1 mile from the trailhead, drops steeply to cross Washington Creek. A sign at the crossing points to Mac Rae Creek, which flows into Germania Creek from the other side of the canyon. There is no trail up Mac Rae Creek. The Washington Creek sign is on the back side of the post. Three tenths of a mile east of the crossing, the Washington Creek Trail to Chamberlain Basin turns north. You will be coming back past here to complete the loop.

Below the trail junction, the Germania Creek trail stays well up on the north side of the canyon for .5 mile, then turns and climbs steeply north over a volcanic outcrop. This trail is open to trailbike use, and this steep pitch has been badly worn by both trailbike and horse traffic, even though traffic is quite light. On the other side of the volcanic ridge, you drop down a ravine and come out on steep sagebrush slopes leading to a wide meadow on the floor of Germania Creek canyon. Excellent campsites are in lodgepole pine and aspen groves on the north side of the meadow. Noises in the night are grazing cattle, not bears.

Eight tenths of a mile of level walking beside the creek beings you to the lower end of the meadow and a slight climb over an alluvial fan as the creek veers away to the south side of the canyon. The trail down from the fan is not very clear and, because of crisscrossing cattle trails, might appear to cross the creek. Actually it squeezes between the creek and a steep slope on the north side. A half mile farther on, below a volcanic outcrop, the trail does ford to the south bank of Germania Creek, then descends moderately through a steeper-sided stretch of canyon to the head of another, smaller meadow. In this meadow, 1.5 miles from the first crossing, a trail sign points south to Bowery Guard Station. Excellent campsites are near the trail junction.

Cross to the north bank of the creek again wherever it's convenient. The trail is not very clear in the meadow, but is obvious again on the north side, where it climbs steeply over a glacier-worn volcanic dike. On top of the dike, take time to walk over and look down at Germania Creek Falls in the spectacular gorge the creek has cut through an old lava flow. Descend northwest off the dike, then east again over some small ridges to cross Chamberlain Creek and come to a junction with the trail to Chamberlain Lakes. A sign, facing east, is 50 yards up this trail from the junction.

The Chamberlain Creek trail is nonvehicular, little used and not often maintained. The steep canyon is also pristine and quite beautiful. Unless you run into a thunderstorm, the loudest noise you're apt to hear is the scolding of chickarees (pine squirrels).

Start climbing northwest at a moderately steep rate past Douglas firs, aspen groves and open slopes, some grass and some loose rock. The first mile of trail stays up on the northeast side of the canyon, then comes close to Chamberlain Creek in a lodgepole-pine-forested flat. As you come out of the trees into a meadow, the indistinct trail turns north uphill and crosses the top side of the meadow. Blazes mark the trail where it re-enters heavier forest.

Continue climbing up the side of the canyon, and then very steeply up a tributary canyon, to top out on a rim overlooking Chamberlain Creek Falls in a chasm carved out of volcanic rock. From the canyon rim, climb northwest up a steep ridge, through a gully and around the north side of a knob to a meadow. A few rock cairns mark the indistinct route across the meadow. Stay northeast of a line of trees and climb a steep, open slope directly toward the tip of Castle Peak, showing on the horizon. At the top of the climb, two definite cairns mark a turn southwest to a bench far above Chamberlain Creek. From there, you cross a series of low ridges in open country with a few whitebark pines, then descend gradually to a junction with the Livingston Mill-Castle Divide trail, 9.8 miles from the trailhead in Germania Basin.

This trail climbs around the massive limestone east shoulder of Castle Peak, then forks to run down either Wickiup Creek or Little Boulder Creek to the East Fork of Salmon River road. Another branch farther north goes to Boulder Chain Lakes, Frog Lakes, Big Boulder Creek and the trailhead at Livingston Mill.

A quarter mile west of the Livingston Mill-Castle Divide trail junction, our trail is close to

Germania Creek Falls slowly wears away an ancient volcanic dike

the north bank of Chamberlain Creek again, approaching the first and lowest lake in Chamberlain Basin. Directly north of this small lake, the textured wall of Castle Peak rises to 11,815 feet. The east side of Castle Peak is limestone, light gray, rounded by erosion and buttressed by long slides of talus. West of a sharp dividing line, harder, uptilted strata of red-brown sedimentary rock break at the top to form the highest crests. suggesting battlements and giving the peak its name.

Patches of subalpine fir and whitebark pine are interspersed with verdant meadows around the lakes on the floor. Tall stalks of green gentian punctuate the meadows, and other alpine flowers are abundant in season. Good campsites are around the lower lake and between it and a larger lake, one half mile northwest. Bare rock cirques hold two more smaller lakes at the northwest end of the basin.

As the trail turns south to cross Chamberlain Creek below the outlet of the first lake, a fork leads around the north shore of the lake and, eventually, to the second lake, higher in the basin. South of the creek, our trail to Germania Basin climbs moderately over low ridges of glacial debris, then runs around the east rim of a perfectly round bowl containing a pond that varies in size with the season. Now climb more steeply southwest over a ridge and southeast up the side of the very steep, 9,800-foot ridge on the southeast side of the basin. A few zigzags

Golden aspen leaves brighten Germania Creek Canyon in September

relieve the strain a little before the final push to a saddle on the crest.

The view from among the twisted whitebark pines on the narrow crest is one of the most spectacular in the White Clouds. To the north, the entire south face of Castle Peak looms above Chamberlain Basin. Chamberlain Creek canyon drops off to the southeast, and a panorama of varicolored peaks and ridges extends from Castle Peak around to the west. Germania Creek canyon and the Boulder Mountains complete the view to the south.

From this saddle the trail drops very steeply west, diagonally across the almost vertical slope on the southwest side of the knife-edged ridge. It then turns south around the head of Jack Creek canyon and west around the nose of a ridge to overlook Germania Creek canyon to the south and Washington Basin to the west. To this point, the trail from Chamberlain Basin has been in fair-to-good condition in spite of steep grades, but now a very steep pitch, badly worn and eroded, descends to a junction with the Washington Lake trail. This junction is 2.4 miles from Chamberlain Lakes. Washington Lake is 2.6 miles north up the canyon (see Backcountry Trip 17).

From the Washington Lake trail junction, descend moderately southwest through lodgepole and whitebark pines for a quarter mile to a rim overlooking Washington Creek canyon and Washington Basin farther west. The next .6 mile down to Washington Creek junction is one of the worst pieces of trail in the SNRA—very steep, rough, torn up, dusty and lacking any semblance of switchbacks. A side trip of 100 yards on the Washington Creek trail will take you to Washington Lake Creek, the first drinking water since leaving Chamberlain Basin and the last until you get to the bottom of Germania Creek Canyon.

Back on the trail, our route southeast down Washington Creek descends moderately on a series of benches far up from the creek. After almost a mile of easy walking through open grassland and aspen groves, the trail goes down more steeply around a shoulder and through a side canyon to intersect the Germania Creek trail .3 mile below its crossing of Washington Creek. Three Cabins trailhead, starting point of our trip, is 1.3 miles west up Germania Creek.

17–Fourth of July Creek to Chamberlain Basin

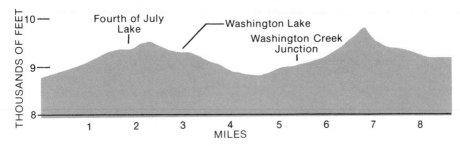

Starting point for this 17.5-mile, two-to-four-day round trip among the highest peaks of the White Clouds is at 8,800 feet elevation. That's the lowest point of the trip. The entire color-banded ridge (vertical strata of light gray limestone and red-brown sedimentary and metamorphic rocks) east of Fourth of July and Washington lakes reaches above 10,000 feet. Around the other side of the ridge above Chamberlain Basin, Castle Peak is even higher.

Fishing is surprisingly good in Fourth of July and Washington lakes, in spite of their being easily accessible. Motorized trail connects the trailhead to Washington Basin, but does not go around to Chamberlain Basin.

You will need a high-clearance vehicle to get closer than 2 miles to the trailhead at the end of the Fourth of July Creek road and, depending on the condition of the road at the time, four-wheel-drive may be required to get up a steep pitch approximately 1.5 miles from the trailhead.

Topo Maps—*Washington Peak* and *Boulder Chain Lakes* quadrangles include all the trails involved in the trip, plus 6 miles of the Fourth of July Creek road.

STARTING POINT

Fourth of July Creek road leads east from Highway 75 south of Fourth of July Creek, 48 miles north of Ketchum. Details of the location of the junction and of the drive to the trailhead are in Motor Trip 4. If you're able to drive 10.5 miles east to the cluster of miners' buildings at the end of the road, park west of the buildings clear of any turning areas or access tracks.

The register and starting point of the trail to Fourth of July Lake are south of the buildings near the creek.

DESCRIPTION

The trip begins with a moderate ascent east around the shoulder of a ridge south of Fourth of July Creek. A few almost-switchbacks on the excellent trail, rebuilt in the late '70's, bring you to a bridge over the creek a half mile from the trailhead. After less than a quarter mile of moderate climb above the north bank, cross to the south bank again just above the confluence with a tributary and make a short, climbing half-loop to cross back to the north bank again. Zigzag north to the foot of a ridge, then climb, still moderately, east beside a tiny stream through open forest to a small meadow with a talus slope on the north side.

Skirt the meadow and turn south on a short, steep climb to a flat and, 300-400 yards farther south, a junction with a trail going over the ridge to Ants Basin and Warm Springs Creek. Southwest from the junction dip slightly through open lodgepole pine and subalpine fir forest to the outlet of Fourth of July Lake, 1.7 miles from the trailhead. Most of this section of trail has been relocated from the route shown on the *Washington Peak* quadrangle.

Fourth of July Lake is an exquisite little 10-12 acre lake, set in a grassy, shallow basin, surrounded a short distance back from the shore by symmetrical spires of subalpine fir. To the south, west of the gap leading to Washington Lake, a pyramidal peak rises to 10,713 feet. North and east of the basin, a 10,000-foot-plus knife-edged ridge is topped by 10,872-foot Patterson Peak and an unnamed peak of 10,707 feet. Snow lingers in cols and cirques above timberline throughout most summers.

Seen from the trail near the outlet, the lake looks deceptively shallow. It is much deeper in the middle and toward the east shore. Flyfishing is an absolute delight from grass hummocks on the shoreline, even during the middle of the day. A cast toward one of the deep blue-green holes offshore can inspire a startling burst of action as 12 or 13 inches of beautiful cutthroat trout catapults clear of the water, fly in mouth. In a couple of hours, we lost six or seven before getting them close to shore, and released that many more from barbless hooks. Another four went into the frying pan for dinner.

Many excellent campsites are east of the trail before you get to Fourth of July Lake and west of the trail after you cross the outlet. Wildflowers bloom everywhere in the grasslands around the lake at the end of July.

The trail to Washington Lake climbs moderately south from Fourth of July Lake, then turns southeast to climb more steeply across a rocky slope toward a gap east of dark-brown, pyramidal Peak 10713. Most of the trail has been rebuilt, but it follows closely the route on the *Washington Peak* quadrangle. A few lodgepole and whitebark pines hang on in the rocks beside the trail as it skirts the northeast shore of a small tarn nestled under a talus-covered buttress, southwest of the gap.

We turn east to start the descent toward Washington Lake, now in sight in the basin below. This section of trail has been rebuilt and relocated from the route on the *Boulder Chain Lakes* quadrangle. It makes a loop east, then turns back west and circles around the head of the basin, descending moderately steeply across a number of seeps and small springs to the west shore of the lake.

Talus slides, falling from a 10,000-foot-plus ridge, form most of the east shore of quarter-mile-long Washington Lake. The northwest and west shores are bordered by marshy flats, kept wet by springs and seeps flowing from the basin walls. A few good campsites are in the trees on the rocky rim west of the trail. The lake harbors plenty of 12-inch cutthroats, as well as medium-sized brook trout, but is not as easy to fish as Fourth of July Lake.

10,000-foot-plus White Clouds ridge rises behind Washington Lake

When you've seen enough of the spectacular scenery, continue descending moderately on good trail down the wide valley below Washington Lake. A half mile through meadows and sparse forest leads to a steeper drop to a flat between two forks of Washington Lake Creek, and a junction with the vehicular trail going over the west ridge to meet the jeep road below Washington Basin. This trail is not on the *Boulder Chain Lakes* quadrangle.

Our nonvehicular trail crosses the east fork of the creek and follows down the east bank of the combined streams in heavy forest for a quarter mile. Then, as the creek drops into a steeper, **V**-shaped canyon, the trail turns and contours almost level on the very steep east slope for 1.5 miles to a shelf, on which it meets the Chamberlain Lakes trail. Descriptions of this trail (in the reverse direction) and Chamberlain Basin are in Backcountry Trip 16.

Rather than returning to this junction from Chamberlain Lakes, a loop of approximately 18 miles could take you down Chamberlain Creek, up Germania Creek to Washington Creek, up again to the jeep road below Washington Basin, and then over the ridge to the trail junction near Washington Lake. It would take two more days, without layovers, and you would have to backtrack only a little over 3 miles of trail. Most of the trail is described in Backcountry Trip 16.

Storm clouds gather over Chamberlain Basin and 11,815-foot Castle Peak

18–Fourth Of July Creek To Robinson Bar

At 10,000 feet on a hot afternoon, packs weigh heavily, knees wobble and thin air sears the lungs as you finally reach a saddle. One glance over the other side, however, and all that is forgotten. Ants Basin hangs above the edge of Warm Springs Creek canyon as if suspended in air. As the day wanes, the already bright colors of the ridges and peaks across the canyon are intensified by the rays of the lowering sun.

Later, on the floor of the basin, mist wraiths drift above the lush grass as the sun's last rays reflect orange and red from the highest snow patches on the eastern skyline. Starlight reigns for an hour, only to be dimmed by the searchlight of a full moon rising above the ramparts to silhouette a file of deer on their graceful way to drink at the pond

Ants Basin in the center of the White Clouds

below your tent.

This is your reward for the first-day climb over the ridge south of Ants Basin on this four-or-five-day, 34-mile transect from south to north through the center of the White Cloud Mountains. From the top of the ridge, the rest of the trip is all downhill to Robinson Bar at 5,900 feet elevation on the Salmon River. For a change from all that downhill, add a day to your excursion by making a 4-mile side trip up to Born Lakes at the head of Warm Springs Creek canyon.

Fishing is excellent for good-sized brook trout at Born Lakes, and for cutthroats, brooks and rainbows in Fourth of July Lake and Warm Springs Creek.

The one-way trip requires a car-

shuttle or a pick-up. Of course, you can walk part or all of it as a round trip if you wish. Do not attempt this trip too early in the season; high water will make crossings of lower Warm Springs Creek impossible. As in Backcountry Trip 17, you will need at least a high-clearance vehicle to get all the way to the trailhead on Fourth of July Creek.

Topo maps needed for the trail portion of the trip are *Washington Peak* and *Robinson Bar* quadrangles.

STARTING POINT

The starting point is somewhere on the Fourth of July Creek road, the same as for Backcountry Trip 17.

Robinson Bar, the north end of the trip, is 15 miles east of Stanley in the Salmon River canyon. The turnoff, on the south side of Highway 75, is signed "O'BRIEN CAMP-GROUND." Drive 1.5 miles, past two camp-grounds, to a locked gate at Robinson Bar Ranch. Please park off the road and clear of the gate.

Access to the Robinson Bar trailhead may still be a problem when you read this. Check with an SNRA office before you make the trip.

DESCRIPTION
Fourth Of July Lake To The Meadows

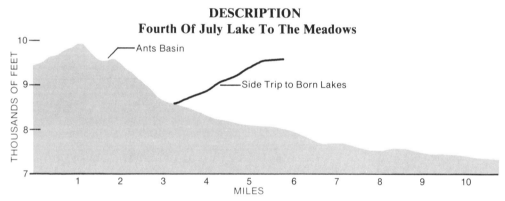

The first 1.5 miles to the trail junction near Fourth of July Lake is described in Backcountry Trip 17. It's a good idea to drop your packs and rest, or fish a while at Fourth of July Lake, before starting the climb toward Ants Basin.

The first quarter mile of new trail from the junction north of the lake climbs gradually, a little north of east, across glacier-sculpted rock shelves and through meadows and pockets of lodgepole pine and subalpine fir, to the foot of a steep ridge. Another quarter mile of steep, rough, twisting trail leads northwest to a pond on a bench. You level off temporarily past this murky tarn, then turn more westward to climb moderately steeply along the side of the ridge. This transect offers striking views across to huge Peak 10713 south of Fourth of July Creek, and down to the trailhead, where vehicles and mine buildings now look like toys. After a half

mile on fair trail, level off and dip down through a ghost forest of dead whitebark pines to a saddle where the trail turns north across the ridge.

Across Warm Springs Creek canyon from the saddle, a long file of peaks and ridges marches north to end at the deep trench cut by the Salmon River. An unnamed, 11,342-foot limestone peak dominates the long line, its almost white color contributing to the White Clouds' name. Directly below the saddle, unbelievably green Ants Basin spreads like a relief map—every tiny, meandering stream etched in utmost detail; ponds washed in pale, transparent blue, revealing bottom contours; every tree, rock and grove precisely overlaid in darker greens and browns. Relax and enjoy the visual feast for a while before beginning the steep descent on the north side of the ridge.

From the saddle the trail descends diagonally, with a few rudimentary switchbacks in the steepest places, across northeast-facing talus slopes to level off and disappear in the middle of mile-long, quarter-mile-wide Ants Basin. Clumps of whitebark pine and subalpine fir on the floor of the basin shelter many excellent campsites. Small streams, springing from the base of the ridge and meandering across the basin, provide marvelous, ice-cold drinking water. Three beautiful, flower-lined ponds are too shallow to contain trout.

Although a number of large rock cairns seem to point the way, there is no trail across Ants Basin, and the trail beyond the basin, leading north into Warm Springs Creek canyon, is very difficult to find. The best way to find it is to go directly northwest to the edge of the "basin"; from there you descend, still northwest, to the edge of a large flat, then turn east and look for a small meadow at the top of a ridge running north into the canyon. This 15-20-acre meadow is the key to finding the trail again. A small creek runs across the south side of the meadow. Pick your way down beside its north bank until you find a large rock cairn. The trail drops steeply east from the cairn down an open, rocky slope, then is well-defined through a grove of trees. Continue east down another open slope and look for blazes where the trail enters more forest and turns north down the side of the

ridge. Descend moderately from this point, on good, well-defined trail through heavy forest and occasional open slopes, to a junction with the Warm Springs Creek trail at the bottom of the canyon.

A sign at this junction, pointing toward Ants Basin, indicates: "4-FOURTH OF JULY LAKE" and "1-STRAWBERRY BASIN." However, the topo map shows no trail to Strawberry Basin from here, and Fourth of July Lake is only a little over 3 miles by way of Ants Basin. Another sign, pointing up the canyon, is more factual, showing a distance of 2 miles to Born Lakes, which are nestled under the high peaks at the head of the canyon. This is a very pleasant side trip with good fishing—if you have time.

Good trail, well-defined except where a slide has wiped it out for a short distance, descends gradually north, well away from Warm Springs Creek. After coming in view of a waterfall foaming down the east wall across the canyon, turn to cross the creek on a log jam .6 mile from the Ants Basin junction. This crossing could be uncomfortable in high water, but should not be dangerous.

Below the crossing, Warm Springs Creek canyon and the trail turn northwest. You cross a rocky outwash flat and a meadow northeast of the creek and enter a grove of large spruce and fir containing an elaborate sheepherders' or stockmen's camp with tables and benches. For

A short stop-over at Fourth of July Lake can produce a 10-inch cutthroat trout

2.5 miles beyond the camp, the trail stays well up on the northeast side of the canyon, descending moderately across alluvial fans and open slopes, and through patches of forest while the creek drops steeply down a narrow gulch. As the canyon turns westward, the trail makes a steep descent through heavy timber to come close to the creek again.

The canyon soon widens to a valley with meadows and willow flats along the creek, and the trail alternates between the flats and benches on the north side. A moderate ascent leads to a crossing of an unnamed tributary tumbling out of a canyon from the north. A little-used trail runs up this canyon to Ocalkens Lake. The trail is no longer maintained, and will probably not be signed when you get there.

Our trail continues west across a flat, then up behind a knob and over a low spur ridge as the creek plunges through a narrow defile. We skirt the side of a lush meadow, where an abandoned cabin is sheltered by a grove of trees, then climb moderately again to the shoulder of a ridge overlooking Warm Springs Creek as it turns northwest. A small, marshy lake across the creek is at the lower end of Mountain Home canyon. Fair campsites are on a bench between the trail and the creek.

Alluvial flats and a long, log drift fence mark the upper end of The Meadows. The Meadows is really one huge meadow, once a lake, 5 miles long and up to 1 mile wide. It is all grass, except for a few willow thickets, and large herds of cat-

tle graze it every summer. Warm Springs Creek meanders through The Meadows in a number of channels, blocked by beaver dams where willows provide food and building material. Strangely dull-colored brook trout, without the usual markings, hide under cutbanks and in the deeper spots in the sandy-bottomed channels. They rise avidly to dry flies in the evening, and a 10-incher will give you a battle. Be careful not to hook a steer on your backcast—he'll give you more battle than you want.

The *Washington Peak* quadrangle shows the trail running along the base of the steep east slope to a point well below the drift fence before turning to cross to the west side of The Meadows. On the ground it's pretty hard to tell where the trail goes. The creek has shifted its course through the alluvial flats above the fence a number of times and has washed out parts of the old trail. There is trail on the west side at least to the west end of the fence, so cross where it looks easiest and pick up the trail at the base of the west slope. A mile and a half of level walking from the drift fence will bring you to a junction with the Pigtail Creek vehicular trail. Trailbikes are authorized on this trail and on the Warm Springs Creek trail from this junction north to Garland Creek.

Many campsites, badly abused by people and cattle, are in lodgepole-pine groves near Pigtail Creek and .8 mile farther north, near Martin Creek.

Beaver house in The Meadows

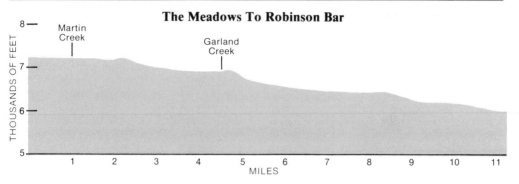

The Meadows To Robinson Bar

Martin Creek

Garland Creek

From the Pigtail Creek trail junction north to Martin Creek, the trail follows an old jeep road. You cross Pigtail Creek in less than a half mile, then Martin Creek in another half mile. We crossed on footlogs, but high water may have washed them out.

After skirting more lodgepole pines sheltering better campsites, the trail turns into the center of the meadow and fords Warm Springs Creek half a mile from Martin Creek. It is a good-sized stream here, and could be dangerous in early season.

You continue across the meadow and into a sparse stand of small lodgepole pines on the east side as the meadow narrows and is finally choked with willows. As the creek plunges down a narrow granite canyon, the trail climbs moderately to the top of a small ridge to the east and passes through a drift fence put there to keep cattle from wandering down the canyon from The Meadows. Be sure to replace the poles of the gate behind you. Three steep switchbacks take you down the north side of the ridge to a crossing of Bear Lake Creek. You descend moderately beside Warm Springs Creek for a short distance, then climb slightly along the side of the canyon to stay above a swampy area.

As the canyon widens to a flat-floored valley again, the trail winds through lush grass under the trees of a parklike forest. Farther on, the trail is squeezed between the creek, now lined with tall alders, and a slide. As the creek curves away again, the trail enters an old burn, thickly overgrown with young lodgepole pines. The pines give way to willow thickets and, 4.5 miles from Pigtail Creek junction, the Garland Creek trail branches west. A good campsite, with crude table and bench, is near the junction.

You turn east from the Garland Creek junc-

tion to climb moderately over the shoulder of a ridge and drop down to Swimm Creek. Pass a poor campsite near the crossing, then circle farther east around a swampy area to three new switchbacks down the steep north face of the ridge. For the next 2 miles, the narrow valley twists around spur ridges, sometimes forcing the trail up on the slopes away from the creek. A

A quiet stretch of Warm Springs Creek below The Meadows

145

few sandy flats harbor good campsites, and fishing is good wherever you can get to the creek.

As you turn east around a spur ridge 2.5 miles below Swimm Creek, a beautiful, wide flat opens up. Grass carpets the upper part of the flat, sagebrush the lower end. Clumps of Douglas fir and lodgepole pine shelter many excellent campsites. Warm Springs Creek, almost a river now, winds east, then north, in a wide bed of gravel and boulders. Flyfishing is marvelous here for three species of stream-bred trout—rainbows, brooks and cutthroats. Not very many of them will snap your leader off, but they are all very active.

In thick lodgepole forest, a half mile below the flat, an oldtime miner's low cabin sits beside the trail, part of its sod roof still intact. Within a quarter mile, the trail turns west to cross the creek. The crossing is a good half mile above Prospect Creek, not close to it, as indicated on the *Robinson Bar* quadrangle. The creek is really a river at this point, and the ford would be very dangerous, if not impossible, in high water.

Warm Springs Creek makes a wide turn east a quarter of a mile below Prospect Creek as the trail climbs around a rocky shoulder to continue north on benches and flats away from the creek. You come close to the creek again a mile farther north, then turn almost east, well north of the creek, for .8 mile through Douglas fir and lodgepole pine before turning north around a spur ridge. As you make this turn, mountains north of the Salmon River loom up at the end of the valley—only 1 mile left to the trailhead!

Soon after turning north, the trail drops down to a ford to the east side of the creek. Do not cross the creek here. Unless access to the trailhead has been established through Robinson Bar Ranch or around the east side of the ranch, you should stay on the west side of the creek. After wandering over benches away from the creek and close again for .6 mile on a poorly defined tread, you come to obviously constructed trail leading up through talus and over a shoulder of rock that overlooks Robinson Bar Ranch on the other side of Warm Springs Creek. Well defined tread runs 300 yards down the north side of the ridge to the road just outside the locked ranch gate.

Early miners must have been very short people, or they had a lot of knots on their heads from bumping the rafters in this cabin on Warm Springs Creek

19–Aztec Mine To Garland Basin, Casino Lakes And Big Casino Creek

Although all 18.5 miles of this trip are open to trailbikes, only the first 4.5 miles into The Meadows are heavily used. People are very scarce on the Martin Creek section, and not often seen in Garland Basin or around Casino Lakes. This is a low-altitude excursion, considering that it is in the White Clouds—the highest point on the trail is 9,100 feet, at the top of the pass south of Casino Lakes. Without side trips or layovers, the one-way trip is easily completed in four days.

Panoramic vistas are a bit limited because much of the country is heavily wooded, but secluded lakes and moss-bordered creeks offer a different kind of beauty. Wildflowers are everywhere. The Garland lakes, Casino lakes and Rough Lake (a 3.5-mile side trip) all provide excellent fishing.

If you don't have a high-clearance vehicle to get up the Fisher Creek road to Aztec Mine, a very pleasant walking alternative is the Williams Creek trail. The other end of the trip, at Salmon River Campground, is accessible to any vehicle. The last crossing of Big Casino Creek, near the end of the trip, can be dangerous during high water. Alternate routes are via Rough Creek and Boundary Creek.

Two **topo maps**, the *Casino Lakes* and *Washington Peak* quadrangles, contain almost all the trails involved, if you start from Aztec Mine. A mile and a half of trail in The Meadows is on the *Robinson Bar* quadrangle, and the lower parts of the Fisher Creek road and the Williams Creek trail are on the *Obsidian* quadrangle.

Somewhat newer log buildings at Aztec Mine

STARTING POINT

The Fisher Creek road turns east from Highway 75 about 2 miles south of Obsidian, near milepost 175. The first mile of the road is good gravel surface, but then, beyond a group of summer homes, the surface deteriorates rapidly as the road comes closer to Fisher Creek. In 1986 a large washout closed the road completely 2 miles from the highway. The road was supposed to be repaired by the summer of 1987. If it has been rebuilt, the first two or three miles of the road will probably be in better condition than they have been for years. After traversing 5 miles of rough road, however, you still have to face the last half mile up to Aztec Mine, which is very close to being four-wheel-drive only.

A pleasant alternative to the difficult drive to Aztec Mine is to walk or ride 7.2 miles on the excellent Williams Creek trail to a junction with the Pigtail Creek trail in the canyon below Aztec Mine. The Williams Creek trailhead is clearly signed on the east side of Highway 75 just north of Obsidian. (The trail and trailhead have been relocated from the route shown on the *Obsidian* quadrangle.)

The car-shuttle or pick-up point at the end of the trip is the Salmon River Campground, 4.5 miles down the Salmon River from Stanley. The bridge to the south bank of the river is downriver from the campground. The trailhead is on the west side of Big Casino Creek at the south side of the campground.

If you should decide to go out the Rough Creek trail, the route to that trailhead is described in Backcountry Trip 20.

A shorter alternative ending, the Boundary Creek trail, brings you to a trailhead 1 mile east of Highway 75 near the north end of Sawtooth Valley. The signed turnoff for this trailhead is between mileposts 183 and 184, opposite the Sawtooth Fish Hatchery.

DESCRIPTION
Aztec Mine To Garland Basin

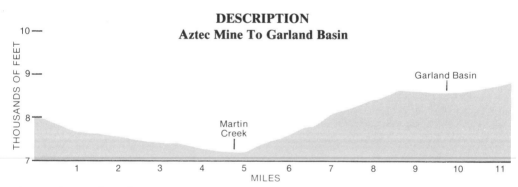

Aztec Mine consists of two or three log cabins and a dilapidated log headframe on top of the divide between Fisher Creek, draining west, and Pigtail Creek, draining east into The Meadows. The mine seems to be abandoned, but the cabins appear to have been recently inhabited.

The Pigtail Creek trail, actually a jeep road, begins at a locked gate north of the buildings. The trail register and various signs, including one that limits vehicular travel to two-wheel machines, are by the gate. Start the descent by looping west around a ridge shoulder, then turn northeast down a ravine. Within the first quarter mile, a mine-car track crosses the road from a fairly recent prospect tunnel. Stay out of the

tunnel; it's not only dangerous, it's private property.

The ravine soon becomes a narrow canyon, with a tributary creek in the bottom, turning northwest and descending to a flat and, 1.4 miles from the trailhead, a junction with the trail coming over the ridge from Williams Creek. A roofless log cabin, now used primarily as an outhouse by frequent travelers, sits near the junction. Two creeks come together below the flat to form Pigtail Creek.

A confusing sign at the Williams Creek junction points down the canyon .3 mile to Big Meadow. This is not the The Meadows, through which Warm Springs Creek flows; it is a meadow .3 mile down this canyon, just as the sign says. The trail (road) descends moderately down the canyon on the east side of the creek, mostly in sparse lodgepole pines and Douglas firs except for "Big Meadow." Glacier-rounded knobs of solid, light gray Idaho granite rise above the walls of the narrow canyon.

As the canyon widens and other streams join Pigtail Creek, there is good fishing beside the trail for native cutthroat to 8-9 inches.

Three and three quarter miles from the trailhead, you come to a **Y** in the trail on the edge of The Meadows, a 5-mile-long by 1-mile-wide expanse of luxurious grass. Take the left fork north a half mile to cross Pigtail Creek, then .4 mile farther through the grass to a log drift fence running all the way across the meadow. Look for a gate in the fence near the trees on the west side of the meadow. Please close the gate after going through it if you found it closed. Now head northwest until you find Martin Creek within .3 mile. The trail is not defined nor marked here in the meadow. An icy ford will take you to the north bank, where you can pick up the Martin Creek trail headed west in a lodgepole-pine grove. Trailbikes are allowed on this trail, but it is not heavily used.

You climb moderately west into a steep-sided canyon beside cascading Martin Creek, then make a steep turn north around a granite knob. Level off for a short distance before climbing steeply west again to the lower end of a wide, glaciated valley. The trail approaches the creek again at an idyllic spot for a rest. Logs have dammed a grassy-banked pool, shaded by Douglas firs and lodgepole pines. A few minutes of soaking in the icy water will anesthetize those aching feet. Pan-sized cutthroat trout rise

eagerly from under logs and from beneath cutbanks in the narrow stream above the pond.

A half mile of good, almost level trail, leading west in the lush valley, brings you to a junction where a sign points north to Garland Creek. The trail on up Martin Creek deadends within a short distance.

On the way to Garland Basin, and eventually Garland Creek, our trail climbs moderately, then moderately steeply, northwest up the side of the Martin Creek valley. You cross a sagebrush slope above lodgepole forest and enter the valley of a small tributary stream. The valley soon narrows to a steep-sided canyon, and the trail turns west up a side gully to climb steeply over a ridge. A quarter mile farther on, and 1.3 miles from Martin Creek, an open bowl is at the head of the canyon. An elaborate campsite, with chain-sawed chairs, table and lean-to frames is in the edge of the trees on the lower side of the bowl. Feeder streams trickle through the grass, watering wildflowers before combining to plunge down the canyon below.

The trail skirts the west edge of the bowl and soon begins a steep climb north to the top of the ridge between Martin Creek and Garland Basin. Among the sagebrush on the open slope, many wildflowers bloom, including lupines, phlox, a light-blue larkspur and a very dark purple one. Soon you level off and turn west across the top of the ridge to overlook Garland Basin.

North of the heavily forested basin, a 9,000-foot-plus ridge builds up northeast to 9,954-foot Lookout Mountain, highest peak in the area. Only one of the many Garland Lakes can be seen through the trees on the basin floor. The rest are hidden around the ridge to the west or in the forest below.

From this overlook, contour west almost level on the side of the ridge for .6 mile to the outlet creek of the first Garland Lake. The lake is out of sight a quarter mile west above the trail. To get to it, cross the creek, climb the small ridge above the west bank and turn south across its crest toward the main ridge. Where the spur ridge approaches the main ridge, the outlet creek flows through a gap. Follow the creek west to the 12-15-acre round lake, completely surrounded by heavy forest. Tiny pink and white heather blossoms color the shoreline, and beautiful cutthroat trout will rise to a well-placed fly.

The Meadows

Back on the trail, you continue, with a few minor ups and downs, around the south side of Garland Basin in lodgepole pines and subalpine firs. Pass a spring and a small creek before skirting the north edge of a large meadow and the south shore of a small pond. The trail has been relocated here; the topo map shows it going directly across the meadow.

Now turn a little southward around a shoulder, cross another small creek and climb moderately up a bare hillside to the edge of a cup holding the next Garland Lake. This lake is a little more open, smaller and deeper than the first, and contains a good population of 9–10-inch cutthroat trout. Excellent campsites are around the east side of the lake, away from the shoreline.

A small creek a quarter mile west of the second lake is the last sure source of drinking water this side of Casino Lakes, 1.5 miles west over the ridge. A moderate climb of .8 mile, wandering a little north of west through thick forest, brings you to a four-way trail junction at the top of the ridge on the west side of the basin—11.2 miles from Aztec Mine. The trail crossing our trail goes northeast around the head of Garland Basin past a junction with the Garland Creek trail at .7 mile, then up the north ridge to another junction with a trail to Lookout Mountain before continuing across the ridge to Rough Creek. In the opposite direction, the cross-trail connects with the Boundary Creek and Little Casino Creek trails. Casino Lakes are straight ahead across the intersection.

Side Trip to Rough Lake

A sign at the Casino Lakes junction points northeast to Garland Creek Trail. This is also the route to the north ridge and Rough Creek. The trail descends moderately around the head of the basin .7 mile to a meadow with a beautiful little lake in its center. In the third week of July, shooting stars and alpine buttercups saturated the meadow with color, contrasting with remnant snowbanks in the thick stand of surrounding firs. Skirt the west side of the meadow to a junction with the Garland Creek trail—6 miles down to Warm Springs Creek and the trail described in Backcountry Trip No. 18.

Beyond a small hump to the north, you turn east around another small lake and begin a steep climb of .3 mile to the ridgetop north of the basin. North of the crest, Rough Creek flows north to the Salmon River through a wide valley. To the southeast the view extends across Garland Basin and The Meadows to the highest White Cloud peaks, including Castle Peak. Rough Lake is out of sight in a cirque to the northwest.

The off-trail route to Rough Lake begins with a steep climb west through gnarled whitebark pines along the brow of the ridge. After a quarter mile, angle over to the north side of the ridge and look for a faint trail contouring north around a shoulder. You must stay above some cliffs on your right, then descend steeply northwest into the cirque containing the lake. If you go more than a half mile from the trail without finding the lake, you should backtrack rather than take a chance by climbing down the cliffs.

Subalpine firs, spruce and whitebark pines line most of the shoreline of 6-acre Rough Lake, but there are plenty of open places for flyfishing. The deep lake boils with pan-sized brook trout hitting anything that touches the surface of the water. There are also rumored to be large cutthroat trout in Rough Lake, but we didn't find any. Excellent campsites are in the trees near the outlet.

Mostly open shoreline of Rough Lake offers easy fishing

150

Garland Basin To Salmon River Campground

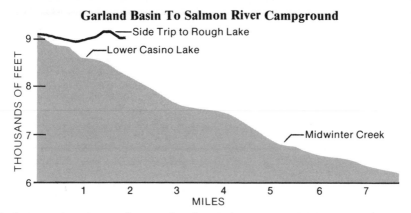

From the four-way junction on the west rim of Garland Basin, the Casino Lakes trail descends steeply northwest, first in a gully, then zigzagging on badly worn tread down a rocky slope. In less than a half mile, the trail levels out in a boggy flat and passes east of the first Casino Lake. This marshy lake is surrounded by spruce bog and is almost unapproachable.

Another quarter mile of moderate descent beside a small stream in thick forest brings you to Lower Casino Lake. Although this lake also has a swampy shoreline, a good campsite sits on a shelf above the west shore near the trail. Excellent fishing for brook trout to 12 inches makes wading the swampy shores worthwhile.

As you continue north, a good campsite is near the outlet of Lower Casino Lake. Rustic benches and table attest to saws and axes carried by horses or trailbikes. Two or three hundred yards farther down, you cross a tributary of what is now Big Casino Creek. Continue for a half mile on a moderate descent through open lodgepole pines on the west slope to a crossing of Big Casino Creek on adequate footlogs. You cross the creek four more times in the next 1.3 miles of descent down steeper canyon. Some of these crossings would be difficult during high water.

On the east side of the canyon, the trail descends moderately through open forest, well up from the creek. In the next 2 miles, Douglas firs replace the subalpine firs of higher altitudes and alders begin to appear along the creek. Grass, prostrate juniper, Labrador tea and red heather form a verdant understory, liberally sprinkled with wildflowers—arnica, lupine, monkshood and an intensely scarlet Indian paintbrush.

Below an area of dying lodgepole pines, 3 miles from Casino Lakes, the trail comes close to the creek again in a flat that is a veritable jungle of spruce, fir and alder.

Now you ascend moderately away from the creek, round a shoulder, and struggle down the next three quarters of a mile on the worst piece of trail on this trip. It is not a steep slope, but the trail has been cut in a straight line through a fairly thick stand of lodgepole pines, and has since washed out to become a ditch filled with boulders and crisscrossed by fallen trees. The Forest Service plans to reroute this section of trail when funds are available. Meanwhile, the obstacle course ends at the crossing of Midwinter Creek—an excellent rest stop.

Half a mile below Midwinter Creek, in a wider valley, beavers have successfully dammed the creek above the washed-out remains of a man-made dam. From the dam, you climb slightly in sagebrush past the remains of a cabin, and drop down by some old mine workings. Below the diggings, beavers have built another large dam completely across the creek. Within a short distance below the beaver dam you should cross to a jeep road on the creek's west side. This would be a very dangerous crossing in high water, but the trail on the east side soon gives out. No sign tells you where to cross.

A mile of moderate descent on the jeep road, washed out by the creek in places, brings you to the trailhead and the Salmon River campground.

20–Rough Creek To Garland Basin

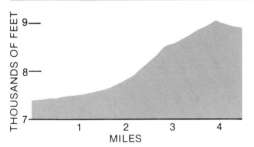

THOUSANDS OF FEET

9—

8—

7—

1   2   3   4

MILES

You can make this trip, as far as the upper end of Garland Basin and back, in one day if you want—it's only 4.5 miles one way. If, on the other hand, you want to enjoy a more leisurely pace, identify the wildflowers, explore more of Garland Basin, and make a side trip to good fishing in Rough Lake, plan on a four-day trip and a total of 20 miles or more.

Two alternative semiloop trips are possible: (1) Down Garland Creek from Garland Basin to Warm Springs Creek and out to Robinson Bar, and (2) back to the Salmon River campground by way of Casino Lakes and Big Casino Creek. Trails and car-shuttle or pick-up points are described in Backcountry Trips 18 and 19.

Except for the possibility of snow on the north side of the ridge between Rough Creek and Garland Basin, the round trip is an excellent early-season excursion. Crossings of Rough Creek are not dangerous.

Topo maps—The trail to Garland Basin and the semiloop back down Big Casino Creek are on the *Casino Lakes* quadrangle. Part of the semiloop to Robinson Bar is on the *Robinson Bar* quadrangle.

STARTING POINT

Rough Creek is one of the few trailheads in the White Clouds that can be reached in a modern sedan. Four miles of narrow but good gravel road climb up the lower canyon from a Salmon River bridge 9.5 miles east of Stanley and 1.5 miles below the Basin Creek campground.

No sign marks the turnoff and bridge to the Rough Creek road. Upper Harden Creek, on the north side of the highway and directly across from the turnoff, has a sign but it is legible only from the east.

Across the bridge the road turns west and makes a series of switchbacks up the side of the Salmon River canyon before turning south up the west side of narrow Rough Creek canyon.

Two and a half miles up the canyon a reasonably modern building appears above the road on the right and the road turns to cross the creek on a high fill over a culvert. After climbing a short distance up the east side of the canyon, the road turns south again up a side canyon, goes around a hump and enters a wide valley where Rough Creek meanders through a thick forest of lodgepole pine and subalpine fir.

The end of the road and the trailhead are at the lower end of the valley. Excellent campsites are near the trailhead, and the creek has small cutthroat and brook trout.

DESCRIPTION

Start walking south on excellent, almost level trail east of Rough Creek for the first quarter mile, then cross to the west bank on good footlogs. Continue south through a marshy area, accented with marsh marigolds, shooting stars and globeflowers in early summer. As the sides of the valley close in, the trail moves up on the west slope and ascends at a moderate rate, still in heavy forest of lodgepole pine and mixed firs.

As you come close to the creek again a mile above the first crossing a relatively recent mining claim is on the east bank. Part of the sod roof is still on the miner's cabin, and rusted remnants of his equipment, including a hand-cranked winch, are strewn about. A diversion ditch from the creek and a water-filled shaft are the total existing result of what must have been years of effort.

On the west slope, the trail climbs moderately again and, 2 miles from the trailhead, crosses an open, grassy slope before dropping down to cross to the east bank of Rough Creek. An excellent campsite is under the trees at the lower edge of the slope.

Rough Creek turns southwest from the crossing, and the trail makes a steep ascent in two long switchbacks to the brow of a ridge to the southeast. Continue at a moderately steep rate of climb south to the top of this spur ridge, then level off for a short distance to reach a trail junction to Lookout Mountain. The fire lookout tower at the top of Lookout Mountain is 2 miles east and 1,500 feet higher. It's a very steep trail and in most years isn't free of snow until late July.

Our trail to Garland Basin turns southwest along the side of the main ridge, then climbs through a steep ravine to a bench before starting the final steep diagonal on rough tread to the pass at the top of the ridge. Your climb to the thin row of weather-beaten whitebark pines on the crest is rewarded by a magnificent panorama south and east across Garland Basin to the highest peaks of the White Cloud range.

Since you are already on top of the ridge, this is a good time to make the side trip to Rough Lake described in Backcountry Trip 19. It has the only good fishing in this area—Garland Basin has no fish.

If you plan to go to Robinson Bar, the Garland Creek trail branches east at the second lake in the basin below you. Garland Basin invites your exploration and has beautiful lakes, campsites and excellent fishing. The alternative return trip down Big Casino Creek, including good fishing at Casino Lakes, is described in Backcountry Trip 19.

Garland Basin from the ridge above Rough Creek

21–Boulder Chain Lakes

A dozen crystal-clear lakes, set in solid rock, form giant, watery steps to the base of the 11,000-foot-plus main ridge in the remote interior of the White Cloud range. More than a thousand people may travel the 8 miles of rebuilt trailbike trail over Red Ridge as far as Frog Lakes during a summer season. But trailbikes are barred above Willow Lake, and probably not more than a dozen people a year walk the next 5 miles of rougher trail all the way to Lonesome Lake at the top of the Boulder Chain.

Fish are easy to catch in all lakes of the chain, but the lakes are so over-populated with rainbow and cutthroat trout that few of the fish ever grow to be more than 8 or 9 inches long. Frog Lakes, although much more heavily fished, harbor magnificent, fat cutthroats to 16 inches or more.

You can continue on a north-south traverse of the high White Clouds past Castle Lake, Castle Peak and Chamberlain Basin to trailheads in Washington or Germania Basin, but it's a very long way around for a car-shuttle. If access problems to trailheads on the upper East Fork of Salmon River road have been resolved, you can plan a semiloop trip down Little Boulder or Wickiup creek. Otherwise the trip to Boulder Chain Lakes is a round trip of three or four days. Or you can combine it with Backcountry Trip 22 to Big Boulder Lakes for a trip of up to a week and 25 or 30 miles.

Early-season travelers will not have much trouble with stream crossings, but are apt to find a great deal of snow on the north slope of Red Ridge and around most of the Boulder Chain Lakes. In most summers, the snow will be gone by the middle of July.

You can drive to the trailhead in a modern sedan, but it will be very dusty by the time you get there.

All but .8 mile of the trail is on one **topo map**, the *Boulder Chain Lakes* quadrangle. The other .8 mile and the trailhead are on the *Livingston Creek* quadrangle.

STARTING POINT

First find the East Fork of Salmon River road. It turns south from Highway 75, 4 miles east of Clayton and 37 miles down the Salmon River from Stanley.

The first 10 miles up the wide valley are paved. The remaining 8 miles to the Big Boulder Creek road are well-graded gravel, but dusty unless it has rained recently. Many picturesque clusters of log ranch buildings sit beside the road, and herds of cattle and sheep dot the vivid green pastures on both sides of the river. If you're making the trip in late July or August,

Window rock beside the Big Boulder Creek road

Lake 9755, near the top of the Boulder Chain—Lonesome Lake is in the cirque to the right

take time to stop at one of the bridges and watch the spawning salmon swim up the river, over 700 miles from the Pacific Ocean. Because it is a salmon spawning stream, the East Fork is closed to all fishing until early September.

The Big Boulder Creek road, turning west, is just beyond the bridge over the creek. Unless there has been a recent change, you won't need to worry about mistakenly going very far beyond the junction—a local rancher has put a locked gate acrosss the road less than a mile above Big Boulder Creek.

The road recrosses the creek less than a half mile from the junction, and climbs steeply on the north side of a narrow canyon. The Forest Service maintains the road and, although some of it is one-lane, it is usually in good shape.

Above the road, 2 miles from the junction, a window rock stands against the sky—an old volcanic plug with a hole eroded through it, almost gothic in shape. At 4 miles, the canyon widens to a flat-floored valley and Livingston Mill comes into view at the confluence of Big Boulder and Jim creeks.

Just before you get to a wire gate across the road, a dirt road turns left (south) past an old tailings pond to the trailhead close to Big Boulder Creek.

The unlocked gate will not prevent you from continuing through the Livingston Mill property and on up the Jim Creek road to the top of Railroad Ridge, if you so desire. Jim Creek road

beyond the mill is impassable to anything but four-wheel-drive vehicles or trail-bikes, however.

It is worth driving beyond the gate to look at the dilapidated mill buildings and the residential area south of Jim Creek. Twenty or so houses line both sides of "Main Street," and a former manager's grand log house is on a knoll to the west. A diesel generator at the mill has not run for at least 30 years, so the wires still draped from leaning power poles are useless. At least two of the houses are still occupied by the present owners of the property. Do not enter the mill buildings or cross Jim Creek to the residential area. It is all private property.

The "Castle Peak" trailhead is east of a fence along the side of the broached tailings pond below the mill. A leveled space beside a dike along the creek provides space for two portable toilets and parking for 15 to 20 vehicles. Besides listing distances to various points, a sign at the trailhead reads, "TRAVEL WAY OPEN TO FOOT AND HORSE TRAFFIC, TWO-WHEEL VEHICLES. CLOSED TO ALL OTHER TYPES OF VEHICLE TRAVEL BEYOND THIS SIGN."

Although we caught native cutthroat trout in Big Boulder Creek below the trailhead in 1979, no fish rose during our visit in the summer of 1986. A spring flood in 1986 that changed the course of the creek may be responsible for the change.

Livingston Mill in 1979

DESCRIPTION
Livingston Mill To Little Redfish Lake Junction

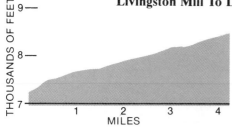

Good, recently constructed trail ascends gradually west from the trailhead on a dike for .2 mile before crossing Jim Creek where it flows out of the Livingston Mill property. Another .3 mile of gradual climb on a bench between Big Boulder Creek and an old rail fence brings you to the southwest corner of the mill property. The next half mile of moderately steep ascent up the ridge between Big Boulder and Jim creeks is on an old jeep road. The road disappears at a slide, and good trail goes around the slide to a bench far above cascading Big Boulder Creek in a narrow canyon. Another quarter mile of gradual climb brings the trail beside the creek in mature spruce-and-lodgepole-pine forest.

Then you come out into an open willow flat and follow the northwest side before turning to cross the creek on a new bridge in the middle of the flat. At the upper end of the flat, the Livingston Mill-Castle Divide trail branches left up the hill just before the Big Boulder Creek trail crosses the creek again. The *Boulder Chain Lakes* quadrangle shows the first creek crossing and the trail junction at the lower end of the flat.

The wide new trail ascends three moderate switchbacks south to the top of a spur ridge, then climbs back and forth across the brow of the ridge in open forest to a saddle where the Little Redfish Lake trail branches left.

Side Trip To Little Redfish Lake

This Little Redfish Lake is almost a mile up the north side of Red Ridge from the trail to Frog Lakes—obviously different from the other, crowded Little Redfish Lake far to the west on the other side of Sawtooth Valley. The trail is closed to trailbikes.

The trail starts east, crosses a tiny creek, and then turns south to climb steeply, sometimes

very steeply, through a series of grassy swales, bordered by lodgepole pines, subalpine firs and spruce. When you stop to rest, which you surely will, you will discover wonderful close-up and distant views. Underfoot, gilias, forget-me-nots, globeflowers and yellow-red columbines bloom in the grass. Looking up to the west, a white wall of limestone looms above the flat-floored upper valley of Big Boulder Creek. Away to the north, dark red Railroad Ridge fills the middle distance, topped by purple crests north of the Salmon River canyon.

As you level out somewhat, you come close to the outlet creek and follow it up to the lake. Except on the south side, 100 yards of lily pads and marshy grass surround 40-acre Little Redfish Lake inside a wall of trees. The south shore is steeper and firmer, with trees reaching the shoreline in a couple of places. A rough trail goes all the way around the lake in the edge of the trees. Excellent campsites are sheltered by large subalpine firs near an inlet stream on the southwest side.

We didn't fish, but we did see a lot of trout—rainbows or cutthroats to at least 10 inches. It's a marvelous, isolated spot to spend a day or two.

Rebuilt trail below the
Little Redfish Lake junction

Little Redfish Lake Junction To Frog Lakes

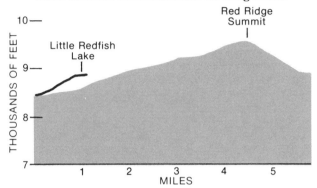

All the trail from Little Redfish junction to the top of Red Ridge has been rebuilt and relocated from the route on the *Boulder Chain Lakes* quadrangle. Only a few short sections of the new trail are steeper than a moderate climb.

We begin with a half-mile-long traverse west along the very steep slope above Big Boulder Creek valley to a crossing of a tiny creek. Although the trail crosses this stream seven more times on the way up, the higher crossings may be dry in late summer, so this may be the last drinking water for 3 miles to the other side of Red Ridge. A short distance past the cross-ing, we begin a series of long switchbacks to climb south through mixed forest and flower-decked open slopes.

At the top of this set of switchbacks, turn directly south across a flat shelf to a small, round, pothole lake at 9,250 feet. The water is not more than 4 or 5 feet deep (less in late sum-mer), so the sun warms it to swimming tempera-ture. You can get wet and wash off some sweat, but the bottom is muddy.

Turn east beyond the lake to begin the final set of switchbacks to the top of the ridge. On the third switchback you come out of forest onto an open, grassy slope, dotted with alpine flowers—phlox, alpine buttercups, asters and red and white heathers. Panoramic views of most of the northern White Clouds stretch away north and west.

From among the stunted whitebark pines on the summit, you get a first look at the majestic north face of Castle Peak, 4 air miles south. Below to the southeast, two Frog Lakes reflect the sky inside their borders of brilliant green grass. West along the ridge, a magnificent group of varicolored peaks top 11,000 feet.

An unusual, exclusively whitebark pine for-est extends almost a half mile down the north face of Red Ridge before giving way to sage-brush. The trail descends south at a moderate grade in a series of long switchbacks. At the bot-tom of the third traverse, as you turn east, a small stream offers the first drinking water on this side of the ridge. During two more traverses across the sagebrush slope, look for wildflowers that grow best in this habitat—sulfur flower, beeplant, wallflower and silky phacelia, for starters.

Red and yellow columbine blooms at 9,000 feet in August

Two more short switchbacks dip down to the head of Spring Basin, where the trail crosses to the southwest side and then descends moderately southeast through the edge of the bordering forest. Less than a half mile in the trees brings you to a small pond west of the larger of the two Frog Lakes, 9 miles from Big Boulder Creek and 10.7 miles from Livingston Mill.

Frog Lakes are surrounded by grassy marshes and lily pads except for short stretches of firmer shoreline around the northeast side of the big lake. Badly abused campsites are on a knoll beside the small pond west of this lake. Excellent campsites are on a low ridge above the southeast shore of the big lake. The little lake

has a wide border of marsh all around and no campsites. The lake water is drinkable, but you may feel better about it if you boil it first.

The name and the froggy appearance of the lakes is deceiving. Frogs frequent the marshy shores, true enough, but a little farther out, beautiful, fat cutthroat trout make solid "whops" as they leap all the way out of the water after airborne insects. You may land a trophy if you can keep him from breaking off in the lily pads. If you have your camera with you on the northeast shore as the sun drops behind the west ridge, you will be able to record a magnificent reflection of the brilliantly lit north face of Castle Peak looming up in the southwest.

Frog Lakes To Boulder Chain Lakes

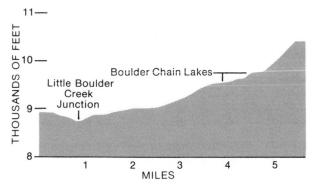

The trail from Frog Lakes still follows the route shown on the *Boulder Chain Lakes* quadrangle around the head of Little Boulder Creek valley. It is an almost level contour .8 mile around to the outlet end of Willow Lake, lowest of the Boulder Chain.

The trail forks just beyond Little Boulder Creek, the outlet stream from Willow Lake. A good campsite is in the trees north of the outlet. The east fork divides again within 1.3 miles— one trail runs down Little Boulder Creek and the other climbs up to Castle Peak Divide. Our west fork to the Boulder Chain Lakes climbs steeply southwest across the heavily forested side of a knob south of Willow Lake.

You continue climbing around the west side of the knob, then dip down to cross the log jam at the outlet of Hatchet Lake, larger than Willow Lake. (These lakes are named on the Sawtooth National Forest map, but not on the topo map.) A steep scree slope drops from a peak into the southwest side of Hatchet Lake. Excellent campsites are on a flat northwest of it. Starved 8-inch rainbow trout rise avidly to flies even in mid-afternoon.

The next rocky basin, a quarter-mile climb west over jumbled boulders, holds three beautiful lakes in a row. These aren't named anywhere, so they go by their elevations on the topo map—8939, 8978 and 9008. Beside the first lake, 8939, the trail gets rougher and harder to follow. Cross the outlet creek below Lake 8939 and go halfway around the south shore, then turn uphill beyond the butt of a very large rotted snag that fell long ago. Climb steeply through a ring of subalpine firs and you will find the trail running west between the trees and the talus slope above. The trail is clear past some good campsites on the top of a moraine between the first two lakes and on across the talus slide on the south shore of Lake 8978. It then turns north to cross the connecting stream between Lake 8978 and Lake 9008, just below a scenic cascade.

Now you climb over a low moraine and dip down to the north shore of Lake 9008. A gorgeous meadow, packed with wildflowers, lies between the trail and the shore as you continue northwest. A partial list of flowers includes Indian paintbrush, violets, alpine buttercups, parrot's beak, shooting stars, heathers, elephant's heads, veronica, marsh marigolds, strawberries and Labrador tea. Excellent campsites are near where the trail turns south beyond a marsh at the northwest corner of the lake. All three lakes have large populations of rainbow trout. The fish in Lake 9008 are a little larger than those in the other lakes. As you turn west away from the lake, signs request that you build no campfires higher in the basin.

A mile of fair trail climbs, first moderately and then steeply, to the next group of five lakes and a pond. The route follows the connecting stream, crossing it three times as it cascades down through jumbled rocks. The last crossing is just below the outlet of Hourglass Lake, first of the higher group of lakes.

The upper level of the basin is magnificently alpine—snow persists in sheltered locations in the middle of July, contorted whitebark pines are the predominant trees and the most arctic of wildflowers, moss campion and Townsendia, appear. A crescendo of awesome peaks and ridges forms a backdrop on three sides of the incredibly blue lakes, in basins scooped out of solid granite by ancient glaciers.

You continue west in a gradual climb past the south shore of Hourglass Lake and a small pond in the creek, then turn southwest on a scree slope past Hammock Lake. Hidden Lake is hidden, as its name implies, around a rocky shoulder to the northwest. Three rough, steep switchbacks lead up a bare rock escarpment to Scoop Lake at 9,643 feet elevation. Scoop Lake is aptly named, since it appears to have been scooped out of the side of a huge ridge, leaving long streams of talus extending into the water from the south and west slopes. The north side is more hospitable, being lower and harboring pockets of soil and some whitebark pines. The trail leads to sheltered campsites near a stream falling from Lake 9755 above to the west.

A faint trace of trail snakes up the wall of talus directly south of Scoop Lake to a basin at the head of Slickenslide Creek. Shallow Lake, Scree Lake, Quiet Lake and Noisy Lake are up there, right under the north face of Castle Peak; however, the way is blocked by snow in July.

You have run out of trail, but Lake 9755 is an easy climb up beside the outlet creek. Another half mile and 800 feet of elevation west, Lonesome Lake (really lonesome) perches in its private cirque under an 11,203-foot, unnamed peak. Lonesome is the highest lake of the chain at 10,435 feet. If the snow is too deep, go back down and see if you can find Hidden Lake. It has trout in it.

Cinquefoil beside a connecting stream in the Boulder Chain Lakes

22–Big Boulder Lakes

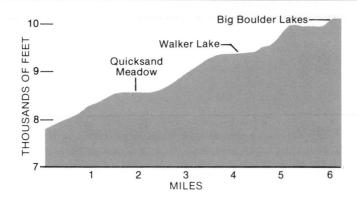

The trail goes as far as Walker Lake. From Walker Lake it's a 700-foot off-trail climb in less than a mile to the east rim of the Big Boulder Lakes basin. The view from the rim is worth the climb even if you get no farther— Walker Lake almost directly below, vividly green Quicksand Meadow farther away in the wide valley of Big Boulder Creek, and a row of magnificent peaks leading away south to Castle Peak on the skyline.

In the basin ahead, three large lakes, almost at timberline, are surrounded by snowcapped peaks reaching above 11,000 feet. Many smaller lakes are in higher cirques or in cups gouged from the floor of the basin. Wind-and-ice-sculptured whitebark pines persevere—growing no more than 10 feet in 100 years. Pockets of grass, red heather and other vividly colored arctic flowers live their short summer lives to the utmost before the snow returns. In the small streams connecting the lakes, surprisingly large cutthroat trout conduct their spawning rituals. Fishing is good in all but the highest lakes.

From the Frog Lakes junction, the trail is nonvehicular and not as easy as the new Livingston Mill-Castle Divide trail, so fewer people come this way. It's possible to walk the 7-plus miles from Livingston Mill to Big Boulder Lakes in one day, but it would be a long and strenuous day. Plan on three or four days for a comfortable round trip and some time to fish.

This is a round trip unless you are prepared to do some rugged mountaineering to come out down Livingston Creek or go over the main ridge to Warm Springs Creek.

The only **topo map** you will need is the *Boulder Chain Lakes* quadrangle.

STARTING POINT
The trailhead is at Livingston Mill, the same as for Backcountry Trip 21.

DESCRIPTION
The trailhead sign shows 7 miles to Walker Lake. The first 2 miles of trail to the Big Boulder Creek junction are described in Backcountry Trip 21.

A bridge across Big Boulder Creek just west of the junction is planned, and may be in place by the time you read this. If not, it is a difficult crossing when the creek is high. After the runoff diminishes each summer, hikers or a trail crew usually place footlogs across the creek. On the other side of the creek, begin climbing at a moderately steep to steep rate up the north slope of the valley in lodgepole forest mixed with occasional spruce and aspen.

Forest gives way to open sagebrush slopes within a half mile, and the trail comes close to the creek again along the north side of a large, triangular meadow. Excellent campsites are along the edge of the meadow before the trail climbs again over glacial debris to a pleasantly forested shelf north of the creek. An old burn takes the place of forest for a half mile as the trail continues to climb over rough terrain above the creek, foaming down a narrow canyon cut through volcanic rock. After turning south around a spur ridge, the valley opens up again and the trail dips down into the unbelievable green grass of Quicksand Meadow.

Quicksand Meadow is a gorgeous, flat expanse of 200-300 acres, overlooked on the south side by the 11,202-foot peak at the top of the ridge west of Frog Lakes. Strangely, although it has been here for a long time, the meadow is not named or indicated at all on the topo map. The area it occupies on the map is colored solid green for forest.

Excellent campsites are under large lodgepole pines in the angle between Big Boulder Creek and a tributary flowing across the meadow from the west slope. Big Boulder Creek offers marvelous opportunities for flyfishing where it meanders along the east side of the meadow. The native cutthroats aren't really big, but they certainly are active.

A sign across the tributary creek warns "WET AREAS IN THIS MEADOW ARE QUICKSAND DANGEROUS TO LOOSE LIVESTOCK." A 40-acre area in the upper meadow has been fenced with logs sometime in the past, apparently to keep livestock out of the quicksand. No cattle have been in the meadow for several years.

From the sign, the trail follows the bank of the tributary creek for a short distance, then turns across the meadow at a blazed tree. The route through the grass is marked by two posts in the meadow and blazed trees at the edge of thick lodgepole pine, spruce and subalpine fir forest on the far side. Make a loop through the trees around the meadow to cross Big Boulder Creek, flowing north at this point. Climb 100 yards up the east bank and recross to the west side below a talus slope. These crossings do not appear on the *Boulder Chain Lakes* quadrangle, although the rest of the route is fairly close to the mapped trail. A series of moderately steep switchbacks take you to a bench above the talus, where the trail continues south on the west side of a narrow gorge through which the creek cascades.

You come close to the creek again as the valley widens, then climb steeply up a rocky slope to level out again on bare granite just below a waterfall. The creek turns west above the fall and the trail makes a moderately steep ascent farther north to more bare granite. The trail then turns south to cross the fork of the creek coming from Walker Lake, then the fork coming from Island Lake. Turn west to recross the Island Lake fork and ascend gradually through heavy forest for a quarter mile to a trail junction.

The left fork continues up beside the creek to Island Lake, less than a mile southwest. Island Lake is in a narrow slot between two granite ridges—a deep, dark little lake with good fishing but virtually no campsites. It is possible to scramble up the very steep ridge northwest of Island Lake and cross over into the Big Boulder Lakes basin, but the easier route is by way of Walker Lake.

Quicksand Meadow

Although it has obviously been there for a long time, the trail to Walker Lake is not on the *Boulder Chain Lakes* quadrangle. The rough but well-defined trail turns north at the junction, ascends two steep switchbacks west, and then levels off northwest on a bench for a short distance before climbing steeply again, north and northwest toward a bare granite knob. You pass the south side of the knob and climb north over a steep little ridge to overlook an idyllic little valley containing two small lakes between which the creek from Walker Lake cascades. After a quarter-mile delightful saunter beside the lakes, the trail disappears in a low talus slope at the upper end of the valley. Look for it on the north side of the creek. Where it crosses is anybody's guess. On the north bank, 200 yards of easy walking through heather and Labrador tea bring you to the outlet of Walker Lane.

Walker Lake is a beautiful alpine lake, between a quarter-and a half-mile long and 300-400 yards wide. Talus covers the lower slopes of the ridge above the south shore, running into the water in some places. The remainder of the shoreline has open forest of subalpine firs and whitebark pines, interrupted by shelving rocks that appear to have been placed just for the convenience of flyfishermen. A number of excellent campsites are back from the east and north shorelines. Unless you are a confirmed masochist, you are well-advised to camp here and make the final climb to Big Boulder Lakes with a minimum dayhike load.

The best route to Big Boulder Lakes begins around the north shore of Walker Lake. Two hundred yards east of an inlet stream, you climb northwest up a steep slope of broken granite for a little less than a quarter mile before turning west at a more level spot to cross the creek. Climb again, west beside a smaller creek, to a small, flat marsh in a cirque. This marsh is a key point—you must find it in order to find the way up to Big Boulder Lakes basin.

Look for rock cairns on the southeast side of the marsh marking the beginning of a faint trail. The track climbs very steeply, a little east of south, snaking directly up the nose of a ridge. Near the top of the ridge, turn west over a small spur and cross the top of a talus slope to the base of a 20-foot escarpment. Continue west to a saddle in the rim and cross south to overlook a shallow, hook-shaped pond. You must find this pond again to return. Do not attempt to descend from the rim anywhere else; your way will be blocked by cliffs.

Cove Lake, lowest of the three large lakes, is a quarter mile south, A small, unnamed lake, lower and farther east, contains the largest trout. Sapphire Lake is the next lake west, and Cirque Lake is at timberline, northwest of Sapphire at the upper end of the basin. More smaller lakes are in higher basins to the south.

As you climb up to Cirque Lake, turn to look south across the basin at the majestic skyline of the highest White Clouds peaks. That view alone is worth the trip.

Big Boulder Lakes basin

Winter Activities

By the first week of December in most winters, or sooner if there is a good snow storm, activity picks up to a frenetic pace in Sun Valley/Ketchum and on the slopes of Bald and Dollar mountains. The lifts crank up and deposit their cargo at the tops of the many barbered and manicured downhill runs. From the lift landings, warming huts and restaurants at the tops of the runs, the skiers spread out in multicolored dots and dashes on their way down to start the cycle over again.

Down in the valley the ski buses and ski-racked autos scurry to and fro between lodges, stores, restaurants and lift parking lots. After dark on the slopes, lights pierce the night as grooming machines crawl up the mountains to prepare the runs for tomorrow's skiing. Below in Sun Valley, Elkhorn and Ketchum, bright colored lights splash on the snow and music throbs from the discos and bars. Thus begins the "SEASON" as contrasted with the "slack," the period between the summer "season" and the "SEASON."

A few miles to the north in the Sawtooth National Recreation Area, however, man's activity is hardly noticeable at all. With the coming of winter, beauty moves down from the unpeopled mountains to the edge of the highway. Roadside ditches, cuts and culverts are filled and rounded by the pristine white blanket. Fences disappear, leaving only white-capped

Heyburn Mountain looms above the snow-covered ice on Redfish Lake

165

tops of the posts as evidence of their existence.

The rustic building style mandated by the SNRA comes into its own when a layer of frosting is added. Probably nothing else in the world can match the image of cozy warmth projected by the firelit windows of a snow-covered log cabin on a cold winter evening. This image is further enhanced by a mile-high backdrop of snow encrusted mountains behind the cabin. Even a Forest Service pit toilet has a certain whimsical charm when it's sitting up to its doorknob in snow and wearing a tipsy 4-foot white chef's cap on its roof.

Plowed highways 75 and 21 and their accompanying power and telephone lines are the only obvious evidence of man's intrusion in the winter

... even a Forest Service pit toilet
has a certain whimsical charm ...

landscape of the SNRA. All other roads, buildings and campgrounds, except for a large parking area across from Baker Creek, are covered in universal white and closed to automobiles. The State Highway Department does make a determined, and generally successful, effort to keep Highway 75 and Highway 21 open all winter.

WINTER CLIMATE

Snow can, and does, fall on any day of the year in the mountains of the SNRA, and sometimes even falls on the floor of Sawtooth Valley during the summer months. There is no sure period of frost-free days from Ketchum north to Challis. Still, despite the occasional storm that may deposit a few inches of temporary snow on the ground in September or October, real winter ordinarily starts in November. Then the big gray winter storms build up over the mountains to the west and move quietly across to the east. By Thanksgiving there may be a foot of snow on the ground. That snow will stay in Sawtooth Valley until April or May of the next year, and in the mountains until June or July. By Christmas, even Redfish, the largest lake, is frozen over to a depth of several inches and covered in smooth, pure white, not to thaw again until the next April. By March 1 snow depth on the floor of the valley is normally four to six feet.

Winter temperatures are cold. The average daily high temperature at Ketchum for the three winter months is 33°F. The average daily low is 6°F. Temperatures north of Galena Summit are usually a few degrees lower. Minus 20°F is not uncommon at Stanley and an all-time low of minus 62°F was recorded by Clarence Cole at the Sawtooth Hotel there in December of 1972. Cole at that time operated the U.S. Weather Bureau recording station at Stanley. Potential winter visitors to the SNRA should not be unduly alarmed about the cold, however. Fortunately, when temperatures are very low, there is seldom much wind, and an adequately clothed person can usually be comfortable even on the coldest day.

The generally windless condition, even dur-

ing periods of heavy snowfall, has a definite in
fluence on the winter scene. There is essentially
no drifting of snow at lower elevations, even in
wide-open Sawtooth Valley. The snow lies over
everything in an evenly contoured blanket
building up to astonishing heights on such flat
surfaces as the tops of posts, stumps and highway signs. With each new snowfall there are
also dazzlingly beautiful buildups on the bare
limbs of aspen, cottonwood and alder thickets.

In a mature conifer forest there may be little
or no snow accumulated on the ground next to
the trunks of the trees, since the snow falling
straight down piles up on the branches until
they bend down to such an angle that the snow
falls off to the sides. The remaining snow on the
branches eventually evaporates, and the end
result is a forest of dark green spruce and fir
trees growing out of wells in the deep snow.
Small trees, sagebrush, and the willow thickets
along the rivers simply disappear until the
spring thaw.

At higher elevations there is more wind, and
drifts and cornices build up on the lee sides of
the peaks and ridges. These formations are very
beautiful and also very dangerous, for this is
where avalanches start. Visitors are warned to
stay out of steep-walled canyons and away from
high, steep slopes. Not only the slopes and
peaks are dangerous—a large avalanche can
travel all the way across the floor of a half-mile
wide canyon with devastating speed. Incidence
of avalanches is very high in all of the moun-
tainous areas of the SNRA. Ample evidence of
the force and frequency of these occurrences
can be seen everywhere in the summer months.
Anything that can snap off a quarter-mile-wide
swath of trees 1 and 2 feet in diameter, as if they
were match sticks, deserves to be treated with a
great deal of respect. The U.S. Forest Service
does not practice avalanche control in the back
country.

One other note of caution. Even though the
chill factor may not be bad for you in the SNRA
winter, it can be very bad for your automobile.
Any vehicle driven into the area during the
winter months should be prepared for subzero
temperatures. This preparation should include
adequate antifreeze, a fully charged battery,
lightweight oil, and tuning for easy starting in
high altitude and extreme cold. Not being able
to get a car started or to get it out of a remote

parking area after a long day of cross-country
skiing or snowshoeing can be a very serious
problem. Tire chains and/or snow tires are a
must. There is always some snow or ice on the
highways during the winter months, and sometimes there is a lot.

DOWNHILL SKIING AND SUN VALLEY

Although there is very little downhill skiing in
the SNRA itself (what there is is helicopter
placed), downhill skiing is the reason for approximately eight out of ten of the winter visitors being in the general area. The majority of
these people have come to ski at Sun Valley.

Sun Valley was the first destination ski resort
built in the United States. "Destination" means
that people come there to stay for a period of
days rather than driving in for the day to ski and
then going back where they came from. Sun
Valley was the first and, the present operators
claim, is still the best. There is a great deal of
validity to that claim. Snow conditions are usually ideal with a preponderance of dry powder
most of the winter. Facilities are first rate and

**Most winter visitors come for
downhill skiing at Sun Valley**
SUN VALLEY NEWS BUREAU
167

are constantly being refurbished and upgraded.

Since the world's first two chairlifts were installed on Proctor and Dollar mountains in 1936, Sun Valley's ski facilities have grown exponentially. Currently there are 12 lifts on Baldy (Bald Mountain) and four lifts on Dollar/Elkhorn for a total hourly lift capacity of 22,500 skiers. Since the largest crowd that has ever shown up on a long weekend is less than half that number, and the average number of skiers per day is between 3,500 and 4,000, it's obvious that there are very seldom any long lift lines here.

Sun Valley has a slope for everyone—from the bunny hills at the foot of Dollar to intermediate and most expert runs off the top of Bald Mountain. There are runs specifically designated for "hot doggers," and slalom and racing runs for world class competition. The longest single run is 3 miles with a vertical drop of 3,000 feet. All the runs are patrolled regularly by professional ski patrol members to make safety checks and provide first aid when necessary. Slopes are groomed constantly and snowmaking machinery has been installed all the way to the top of Baldy's Warm Springs runs to help stretch the season and make up for Mother Nature's occasional deficiencies.

Not all downhill skiers are satisfied with groomed slopes, however, For these, the ultimate thrill is alpine skiing on untracked slopes of loose powder or flawless corn snow. Some of these slopes can be reached at times by car from the top of Galena Pass or by snowmobile on the lower open slopes of the Boulders. The only way to reach really remote areas, however, is by helicopter. The U.S. Forest Service, which controls most of the area, including the SNRA, where this type of skiing is feasible, requires that every helicopter ski party be accompanied by a licensed guide. The only group currently providing this service on a regular basis is Sun Valley Helicopter Ski Guides, Inc. They operate from a heliport near the Sun Valley tennis courts.

Learning to ski or learning to ski better is no problem at Sun Valley. Over 200 professional instructors now teach at one of the oldest and best ski schools in the United States. Group instruction and private lessons are available from absolute beginning to advanced, racing and free-style skiing.

Information on downhill skiing in general and specific conditions of the various Sun Valley runs is available from Sun Valley Resort. General weather information and area snow

Skiing Bald Mountain on a typical Sun Valley day
SUN VALLEY NEWS BUREAU

reports are available at the Forest Service Ranger Station on Sun Valley Road.

Downhill skiing equipment and clothing are available at a number of outlets in the area. Names, addresses and telephone numbers are listed in the directory.

Where to Stay—There are rental accommodations during the ski season for approximately 10,000 people in the Sun Valley/Ketchum area and possible 250 more in the Hailey/Bellevue area. This includes the KOA campground on Highway 75 south of Ketchum, which does, believe it or not, stay open year-round.

Reservations may be made through Central Resort Reservations. See page 21 and the directory.

What Else is There to Do?—Not all the winter visitors to Sun Valley/Ketchum are skiing the slopes all the time. As a matter of fact, the lifts don't carry skiers up Baldy after 4:00 p.m., so skiers who complete their runs shortly after 4:00 have a long evening ahead.

There is no shortage of entertainment or things to do. For example, there are outdoor and indoor ice skating rinks at Sun Valley, both regulation size, and another outdoor rink at Elkhorn. A local amateur hockey league plays a regular schedule of games at Sun Valley, mak-

ing up in enthusiasm what they may lack in professionalism. Edelweiss Resort in north Ketchum and Heidelberg Inn in Warm Springs Canyon have covered, heated swimming pools and so do the Alpenrose and the Tamarack Lodge in Ketchum. Sun Valley Lodge and Sun Valley Inn each have an outdoor heated pool. Sun Valley stables continue operations through the winter offering sleigh-rides, day and evening, and riding in an indoor arena. Gymnasiums and saunas are available at a number of locations and the Racquetball Clubhouse in Ketchum rents courts to the public. Eleven miles south at Hailey there are three indoor tennis courts.

Ketchum/Sun Valley boasts over 40 restaurants and 30 bars offering a wide variety of cuisine, libations and entertainment at a wide variety of prices. There are at least a dozen places to dance, and, if the local scene isn't active enough, there's Hailey down the highway. Hailey has a movie theatre, as do Ketchum and Sun Valley. For those who like to shop, there is a wide variety of shops, stores, and galleries offering everything from jewelry through fine clothing and handcrafts to fine art. And if all else fails, there is cable TV.

One of the most popular extracurricular activities being taken up by downhill skiers is cross-country skiing. And just a few miles north

A helicopter can lift you to untracked slopes of fresh powder in the SNRA
SUN VALLEY NEWS BUREAU

is the entire Sawtooth National Recreation Area. More about both of these things follows.

SCENERY AND
WINTER SIGHTSEEING

The winter landscape in the Sawtooth National Recreation Area is breathtakingly beautiful. Snow, frost and ice simplify and cover most over-all textures of forest, rock, grass and brush, but accent details, such as ledges, cracks and clinging trees on a vertical wall of pink Sawtooth granite. Open sagebrush areas are changed to smooth expanses of white, broken here and there by the convoluted courses of small streams with intricately sculptured banks and snow bridges. Leafless aspen groves silhouette their graceful skeletal structure in subtle grays and whites against unbelievably blue skies.

Close-up details are, if possible, even more beautiful than the large scene. There are the fascinating patterns of small animal and bird footprints and the delicate tracings of frost on the branches and the trunks of conifers and lowly willows. Cold blue shadows of the aspens and cottonwoods stretch in needle-sharp detail across smooth snow, colored pastel rose by the late afternoon sun. A fragile, late-falling aspen leaf lies flat at the bottom of a 5-inch-deep shaft melted in the snow by solar heat accumulated by the leaf's less reflective red and yellow surface. The sides of the shaft perfectly match the shape of the leaf; even the stem has cut its own narrow slot.

There are three basic ways to see all this: from the air, from an automobile on Highway 75 or from the surface of the snow away from the highway. Each way is worthwhile and each will be described in turn.

Aerial Sightseeing Tours—Helicopter sightseeing is an excellent way to get a relatively close-up look at some very remote country in the middle of the winter. The machine can hover close to high peaks and ridges for exciting views and photography. Disadvantages are high noise and vibration levels and extremely high cost. From the Sun Valley heliport a one-hour flight is required to make a round trip to even the southern part of the Sawtooth Range. Sun Valley Helicopter Ski Guides provide helicopter tours in addition to lifting skiers to remote areas.

By contrast a four-place, single-engine light airplane can be chartered for less than half the minimum helicopter hourly rate. An early morning 1-1½ hour flight over Wood River Valley, Galena Summit, Sawtooth Valley, and the Sawtooth, White Cloud and Boulder mountain ranges is a memorable experience. Winter sightseeing flights on clear days are much smoother than summer flights because the thermals don't build up as much when the earth is covered with snow. Fixed-wing aircraft can't fly as low as helicopters do, but they're still an excellent buy for sightseeing. Scenic flights are available from a number of air-taxi and air-charter operators in the area. See the directory for more specific information.

Of course, if you're flying into the area in a private or chartered airplane, a little extra air time spent flying over the SNRA will pay large scenic dividends. Neither fixed-wing aircraft nor helicopters may land anywhere within the SNRA, except at the air strips at Smiley Creek and Stanley, without written permission from the U.S. Forest Service management.

Auto Sightseeing—Winter driving in the SNRA is limited to highways 75 and 21 and a few streets that are kept plowed in Stanley and vicinity. None of the public secondary roads in the recreation area are kept open and most of the ranchers and other hardy year-round residents give up plowing their private roads after the second or third storm. From then on, these residents rely on snowmobiles and snow tractors for transportation out to the highway.

South of the recreation area at Ketchum, Sun Valley, Elkhorn and other residential and resort areas, a number of roads and streets are cleared and open throughout the winter. The loop drive from central Ketchum through Sun Valley, Elkhorn and back down to the highway through Elkhorn Gulch south of Ketchum is scenic and interesting. Dollar and Elkhorn downhill ski areas are right beside the road and there are a number of cross-country ski trails over the golf courses between Sun Valley and Elkhorn. There are also good views of the Pioneer Mountains

Stanley and the northern Sawtooths

and Bald Mountain (Baldy) across the valley where the big downhill runs are. Other short scenic drives can be taken up Warm Springs Canyon to the bottom of the Warm Springs lift and down Big Wood River to the River Run lift for close-up looks at the skiers.

As mentioned earlier, the best of the winter scenery and the opportunity to sample some real peace and quiet are to the north in the SNRA. To experience a good variety of winter wonders, you need to go at least as far north on Highway 75 as the overlook on the north side of Galena Summit. If you have time, the drive on down the Sawtooth Valley to Stanley is well worth the effort and the gasoline. Stanley is much less crowded in winter than in summer, and the place assumes a quiet charm, with wood smoke curling from cabins buried to the eaves in the whitest of snow. Highway 75 north to Challis will be open, and Highway 21 to Boise is usually open. It's a good idea to inquire about road conditions, however, before driving west from Stanley. Plan on a minimum of 2½ hours to drive from Ketchum to the Galena Summit overlook and back in the winter, and at least 5 hours to Stanley and back. Of course, that allows for a few stops.

Start by stopping—stopping at the SNRA headquarters 8 miles north of Ketchum. In addition to viewing the river and the snow-choked cottonwood groves along the way, you'll have a chance to guess which of the many big houses along this stretch of highway were designed for winter residents and which for summer or year-round owners. Some architecture looks good in the snow, some doesn't. The U.S. Forest Service architect of the SNRA headquarters building must have had winter in mind. Not a bad idea considering the fact that winters last two or three times as long here as summers do. At any rate, the headquarters building is quite charming in the winter, with its many angles softened by the buildup of snow outside and warm wood textures and light airy spaces welcoming visitors inside.

Reasons for stopping at the headquarters are to inquire about the weather and road conditions and to pick up one of the tour-tape machines to take with you. You'll find that the staff has plenty of time to talk to you and you can take an unhurried look around the exhibits. The immaculate, heated washrooms are important, too. Remember that you won't be able to get to any of the campgrounds or picnic areas along the way and those pit toilets would be mighty cold if you could get into them.

Cross-country ski trail by Big Wood River north of Ketchum

Although the tour-tape narrative was written for the summer tourist, it's interesting and informative for the winter visitor as well. Compare the summer landscape described on the tape with the snow-covered vistas now surrounding you. For example, the reason for the snowplow guide stakes along the highway is now perfectly clear. Fortunately, most of the milepost signs are tall enough and so placed that they can be seen even in winters of heavy snow.

Ideally you'll be making this trip on the first bright clear day after a snow storm. If so, the aspen, fir and cottonwood groves in the river flats above SNRA headquarters will be a scenic wonderland, with each fir bough and bare aspen or cottonwood twig carrying a maximum load of pure white crystals. The shoulders of the Boulders on your right, gray with sagebrush in the summer, will now show smooth white contours, to be etched within a few days with the intricate swirling traces of snowmobiles and cross-country skis. Higher up, the jutting crags will be bare of snow on their steeper faces, but every tiny ledge and crack will be outlined in white against the dark sedimentary rock. All of this is juxtaposed against the bluest of blue skies, turning almost black at the zenith.

After climbing over Phantom Hill and crossing Big Wood River at milepost 143, look for a plowed loop of road on the right. This is Snow Creek/Silver Creek Flat, a major snowmobile access and parking area. The Silver Creek road bridge provides access to the open foothills of the Boulders on the other side of the river. Baker Creek valley, across the highway to the south, is wide and open with no avalanche danger in its lower reaches. If snowmobilers are there you will probably see some races on the flat inside the road loop.

At about milepost 145 and just beyond, where the highway comes close to a bend of the river, look for beaver ponds in the flat between the highway and the river. You will find a small parking area plowed on the river side of the road; it's worth the effort to stop and climb up on the piled snow to get a better look at the beavers' home. Notice that, even though the river is bridged with snow and ice in some places, there is open water in the ponds. This provides an escape route from the built-up "house" which has only underwater entrances and exits and also, a place to breath when the

beavers are reclaiming their underwater stores of willow twigs. You're not apt to see any beavers at work during the day, but the evidence is there.

Farther up the highway, and before you reach milepost 146, a turnoff leads to the Russian John Guard Station. You may see a Forest Service truck and a snowmobile parked at the turnoff, and smoke coming from the chimney of the guard station down by the river. SNRA work crews stop off here occasionally during the winter, although the road to the station isn't cleared. If you see them there, they can help you in an emergency.

Steam rising in the cold air above Russian John's hot springs, makes them more evident now than in the summer. An area around the springs above the highway, and down the hill under and across the highway where the warm water runs, will usually be clear of snow.

At Prairie Creek, a quarter mile before milepost 147, the emphasis changes from snowmobiling to cross-country skiing. Two plowed parking areas provide access to the Prairie Creek XC trail and by a footbridge to trails on the northeast side of Big Wood River. The Forest Service has reserved the Prairie Creek area for cross-country skiers and snow-

Big Wood River near Russian John

shoers only. It is closed to snowmobile use.

Above Owl Creek, Wood River in most winters will be completely bridged and covered by snow and even the head-high willow thickets along the stream will be concealed beneath a smooth blanket of white. To see the subtle sculpturing along the river's course, you will probably have to climb the high bank that the snowplows have thrown up beside the road.

These high banks impair visibility on the many curves of the highway. Since there may also be snow and ice on the pavement in unexpected places, cautious driving is definitely recommended. Late in the season you may encounter frost heaves—sharp dips and bumps in the highway that can be disconcerting and even dangerous if hit at too high a speed. The highway department does put up warnings of frost heaves in the pavement, but can't always keep up with all of them. A leisurely pace will give you a better opportunity to see the scenery anyway.

You're now approaching Galena Lodge, deep in the snow at milepost 152 at the foot of the climb to the summit. The lodge was once headquarters for a very popular cross-country ski complex, but was closed as of the winter of 1986–87.

Proceeding on up the hill toward Galena Summit, you'll find most of the mileposts and even some of the snow stakes buried in the plowed-up banks along the sides of the road. Especially in the cuts there just isn't enough room to plow the snow on the sides and eventually it has to be scooped up and hauled to a place where it can be dumped down the hill. Many of the curve and caution signs will be decorated with long evergreen boughs stuck in the tops of their support posts. This isn't because the Idaho Highway department admires greenery all that much—they do it so the snowplow operators will know where the signs are and to help the crew that digs the signs out so drivers can see them.

If the sun is warm enough to cause melting on this south-facing slope, watch for small slides from the steep snow banks and an occasional rock loosened from the steeper cuts.

There is a plowed turnout just beyond milepost 157 and another on the outside of the large

SNRA headquarters building was designed to look good in the snow

U-turn just below the summit. From both of these places marvelous views extend to the valley below and up to the crests of the ridges all around. If the weather has been very cold. there may be a thick coating of glittering hoar frost on the trees and rocks. You'll see some windblown cornices on the crests of the higher ridges and probably some recent avalanches that have run down established avalanche paths—just a reminder that avalanches can happen any time on these steep slopes. However, be assured that the highway has been carefully routed to avoid avalanche paths, and a constant watch is maintained for any snow accumulations that might topple onto the roadway.

Another plowed parking area at the summit is primarily for the convenience of cross country skiers and to allow motorists and snow removal equipment to turn around without obstructing traffic. There isn't much to see from here unless you're willing to climb up a lot of snow.

The one really "must" stop on this trip, if the weather is clear at all, is the Galena Overlook, slightly less than a mile down the north side from the summit. There will be plenty of room to park at the Overlook, but you won't find the friendly Forest Service interpretive person who presides there in the summer months and the rest rooms are not only locked up, but completely inaccessible under several feet of snow. The view is as great as ever, though—more monochromatic perhaps, but with more definition. In the clear winter air, the serrated tops of the Sawtooth Range march toward you, seemingly close enough to touch. The immense moraines leading out into the west side of the valley from the lower slopes of the Sawtooths stand out in bold relief in the low-angled sunlight, their summer forest textures and colors muffled and subdued by the snow.

Sawtooth Valley is now a wide expanse of white with isolated details of aspen groves, evergreen forests, stream banks, cabins and ranch buildings picked out in grays, blues and muted greens. The thin line of the highway is etched in sharpest black, turning intermittently to gray where it is still snow-covered—the only obvious man-made mark on a vast landscape. Much of this snow will eventually melt and flow into the Salmon River, thence into the Snake

View across upper Salmon River valley from the Galena overlook

Winter Photography

The Sawtooth winter scenery is apt to inspire an overwhelming desire to take pictures. It's not as easy, though, to take good pictures in the snow as it is at other times of the year. Even professionals have problems.

The first, and most difficult to solve, problem is that there is both too much light and not enough light. The difference in light values between direct sun on the snow and the shadow side of a rock, or a pretty girl's face, can be as much as four or five f stops. This is well beyond the recording latitude of either black and white or color films. Therefore, you will have to add light to the shadows or choose between totally black shadows and totally white snow, with no detail showing. For close-up subjects, such as the pretty girl's face, the answer is to use a strobe light to lighten the shadows and bring out detail. Be sure to check the shutter speed for synchronization (synch.) with the strobe. You must also keep the strobe fill exposure less than the overall exposure for the scene. For big scenes, the only answer is to bracket two or three different exposures.

The second, and more easily solved, problem is to understand how light meters and automatic exposure cameras work and to realize that they will be misled by snow scenes. Light meters and automatic exposure devices are designed to read the light reflected from a middle gray subject. This works fine when the subject, skin tones for example, is a middle value or when a number of values average out to middle gray. Snow scenes, however, are mostly white and your meter or camera doesn't know that unless you tell it so. The uncorrected result will be underexposed pictures with gray or blue snow instead of white.

If you are using an instamatic-type camera without any provision for exposure override, try changing the film speed setting to two f stops lower (e.g., ISO 100 to ISO 25). If that can't be done, try to get more shadows or dark objects in the picture. On more sophisticated automatic cameras, set the override exposure control to overexpose one to two f stops depending on the proportions of snow and shadow in the picture.

If you're using a non-automatic, through-the-lens-metering camera or a separate, hand-held meter, meter the palm of your hand or any other middle value object and use that reading for the exposure.

Contrary to what you might have read in the camera magazines, most modern photographic equipment will function very well in temperatures down to zero degrees Fahrenheit without any special "winterizing." The one thing that will deteriorate very fast is batteries. Replace them often.

A few other precautions for very cold weather are: Don't breathe on the viewfinder because it will frost over and you won't be able to see anything. For the same reason, don't attempt to blow snow off the lens — the lens will frost over and the camera will go blind. Wrap your camera in a plastic bag before bringing it in from the cold. This will prevent moisture condensation on lenses and metal surfaces until they warm up.

and eventually into the Columbia, finally flowing more than 800 miles to the Pacific Ocean. No wonder the Salmon is such a big brawling river in the early summer. The Salmon is quiet now, running under the snow blanket in the upper valley and not really coming out into the open until well below Smiley Creek. Its oxbowed course in the flat valley upstream of the Highway crossing is still easily discernible, however.

Take care going down the hill on the north side of the summit since there is almost always snow on the pavement on this side. The highway department tries to keep the surface sanded to provide traction, but sometimes it can't keep up with the snow. There is a cleared turnout at milepost 161 overlooking the upper valley. Then there are turnouts and chain-up areas by the first Salmon River bridge and the Frenchman's Creek bridge. A stop at one of these is worthwhile just to listen for a few moments to the water gurgling out of sight under the snow. There is also a small parking area at the Pole Creek road junction.

The Smiley Creek Resort at Sawtooth City just down the road was not open during the winter of 1986–87. It remains to be seen whether it will be open in subsequent winters.

About four miles north of Smiley Creek, on the east side of the highway a quarter mile past the Alturas Lake road, is the Busterback Ranch Cross-Country Ski Lodge. Busterback Ranch has been a very popular place to cross-country ski for several years and, with the addition of new facilities in 1986, it proposes to be one of the finest destination cross-country ski resorts in the country.

In addition to being a very large operating cattle and sheep ranch in the summer (the animals are moved to lower elevations in the winter), Busterback provides lodging, outdoor recreation and guide services for summer guests. You'll be welcome to drop in at Busterback whether you are skiers or not. There's always plenty of hot coffee as well as other libations and, if you've telephoned ahead and made reservations, you'll get a chance to dig into some really good ranch-style cooking for lunch or dinner. Excellent overnight accommodations are also available in the ranch house and nearby cabins, but during the height of the skiing season it is wise to make reservations well in advance.

"Spring Roundup" at Busterback Ranch in 1978

Incidentally, the porch of the ranch house provides a magnificent view of the White Cloud Mountains to the east. Winter sunsets, with the sun sinking behind the Sawtooths and turning the higher snow-clad White Clouds to rose, gold and lavender, are something to remember forever.

Beyond Busterback Ranch at the Valley View Summer Home road near milepost 170 another fairly large parking area is used primarily by snowmobilers making the road loop to Alturas Lake or racing on the open flats west of the highway. Between here and Obsidian there are three or four more small parking areas where snow-choked side roads meet the highway. At Obsidian the general store and filling station are open all winter, but the cafe and motel are closed from late November until mid-May.

Driving on down the valley, notice that the

A quiet morning in the living room at Busterback Ranch

snow is not quite as deep as it was higher up. The local climate of the lower end of the valley between Obsidian and Stanley is drier, but not necessarily warmer. Stanley is one of the coldest places in the entire area.

If you look west between mileposts 183 and 184, you will notice plumes of steam rising from a group of low buildings and other structures. This is the Sawtooth Fish Hatchery, completed in 1984 to attempt to restore the dwindling salmon and steelhead runs up the Salmon River. It is too soon to evaluate just how effective the effort has been, but the Idaho Department of Fish and Game is giving it a good try. You won't see much fish action here in mid-winter. The visitor center will be open, however, and graphic displays will give you a good idea of what the hatchery is trying to accomplish.

Just beyond milepost 184 you cross the Salmon River again. The Salmon looks more like a river now, although flowing at a low level, with snow encroaching on its banks and piled high on boulders in midstream. It's a good place to shoot Christmas-card pictures, particularly if you can arrange to get a few snow-laden pine boughs in the foreground.

A good-sized parking lot at the Redfish Lake road junction, half a mile north of the Salmon River bridge, will probably contain a number of vehicles. This is a very popular place for snowmobilers and cross-country skiers alike. It is an easy trip from here to the lake, and the winter scenery is magnificent. You will be able to get a distant glimpse of the lake's snow-draped backdrop from your auto a little farther down the highway, but of course you won't have the white expanse of the lake in the foreground.

The Stanley Ranger Station is open during the day, so you will have a chance to warm up in front of their large fireplace, drop off your tour tape and admire the northern Sawtooth crest from the parking lot. Look in the other direction, too, down the valley to Stanley and across the river at the working ranches huddled in the snow with their backs to the looming icy shoulder of the White Clouds. The snowmobiles you see over there will be hauling hay for cattle or bringing children home from school.

You will find a warm welcome in Stanley. Despite concerted efforts to develop the little town as a winter sports resort, the local people who stick out the long winters still aren't crowded off the streets by tourists when the snow is on. Visitation has picked up considerably since 1984–85, however, when the state highway department declared its intention to keep Highway 21 open to Boise every winter.

The Mountain Village Lodge and Restaurant, on the north side of Highway 21 at the Highway 75 junction, offers excellent accommodations and good food year-round. Directly across Highway 21, the Sawtooth Mercantile general store and filling station also stay open all winter. On the west side of town, two blocks off Highway 21, the venerable Sawtooth Hotel & Cafe provides bed-and-breakfast style rooms and delicious home-cooked meals. Indoor recreation, with live music on weekends and food and drink anytime, can be had in downtown Stanley at the Kasino Club Bar and Restaurant. Two more motels, the Valley Creek Motel, a mile out of Stanley on Highway 21, and McGowan's Resort on Highway 75 in Lower Stanley, are open all year. McGowan's also has a filling station.

If you plan to drive from Stanley to Boise on Highway 21, be sure to check road conditions before leaving Stanley. In spite of the best efforts of the Idaho Highway Department, the road is occasionally hazardous or closed. The trip through Lowman to Boise is truly spectacular in mid-winter, and the South Fork Lodge at Lowman offers a very pleasant stopover along the way. In the other direction, Highways 75 and 93 to Challis and Salmon are almost always clear. Of course you can drive back to Ketchum the way you came, and see the other side of the scenery.

Salmon River and Highway 75 make dark traces across the snow at the south end of Stanley Basin

Cross-Country Skiing and Snowshoeing

There are two basic means of travel over deep snow under your own power—skis or snowshoes. The advantages and disadvantages of each have been extolled for many years by many experts. I am not an expert, but I do have a few opinions, based on my own experience, to add to the volumes already expressed:

"Snowshoeing is a lot of hard work to get to places that are fun, exciting and beautiful. Cross-country skiing is a fun, exciting and beautiful way to get to places that are fun, exciting and beautiful, but it does require a lot of energy.

Also:

"Anyone who can walk can learn to snowshoe to almost any place. And anyone who can walk can learn to cross-country ski *on relatively level ground*. Either method of locomotion gives most of us the only opportunity we'll ever have to walk on water.''

Travel on snowshoes and skis isn't exactly new in the Sawtooth area. People around here have been using them to get around in the winters for 100-plus years. The Indians who frequented the area used snowshoes long before that, but they didn't stay anywhere near the Sawtooths in the winters if they could possibly help it. Early settlers and travelers didn't often snowshoe or ski for fun—It was simply the only way they could travel when the snow got too deep for a horse.

Cross-country ski tracks swirl down the face of a ridge being crested by two snowshoers in the background

There are amazing stories still being told of Whiskey Bob, Fred Patterson and Dave Lightheart, who carried the mail on snowshoes from Ketchum to Galena and over the summit to Obsidian and Stanley in the winters around the turn of the century. A number of hardy citizens traveled over the Sawtooth crest between Atlanta, Vienna and Sawtooth City for various reasons during the winters of the mining booms in the 1880's and '90's.

Snowshoes haven't changed all that much over the years except for the materials of which some of the newer models are made. Skis have changed a lot, however. It would be hard for an old-time miner or trapper to believe that anyone could ski on our present-day skinny synthetic sticks when compared with their broad, 9-10-feet-long, solid wood slabs. The new skinny skis do work. In fact, they work very well indeed, as almost everyone who uses them will testify.

LEARNING TO SNOWSHOE

There are no organized classes in snowshoeing in the Sun Valley/Ketchum or Sawtooth areas. Snowshoeing is normally a self-taught skill, although some advice from an experienced practitioner is certainly helpful. The people in the stores that sell snowshoes will give you some tips. Stores in Ketchum/Sun Valley that sell or rent snowshoes are:

> Backwoods Mountain Sports
> The Elephant's Perch
> The Snug Company

Addresses and telephone numbers can be found in the directory.

Snowshoes come in a surprising variety of designs and sizes and are constructed of a number of different materials. Prices vary a good deal also—from a minimum of $50 to over $150 per pair. Bindings may or may not be included. In any case, you have to have them. If possible, it's a good idea to rent and try out several types of snowshoes before buying.

Basically, snowshoes give you webbed feet wide enough to make it possible to walk on top of the snow instead of in it. Refinements in the shape of the shoes and the form of the bindings make them easier to use. For example, the tails on trapper-style snowshoes are there to weight the backs of the snowshoes and tip the fronts up so they don't catch in the snow when you step forward. Better bindings are hinged, and some have a cramponlike device built into them that projects below the bottom of the shoe to prevent slipping on any icy crust.

Walking on snowshoes requires a high-stepping, rolling waddle that will lift each shoe out of the snow and bring it forward around the other shoe. It's anything but graceful and, for the beginner, it's very tiring, but the alternative may be a humiliating fall when you've tripped yourself up by standing on your own shoe.

Beyond the basic gait, there's not much to learn about snowshoeing except a few tricks that will enable you to get on your feet again if you fall in deep soft snow. For this purpose, if you know you're going into deep new powder, it's a good idea to carry and use ski poles. They will help you keep your balance, provide a means of probing suspected deep holes, and help you get up if you fall.

Clothing for snowshoeing is essentially the same as for cross-country skiing and will be covered in more detail in that section. The main difference between the two is that snowshoe bindings do not require special boots. However, comfortable, water-resistant boots and snow-gaiters are highly recommended.

Winter travel precautions apply to snowshoers just as they do to skiers and snowmobilers. Read the *SNRA Cross-country Skiing* folder and the *Winter Recreation Safety Guide*, both published by the U.S. Forest Service. Both are available at the Sun Valley Ranger Station and the SNRA headquarters. A special temptation for some rugged individualists, just because it's possible on snowshoes, is to climb very steep slopes and mountainsides. Don't do it! You're inviting death or injury by avalanche.

Where to Snowshoe—There is practically no limit to where you can go in and around the Sawtooth National Recreation Area on snowshoes as long as you are careful to stay out of avalanche danger areas. Overnight and longer winter camping trips require careful planning and attention to weather forecasts. Permits are no longer required by the Forest Service for winter travel in the SNRA, but it would be the height of folly not to check in at a ranger station or the SNRA headquarters to tell them where you are going and to inquire about snow conditions.

LEARNING TO
CROSS-COUNTRY SKI

Cross-country skiing is by far the fastest growing winter sport in the Sawtooth area, as it is in many other parts of the country. A number of competent and professional instructors in the area teach both beginning and advanced techniques.

Unlike snowshoeing, it's difficult to learn cross-country skiing techniques entirely on your own. Two or three sessions of group or individual instruction to get started are almost mandatory. Then, after some practice on gentle, open terrain, further instruction in downhill, turning and stopping techniques will be most beneficial. Unless you've had previous downhill skiing experience, the downhill part of cross country is the hardest to learn. Even for expert downhillers, it's not all that easy, because the skis, bindings and boots are entirely different.

The Sun Valley Nordic Ski is the best known school in the area. It operates from the golf pro shop at Sun Valley.

Golf courses are excellent places for beginning cross-country skiing, since they have nice open slopes that aren't too steep. Both Sun Valley and Elkhorn maintain groomed trails on their golf courses. Wood River Nordic—Bigwood Ski Touring Center, located on the Bigwood Golf Course north of Ketchum on Highway 75, offers all levels of instruction. Idaho Guide Service and Sun Valley Trekking Co. of Sun Valley provide ski-touring and winter-camping instruction.

In Ketchum the Elephant's Perch, Backwoods Mountain Sports and Snug's Ketchum Co-op arrange for instruction. A tremendous proliferation of types and variation of cross-country skis complicates the beginner's choice of equipment. Talk to the instructors and the sales people and then rent different types you're interested in to try them out before you buy.

Farther north in the SNRA, Busterback Ranch provides instruction and equipment rentals. Addresses and phone numbers can be found in the directory.

Except for the boots, clothing for cross-country skiing is pretty much up to the individual skier. For skiing deep powder in cold weather, snow-gaiters are a big help to keep snow out of the tops of the ankle high boots.

Knickers and knee socks were once the distinctive items of cross-country ski clothing, and are still comfortable and efficient garments for the sport. However, more recently developed clothing, coveralls and full body suits of synthetic fabrics, are rapidly replacing wool knickers. Of course, none of these clothing items are mandatory; you can cross-country ski in any warm clothing you like. Clothing for the upper body should be in layers, rather than one heavy coat or parka. Cross-country skiing uses a lot of energy (1200 calories an hour if you're really moving), so you'll want to peel off layers as you warm up, and put them back on while you rest. If the weather is very cold. light cotton or silk gloves inside insulated ski mittens are a good idea.

At its best, cross-country skiing can be a graceful, exhilarating combination of walking, running, skating, ballet, and downhill runs in pristine surroundings. Even for the rank beginner it's a pleasant way to walk and slide over deep snow, or light snow for that matter. Although we are longtime hikers and backpackers, we had never been on skis before we went to Idaho for background on this book. Now we're outdoors all year around and love the snow we used to think was only good for keeping trout streams running in the summer.

Cross-Country Ski Trips

All the cross-country trips described here are day-trips and are suitable for novice and intermediate skiers. It is possible, of course, to make longer trips involving winter camping along many of the summer trail and road routes. These longer trips should be made only by expert skiers with winter camping experience, and then only after careful checking with local sources of weather and snow condition information. There are a number of very good guides in the area who will take intermediate and proficient novice skiers on overnight or longer trips safely and reasonably. After one or two of these trips, you'll be much better qualified to strike out on your own. But *never* go alone!

"Never go alone" is also good advice for the day trips described here, but isn't really mandatory if you stay on the signed and groomed trails laid out by the Forest Service and touring center operators. Checking the weather and snow conditions before going out is *always* a good idea, however. Also, the safety and rescue precautions listed in the *SNRA Cross-country Skiing* folder and the Forest Service *Winter Recreation Safety Guide* are must reading for anyone skiing outside of a school area. These folders are available at the ranger stations and the SNRA headquarters.

SNRA headquarters is the trailhead for the North Fork trail

The Forest Service, in signing and describing the cross-country ski trails that it has established in the area, has used "easiest," "more difficult" and "most difficult" to suggest the proficiency required to negotiate the trails. These terms are now internationally recognized and replace the previously used "beginner," "intermediate" and "advanced." To avoid confusion, these new terms are used in the trail descriptions.

Distances on cross-country trails are given in kilometers first with miles following in parentheses. This is also international practice. Lesser distances are given in yards or feet, however, because it's really difficult for most Americans to visualize distances in meters.

The USGS topographic 7.5 minute quadrangle maps that include the longer trips are listed. However, the routes of the cross-country ski trails are not shown on the maps.

1–Sun Valley/Elkhorn Trips

As previously mentioned in the "learning" section, there are several kilometers of semi-private, groomed trails on the Sun Valley, Elkhorn and Bigwood golf courses. These trails are mostly "easiest" classification, with some sections of "more difficult." Wood River Nordic also grooms several kilometers of beautiful trails between Highway 75 and Big Wood River south of the Hulen Meadows bridge. All of these trails are fee trails.

There are a number of other excellent cross-country trails on public property in the nearby area, notably up Trail Creek, the East Fork of Wood River and Greenhorn Gulch south of Ketchum. All of these are covered in Leif Odmark's *Sun Valley Ski Touring Guide* and in Ron Watters' *Ski Trails and Old Timers' Tales.* Since these trails are not close to the SNRA and have been publicized elsewhere, they are not described in detail here.

Everyone has to learn sometime—including the author

2–Big Wood River Trails

These trails are not in the SNRA either, but are nearby and were laid out and signed by the U.S. Forest Service. The trails are also close enough to Ketchum that you can take a taxi to the starting point if you don't have an automobile in the area. The Sun Valley Cross-Country Ski Association grooms these trails. Your donation in the box at the trailhead to help defray their expenses will be appreciated.

The trails are a series of three interconnecting scenic loops on National Forest land north of the Hulen Meadows housing development. A permanent map and signs at the trailhead detail the trails, give degrees of difficulty and designate which sections are for skiers with dogs and which for skiers without dogs. There is skiing for everyone here, with about an even division between "easiest," "more difficult" and "most difficult." A complete tour

of all three loops totals 12.5 kilometers (7.5 miles), but almost any shorter distance can be skied.

The area is closed to snowmobiles.

Topo Map for this area is *Griffin Butte* quadrangle.

STARTING POINT
The trailhead is on the west side of the Big Wood River across the new Lake Creek footbridge. To get there, go 3.5 miles north of the Ketchum traffic light and look for a sign and a plowed parking area on the west side of the highway between mileposts 131 and 132. There are toilets and trash receptacles near the bridge. The parking area is screened by trees and may not be obvious, so look closely for the entrance.

DESCRIPTION
The groomed, machine-tracked trail starts off northward beside the river, winding through cottonwoods and willows for almost 2 kilometers (1.2 miles) before doubling back to climb slightly onto a bench to the west. The trail is clearly marked at regular intervals and on both sides with the standard blue diamond cross-country symbols, and it has been cleared

Skiing through the cottonwoods beside Big Wood River

of brush and graded in some places. After reaching the level bench on an old road grade, look for the markers headed north again. In about one half kilometer you will begin to climb moderately and the markers for the middle loop will take off to the left (west).

To this point, the trail, which is the east side of the middle loop, has been all "easiest" classification and will continue to be "easiest" for another kilometer up the east side of the northern loop. If you are concerned about your ability to negotiate more difficult terrain, simply return to the starting point by the same route. Or, for variety, break new trail across the bench to the southwest and pick up the trail on the south side of the middle loop near the houses where it heads east to the trailhead. The rest of the trail system is classified "more difficult" and "most difficult."

After one kilometer of travel north from the junction on a flat overlooking the river, the north loop turns west and climbs rather steeply up an open valley to a saddle on the crest of the ridge below a steep rock formation. This is a good place for a rest stop and a look at the view across into the Lake Creek valley and back down the Big Wood River valley toward Ketchum. The trail then descends at an angle on the west side of the ridge, turns back north down a valley and makes a wide loop westward before turning south again around spur ridges in open lodgepole pines and firs. At about 5 kilometers you will have turned east again around the nose of the ridge and skied out past some scattered aspens to a point where the north loop is completed and there is two-way traffic for a hundred yards or so back south to where the middle trail loop turns westward.

The middle trail loop climbs gradually westward from the junction across the open bench, then more steeply south, crossing a wide gully and climbing onto the side of a ridge west of the bench. At about 1.5 kilometers (1 mile) from the junction with the north loop you will come to the junction of the southwest loop, which runs clockwise for 2 kilometers in rolling, open terrain to the top of the ridge and back. The southwest loop is steeper than it appears at first glance and is classified "most difficult." Views from the top of the ridge are spectacular. The west side of the middle loop, classified "more difficult," drops down the side of the ridge south of the junction, passes through an aspen grove, and turns east beside the fence marking the boundary between National Forest and private land of the Hulen Meadows development, drops off the bench and returns to the trailhead beside the river.

3-North Fork Wood River Trail

More level than any of the other trails, this is a favorite beginners' trail, but it is also one of the most beautiful. It is a short round trip including a small loop at the far end and totaling only 4.5 kilometers (2.7 miles).

The entire trail is classified as "easiest."

STARTING POINT

The starting point of the trail is the north end of the parking lot at the SNRA headquarters building, so it's very easy to find.

DESCRIPTION

The North Fork trail also separates the skiers with dogs from the skiers without dogs. About 200 yards after leaving the parking lot, you'll see a sign designating the left-hand track for dogs and the right-hand one for no dogs. The no-dog track runs along the west bank of the North Fork.

There are delightful groves of quaking aspen and cottonwood along the river bank tracing long and intricate shadows across the sculptured snow. The North Fork is just the right size stream to be especially beautiful in heavy snow. It's narrow enough to be bridged by the snow in some places and wide enough in others to flow dark and clear between modeled banks of snow and ice. To the west, the wide valley, gray-green with sage in summer, is now a smooth expanse of white leading to the first foothill ridge on the west side.

Slightly less than 2 kilometers (just over 1 mile) of travel along the river bank on the groomed and well marked track will bring you to the first road bridge. The bridge will be piled with snow as high as the railings on the sides and the sign for Murdock Creek on the far side will probably be buried. Murdock Creek flows down through a steep canyon from the north-east to meet the North Fork. In the angle be-tween the two streams, the XC trail makes a wide loop about 1 kilometer long. The Murdock canyon and the North Fork canyon both have avalanche warning signs beyond the flat. Heed the warnings. It is unsafe to travel farther up the steeper parts of the canyons.

On the way back to the parking lot you again have the choice of the "with dogs" trail on the road or the slightly longer creek bank trail without dogs. Or you can ski out across the open valley below the bridge.

Total elevation gain on the 4.5 kilometers of trail is only 160 feet—hardly worth considering. Snowmobiles can and do use this area, but it doesn't normally get heavy snowmobile use.

One of a group of winter campers starting out on the North Fork trail

4–Boulder Creek Jeep Road

Involving a climb of almost 1,000 feet in 4 kilometers (2.5 miles) to reach the first group of miners' old cabins in the canyon, the Boulder Creek road is not a ski trail for rank beginners. However, any skier who can handle a few short steep pitches can enjoy a couple of hours of energetic climbing in beautiful surroundings and a long *schuss* back along the same route. It's certainly better than the summer jeep trip that takes 20 minutes to the same place, jars your vertebrae, assaults your ears and fills your eyes and lungs with dust.

Topo map for this area is *Easley Hot Springs* quadrangle.

STARTING POINT

Drive up Highway 75 beyond the SNRA headquarters to the top of Phantom Hill. Just before milepost 141 the highway crosses Boulder Creek; the Boulder Creek road is on the right less than a quarter mile past the creek. There should be enough space plowed out near the junction to park two or three cars. If there isn't, someone will have to ski back from the parking space by the Easley Hot Springs road almost a mile farther on. The plowed snow may be too high for you to see the Boulder Creek road sign, but that doesn't matter. You can start from the north side of the highway just beyond the creek, ski up the west bank of the creek and within less than a kilometer find the road where it crosses the creek.

DESCRIPTION

If you've found the road at the highway, look for a fork in less than half a kilometer. You may find an obvious track here leading north on the west side of the creek to a yurt belonging to Sun Valley Trekking Co. The Boulder Creek road crosses the creek to the east. Be careful crossing the creek—the snow bridge may collapse.

This route is not signed or groomed, but you should be able to follow the trace of the road even in the deepest snow. Obliging snowmobilers may have packed a track for you.

After crossing the creek, the road goes up the east side of the valley, 100 yards or so from the creek, out in what would in the summer be sagebrush-covered slopes. Now the sagebrush is covered over and smoothed out into even contours of white. The climb for the next 2 kilometers (1.2 miles) is moderately steep, with occasional steeper pitches. There are great views of the creek, its bordering aspens and cottonwoods, and the soaring peaks of the Boulders ahead of you to compensate for the hard work.

At about 3 kilometers, after crossing a small gully, you will enter a parklike open Douglas fir forest that covers the floor of the valley. Note the wells in the snow under the trees. This is also a good place to look for grouse and Canada jays. The climb is not so steep here and you will soon come to a trail register beside the road. Sign up so people will know you've been here. Another kilometer of moderate climbing through the forest brings you to some mine workings and two miners' cabins, one on each side of the road. The large two-story log building on the east side was a combination barn and stable, probably used by teamsters who hauled supplies to the mines in Boulder Basin, far above.

Dust off a log, have lunch and contemplate what life was like for the miners who lived through the winters here early in the century. It must have been rugged here—and consider that some of them wintered-over up in the basin, almost 2,000 feet higher.

Within another half kilometer above the cabins, the road crosses the creek again and enters a short, steep, narrow canyon. Heed the avalanche warning signs. Go no farther than the creek crossing. The entire area between here and Boulder Basin has a very high frequency of avalanches.

It's all downhill on the way back, and you'll probably glide down in less than half the time it took to climb up. Have fun! A stop at the edge of the trees is worthwhile for a good look at the view across the Wood River valley and up into the Smoky Mountains on the other side.

5–Prairie Creek West Side Trails

There are two trails in the lower Prairie Creek canyon on the west side of Highway 75: The first is a 7.7-kilometer (4.6-mile) main loop with an alternative cutoff that will reduce the distance to 6.2 kilometers (3.7 miles). The other is the 3.5-kilometer (2.1-mile) "Vista" trail loop north of the main loop at the mouth of the canyon. Almost all of the main trail is classified "easiest," with only a few short stretches of "more difficult." The "Vista" trail is mostly "more difficult." Both loops are groomed and machine-tracked by the SNRA staff.

Dogs are not allowed on the west side trails, but are allowed on the east side "Billy's Bridge" trails. Snowmobiles are banned from the entire Prairie Creek cross-country ski area.

Topo map is *Easley Hot Springs* quadrangle.

STARTING POINT

The trailhead for west side trails is on the west side of Highway 75 at the Prairie Creek road junction between mileposts 146 and 147. Park on the west side of the highway at the trailhead or at a larger parking area on the east side of the highway just north of the Russian John Guard Station. One kilometer (.6 mile) of signed trail through the trees east of the highway connects the larger parking lot to Prairie campground, with winterized toilets and trash receptacle, and east- and west-side trailheads.

DESCRIPTION

Signs, a permanent route map and a contribution box to help with trail-grooming expenses are at the trailhead. The Boulder Mountain Tour trail, usually double-track groomed in February, comes into the trailhead from the north and aligns with the Prairie Creek trail for .5 kilometer (.3 mile) west, where it turns south to cross the creek. This is also the turn south for the Prairie Creek Short Loop, as indicated on the trail map sign at the junction.

Single-tracked Prairie Creek trail climbs gradually from the junction, a little north of west, to where the Vista Loop turns north, 1 kilometer (.6 mile) from the trailhead. The Vista Loop climbs to the shoulder of a ridge to the north with

Skiers' bridge over Prairie Creek

Avalanche warning sign at the upper end of the Prairie Creek trail

191

marvelous views of the Boulder Mountains, then returns steeply to the trailhead, 2.5 kilometers (1.5 miles) from this junction.

Continuing on the Prairie Creek trail, a moderately steep climb northwest up a valley brings you to a low pass and a short downhill run to a wide bench north of Prairie Creek. The track on the bench climbs moderately west, then turns south to a short, steep drop to a flat by the creek and a bridge in thick fir and spruce forest 2.5 kilometers (1.5 miles) from the trailhead. Heed the warning signs here. Don't be tempted to ski farther up the canyon, there is extreme avalanche danger.

The trail runs west for 150 yards on the south side of the creek over a series of hummocks in the trees, then turns south up a draw. At the head of the draw you turn east in a wide loop over a hump, and start downhill between Prairie Creek and a steep ridge to the south. You can see Boulder Mountain on the eastern skyline as you ski down a gradual hill here with a few humps. A short, steep pitch 2.8 kilometers (1.7 miles) from the trailhead drops to a lower bench closer to the creek. After climbing gradually away from the creek, a steeper climb takes you up a draw to the south for 200 yards. Follow the track east over a little knob and across a heavily forested flat, then more north, starting downhill. You turn south, then east down a narrow draw before skiing over a slight rise and out into the open, where you descend moderately to a junction with the combined Short Loop and Boulder Mountain Tour trails, 5.2 kilometers (3.1 miles) from the trailhead.

Pause here to admire the view of the Boulder Mountains across the Big Wood River valley, and decide whether to turn right to complete the long loop or left to shorten the loop by 1 kilometer (.6 mile). A left turn will take you down a long **S**-curve to the bridge across Prairie Creek and the Short Loop junction. A turn to the right will take you down a longer hill southeast and then back north on a trail paralleling the highway to the trailhead.

6–Prairie Creek to Owl Creek

This is the Boulder Mountain Tour trail on a wooded bench west of the Big Wood River, connecting the Prairie Creek trail system with the Owl Creek trail. It's an interesting 3.5 kilometers (2.1 miles) of "more difficult" skiing overlooking the upper Wood River valley.

STARTING POINT

The Boulder Mountain Tour trail coincides with the lower part of the Vista Loop trail at Prairie Creek, climbing northwest 1.6 kilometers (1 mile) to a junction where the Vista Loop turns southwest.

DESCRIPTION

Follow the blue diamond markers as the trail contours from the junction, first northeast and then northwest, around the nose of a ridge in open country. Ski through rolling hills and sparse timber to come out close to the highway at 1.5 kilometers (.9 mile), then climb moderately west in heavier timber to a bench and more open country. Follow the markers on the bench for the rest of the trip above the west bank of Wood River after the highway crosses to the east side. There are a few steep pitches, but it's mostly easy skiing. Stop and look back occasionally for majestic views of the Boulder peaks across the way.

Extend the trip with a jaunt up Owl Creek if you like (see Trip 8).

7–Prairie Creek East Side Trails

Opposite Prairie Creek on the east side of the Big Wood River are three groomed and machine-packed trail loops which the SNRA staff has named "Billy's Bridge" trails in honor of Billy Smith, who built the footbridge across the river. The 1.5 kilometer (.9 mile) up-river loop is flat and is "easiest" classification. The middle and down-river loops, totaling 5 kilometers (3 miles), include some hillier terrain and are classified "more difficult".

Dogs are allowed on all of Billy's trails. **Topo map** for the area is the *Easley Hot Springs* quadrangle, same as for the west side trails.

STARTING POINT

Park at the same parking areas as for the west side trails. Ski east down a short slope from Prairie campground and cross Big Wood River on Billy's bridge to the east bank. The trail in front of you is the west side of the middle loop. The up-river loop is to the left, the down-river loop to the right.

DESCRIPTION

The up-river loop is an elongated loop in the flat northwest of the bridge. Look for the junction after traveling 200 yards northwest on the mid-dle loop. There are no trees, except for a few willows and small aspen, and no notable terrain features, just easy skiing over slightly undulating ground with beautiful scenery above you on all sides.

Start around the middle loop clockwise from the bridge. Take the right fork at the up-river loop junction and climb a hairpin curve northwest to pick up an old roadbed leading up the side of an alluvial fan spreading from the mouth of the small canyon directly across the valley from Prairie Creek. Near the top of the fan, where there are some small groves of aspen, the markers lead south down the fan, with a few turns, to the junction with the down-river loop. To get back to the starting point, follow the river side of the loop back to the bridge as it curves around some tongues of fir and spruce. If snow conditions are right and you want to practice downhill turns in powder, just take off from the top of the fan straight down the open steeper slope toward the river. Then you can ascend the upper half of the loop and run down the hill again. Stay out of the canyon above the fan, however; there is avalanche danger there.

The down-river loop is a distorted figure 8 of 4 kilometers (2.4 miles) extending south almost to Silver Creek. The east side of the loop climbs across another alluvial fan, then drops down beside the river opposite Russian John Guard Station. Follow a quarter kilometer of two-way trail south before a final short loop on a flat near Silver Creek. The west side of the loop returns beside the river all the way to the middle loop.

Wide-open terrain is the main feature of "Billy's Bridge" trails.

8–Owl Creek

This is a popular area for skiers who like their trails unsigned and un-groomed. There is a sign at the lower end of the canyon near Highway 75 designating the area as a cross-country skiing area, but no markers on the trail. If you stay on the road for the less than 2.5 kilometers (1.4 miles) to the avalanche warning sign, this trip is an "easiest" classification with a little more climb than Prairie Creek. There are some open hills at the mouth of the canyon that can be skied safely and that would rate "more difficult" classification.

STARTING POINT

A little more than 2 miles north of Prairie Creek on Highway 75, near milepost 149, there is a plowed turnout on the west side of the highway at the Owl Creek road. Climb the snow bank and look for the cross-country skier sign and tracks leading to a snow bridge over Big Wood River.

DESCRIPTION

One hundred yards from the highway, cross the Big Wood River on a snow bridge. From the crossing the road heads almost directly west on the north side of Owl Creek. Climb moderately for 1 kilometer (1.6 miles) in the open, then enter spruce and fir forest to make some lazy turns a little farther from the creek. Beyond 2 kilometers (1.2 miles) the grade becomes steeper and you will come to an avalanche warning sign. Turn around and coast back to the mouth of the canyon. Some distance and additional scenery can be added to the trip by skiing back and forth on the low hills west of the Big Wood.

"Yurt-style" warming and dinner hut on Boulder Creek

9–Galena Lodge Touring Center

Until 1983, rustic Galena Lodge Touring Center, on the site of the historic town of Galena, operated the largest system of groomed cross-country ski trails in the SNRA, as well as providing excellent meals, libations and a place to get warm in front of a huge fireplace. Since the former operators sold their interest in 1983, Galena has operated only sporadically and not very well. No trails were groomed in the winter of 1986–87. Rumor has it that the present owner wants to build a large destination resort here, but nothing much had happened as of our publication date.

Galena Lodge is, however, the starting point for the annual Boulder Mountain Tour in early February. Hundreds of cross-country skiers ski the 30-kilometer (18-mile) trail from here to the SNRA headquarters on the day of the tour. Some of the skiers are competing in a race, but a lot more do it for the fun of it. The highway department keeps a parking area plowed by the lodge, and you are welcome to ski all, or any part, of the Boulder Mountain Tour any time but the week of the race. The trail runs south from the lodge on the east side of Highway 75 to Cherry Creek, where it crosses to the west side of the highway for the remainder of the run to SNRA headquarters.

The terrain around Galena Lodge has not changed, of course, and you can still ski there, subject to possible restrictions on private land, but you are not apt to find any groomed trails except for the Boulder Mountain Tour trail. There may be skied tracks on the flat west of the highway and on the roads and trails up Senate and Gladiator creeks. These areas are usually avalanche-free, and the scenery is superb. Check with SNRA headquarters about the status of the area and any possible avalanche danger.

Idaho Guide Service guides treks to overnight yurts in the Cherry Creek drainage, 1.5 miles south of Galena Lodge.

The Galena area falls on two **topo maps:** *Galena* and *Horton Peak* quadrangles.

STARTING POINT

Galena Lodge is at milepost 152, 24 miles north of Ketchum on Highway 75. The parking area at Cherry Creek is on the east side of Highway 75, between mileposts 150 and 151.

DESCRIPTION

"Easiest" classification trails are in the valleys of Gladiator and Senate creeks, in the meadows east of Senate Creek and in the flats west of Big Wood River. "More difficult" skiing is higher up the valleys and over the ridges between Gladiator, Senate and North Cherry creeks as well as up Titus canyon west of the Big Wood River.

You can pick up the Boulder Mountain Tour trail at the Cherry Creek parking area where it crosses the highway or at its beginning at Galena Lodge. Between the two points it winds over open ridgetops, through heavy forest and beside tiny, snow-covered streams in open meadows. There are a few steep pitches that probably qualify as "most difficult." If the trail has not been groomed recently, it at least will be marked with the standard blue markers.

10–Galena Summit

Steep slopes of unmarked dry powder, spectacularly beautiful scenery and easy access by automobile are the major attractions here for alpine touring and telemark skiers. There are no developed trails. Expert skiers ski the steep slopes on both the north and south sides of the summit.

There is avalanche danger in almost all of the skiable area around the summit. Unless you are skiing with a certified guide, it is imperative that you check with SNRA headquarters before skiing this area. The information desk has the latest snow condition and weather information, as well as maps of the recommended ski routes. The Forest Service recommends avalanche-awareness training for skiers here, and recommends that all groups carry avalanche survival and rescue equipment. Do not ski this area alone.

If you meet the qualifications, you can enjoy thrilling skiing here in ideal snow conditions.

STARTING POINT

Start from the parking area at the summit or at the wide U-turn one quarter mile below the summit on the south side. Galena Summit is 30 miles north of Ketchum between mileposts 157 and 158.

DESCRIPTION

About all that can be said in the way of description is to arrange for a pick-up somewhere below and head downhill by the safest route possible. Preferably, a certified guide will show you the way. Stop to rest occasionally and look at some of the most beautiful winter scenery you're ever likely to see.

Steep slopes of Galena Summit offer spectacular skiing for avalanche-aware experts

11–Salmon River Headwaters

Half-day and full-day trips as well as overnight snow camping can easily be planned on the gently rolling floor of this wide valley south of Highway 75. Many kilometers of safe skiing beckon tourers who like to break new trail in pristine snow fields. Beaver ponds, aspen groves and the convoluted beginnings of the Salmon River add interest below majestic backdrops of snow-clad peaks and ridges. There are no developed trails.

The Frenchman Creek road just west of the upper Salmon can also be skied safely for 2 kilometers (1.2 miles) south of the highway to add more distance. However, this valley is heavily timbered and not as scenic as the upper Salmon.

All of this area is "easiest" classification except for the extra effort required to break trail in deep snow. There is some snowmobile use.

Topo maps are *Alturas Lake, Frenchman Creek* and *Horton Peak* quadrangles.

STARTING POINTS

Go down the north side of Galena Summit on Highway 75 to a plowed turnout at the upper Salmon River road near milepost 164 or, if you prefer, go a half mile farther west to the chain-up and parking area by the Frenchman Creek bridge.

DESCRIPTION

Head south on the Upper Salmon road and pass the old sheep corrals on your right at 2 kilometers (1.2 miles) from the highway. The road makes a wide loop in low, open hills on the east side of the valley before coming close to the river at 5 kilometers (3 miles) in a beaver pond area. Beware of skiing over beaver ponds, there may be holes in the ice, camouflaged under loose snow.

If you are starting from the Frenchman Creek parking area, two roads lead south from Highway 75 just east of the bridge. One is the Frenchman Creek road going directly south into the timber on the east side of Frenchman Creek. The other road runs east around the nose of a low, forested ridge into the open Upper Salmon valley, then turns southeast along the edge of the trees on the west side of the valley. Beyond a gravel pit at 1 kilometer (.6 mile), this road becomes a trace and then disappears. To get to the Upper Salmon road, cross the river south of the gravel pit and look for the road east of the low hills.

Continue south on the east side of the tiny meandering river through occasional clumps of lodgepole and aspen. Chemeketan campground is in a large grove of lodgepole pine 7.5 kilometers (4.5 miles) from the highway and just beyond a small creek that comes down from the hills to the east. Scrape the snow off a table and have lunch or set up an overnight snow camp if you like.

The large meadow south of Chemeketan is too marshy for comfortable foot travel in the summer, but when frozen solid provides delightful skiing for another kilometer above the campground. Stay off the sidehills, however, and out of the upper canyon above the meadow —there is avalanche danger there. Return to the highway by the route you came, or make a loop down the other side of the valley if you still feel like breaking new track.

12–Busterback Ranch Nordic Touring Center

Forty kilometers (24 miles) of well-laid-out, groomed and signed trails in the Sawtooth Valley and on benches and moraines toward Alturas Lake are the primary attraction at Busterback Ranch during the winter season. Add to that an excellent staff of instructors and guides, very comfortable accommodations, outstanding family-style food service, homey public lounge and warming facilities and wood-fired sauna and hot tub. Now locate all this well away from any other civilization in the midst of some of the world's most spectacular winter scenery, and you have the makings of a first-class cross-country ski resort.

In the summer Busterback has a dual capacity: It is a working ranch with hundreds of cattle, sheep and horses grazing in the irrigated pastures. It is also a guest ranch, offering all types of outdoor recreation. After the livestock has been moved out in the fall and the snow begins to fall, the cross-country skiers take over. The skiing season usually lasts from the first part of December to the middle of April. Snow conditions are usually ideal, and none of the trails even approach avalanche areas.

Busterback offers a variety of ski packages that include lodging, meals, instruction, guided treks and equipment rentals in several different combinations. Day-skiers are welcome to use the trails and the public facilities of the lodge for a moderate day-use fee.

Of course, day-skiers may also rent equipment and arrange for instruction. Non-guests who plan to eat lunch and/or dinner at the ranch should make reservations in advance, but coffee, cookies and sandwiches are almost always available. There is also a well-stocked wine-and-beer bar. With ad-

Poleless skier tops the hump in impromptu obstacle race at Busterback

vance notice, the staff will prepare tasty trail lunches that you can devour in one of the sheep-wagon warming huts beside the trails.

The trails offer something for all classes of skiers, including skaters. In addition, many open slopes offer tele-marking opportunities, and the whole floor of Sawtooth Valley is available for off-trail skiing.

Topo map for the area is the *Alturas Lake* quadrangle.

STARTING POINT

Look for the sign and the ranch buildings on the east side of Highway 75, 40 miles north of Ketchum and a quarter mile north of the Alturas Lake road junction. Starting point for the developed trails is across the highway from the ranch driveway.

DESCRIPTION

Ski the open meadows and along the Salmon River (a little too big to be snow bridged here) as far south as Smiley Creek and as far north as you like. There are no signs and no marked trail, but you won't get lost; you can see forever—the full length of the Sawtooth Range to the west and a lot of the White Clouds to the east. One small caution: Watch for wire fences. The snow will probably be deep enough so that you can easily step over them, but if you ski into one without seeing it, you may be injured.

There are several groomed and tracked trail loops on the flats west of the highway and up on the benches and low, timbered hills between the flats and Alturas Lake Creek farther west. Con-figuration of these loops changes somewhat from year to year depending on snow condi-tions and on what the staff thinks will work best. Trails are well signed and marked and easy to follow using the map provided at the ranch. Generally the "easiest" trails, as might be ex-pected, are on the flat and the "more and most difficult" trails are in the timber on the benches and hills. One large loop of mostly "easiest" skiing turns south almost to the Alturas Lake road, then west to Alturas Lake Creek and north along the creek nearly to the Valley View

road before turning into the flat again and wandering back south to the starting point for a total of 9 kilometers (5.6 miles). An especially beautiful part of this loop along the creek often provides an opportunity to observe wildlife—Canada jays and snowshoe hares predom-inantly. Busterback thoughtfully provides resting benches at especially scenic points along the creek.

At the north end of this loop a track con-tinues west across the Valley View road bridge to connect with a series of trail loops on the west side of Alturas Lake Creek and up onto the moraine south of Pettit Lake. Occasionally groomed trails lead on from these western loops to Alturas Lake and Pettit Lake.

Two sheep wagons, with functioning wood stoves and large enamel coffee pots are stra-tegically placed along the trails for use as warming huts.

New snow on a Busterback Ranch trail

13–Hell Roaring Lake

This trail provides a safe and relatively easy opportunity to get some back-country skiing experience. There is avalanche danger at the upper end of the lake, however. Plan a full day for the trip of almost 17 kilometers (10.4 miles) in and out. Snowmobiles are not allowed beyond the Sawtooth Wilderness boundary.

Topo maps for the trip are *Mount Cramer* and *Obsidian* quadrangles.

STARTING POINT

Hell Roaring Creek road turns west directly across the highway from the Fourth of July Creek road, 4 miles south of Obsidian, near milepost 174. The trailhead is across the Salmon River bridge 1 kilometer (.6 mile) west of the highway.

DESCRIPTION

The trail climbs directly west from the trailhead through jumbled moraines to reach the north side of Hell Roaring Valley below the lake. Hell Roaring Lake is 8.3 kilometers (5.2 miles) from the trailhead. For further description of the trail, see Backcountry Trip 8.

Skiing the shoreline of Redfish Lake—melted spot is a spring on the lakeshore

14–Redfish Lake

There is sometimes heavy ski and snowmobile traffic on the Redfish Lake road in the winter, but nothing like the summer auto traffic. With a foot or more of ice on the lake and three or four feet of snow over everything, swimming isn't very popular, but it is still possible to get a pretty good sunburn on your goose bumps if you take off your shirt on a bright day.

Winter camping is not encouraged in the campgrounds, and Redfish Lodge is usually closed for the season by the first of November. The picnic tables are still there, however, and an easy half or full-day ski trip gives you a chance to enjoy a picnic lunch in the midst of awe-inspiring winter scenery. You haven't seen mountains until you've seen the Grand Mogul and Mount Heyburn in winter dress behind the white expanse of Redfish Lake, or the serrated white wall cutting into the sky at the head of Fishhook Valley. This is all "easiest" skiing, except for some spots of "more difficult" in the Mount Heyburn campground, as long as you stay on the road system or on the north and east shoreline of the lake. Stay away from the steep west side of the lake, where there are avalanche possibilities.

STARTING POINT

The Redfish Lake road junction with Highway 75 is one half mile north of a bridge over the Salmon River and 4.5 miles south of Stanley near milepost 185. There is a large plowed parking area at the junction.

DESCRIPTION

This is not a signed or groomed trail, but the road will be well tracked and easy to follow. At 1 kilometer (.6 mile) south on the almost level road, you will see Little Redfish Lake through the trees to the west. A signed, but not groomed, scenic cross-country ski trail runs around the lake. In January, February and March it's normally safe to ski onto the lake to enjoy the spectacular views. Stay away from the inlet and outlet of the lake; moving water doesn't freeze.

At two kilometers (1.2 miles) on the road, cross the Redfish Lake Creek bridge. In the morning, if the weather is cold, there will be clouds of steam over the water as it runs rapidly between the sculptured banks and snow-capped midstream boulders. This doesn't mean that the water is warm; it's just relatively warmer than the air, and vapor released by the water movement condenses into visible steam. It all combines to make beautiful pictures when the low winter sun strikes through the clouds.

Picnic lunch at Mount Heyburn Campground overlooking Redfish Lake

Another .5 kilometer of gentle climb beyond the bridge brings you to the turnoff west to the backpacker parking lot next to Fishhook Creek. It's safe to ski up Fishhook Creek Valley for 2 or 3 kilometers as long as you stay in the middle of the wide valley on the south side of the creek. There is some avalanche danger from the steep ridge on the north side. Cross on the foot bridge at the parking lot and strike out west up the valley through the timber until you reach open meadows, where you will have a 360° panorama of snow-covered peaks and ridges. Return along your tracks and out beside the Redfish Lodge buildings.

The main road continues south past the visitor center. At the top of the rise, where the lake comes into view, there is usually an established track across the meadow to the road leading east to the picnic areas and campgrounds on the north end and east side of the lake. Ski down the road to cross the outlet creek on the road bridge. Beyond the bridge you can ski the maze of roads through the campgrounds or ski along the shoreline of the lake for 3–4 kilometers (2–2.5 miles) to where there are excellent views of the Grand Mogul and Mount Heyburn at the head of the lake. Be careful of skiing on the ice of the lake where small creeks or springs run in; the ice can be very weak at these points. Return the way you came. The road junction by the visitor center is 3.5 kilometers (2 miles) from the highway.

Expert skiers looking for greater challenges may want to try the "most difficult" Bench Lakes trail up the top of the giant moraine west of the lake. The trailhead is in Fishhook Creek valley near the backpacker parking lot.

15–Stanley Area

As of this writing there are no developed cross-country ski trails in the Stanley area. However, the Stanley Winter Sports Association, combining cross-country ski and snowmobile interests in the Stanley area, does occasionally groom cross-country trails in the Stanley Lake area and may groom other trails in the future. Groomed or not, there are many, many kilometers of excellent skiing on the wide open benches and rolling hills south and west of Stanley, as well as along Meadow, Goat, Iron and Stanley creeks, and across the many meadows adjacent to Highway 75 west of Stanley.

The best place to start in order to enjoy the multitude of cross-country skiing opportunities around Stanley is at the Stanley Ranger Station. The ranger station, open all winter, supplies weather, trail and snow-condition information. A large, plowed parking area gives access to excellent, untracked skiing on open, gentle slopes between Highway 75 and the Sawtooth foothills. In addition, the public information area of the ranger station, with its big fireplace, is one of the nicest warming huts you're ever likely to find.

Guided backcountry treks to overnight huts in the northern Sawtooth range can be arranged with Leonard-Ayer, headquartered near Stanley, and with Sun Valley Trekking Co. of Sun Valley. Unguided backcountry expeditions are not recommended.

Other winter facilities and accommodations in the Stanley area are described in "Auto Sightseeing" on pages 178 and 179. Addresses and telephone numbers are in the directory.

Topo Maps for this area are *Stanley,*

Stanley Lake and *Elk Meadow* quadrangles.

STARTING POINTS

Stanley Ranger Station is on a bench west of Highway 75, 2 miles south of the town of Stanley. In Stanley you can start skiing from any point where it's legal and convenient to park.

Other access points are from Highway 21 headed toward Boise: Iron Creek road junction is 2.5 miles from Stanley; Stanley Lake and Stanley Creek junction, 5 miles; Elk Meadow, 8.5 miles; Sheep Trail campground with toilets and refuse container, 10 miles. There are plowed parking areas at all these intersections.

DESCRIPTION

There are more than 4 square miles of open country south of Highway 21 and west of Highway 75 that can be skied safely and comfortably by novice skiers without ever being out of sight of the buildings of Stanley and the ranger station. You need only turn the other direction to see all of the magnificent peaks of the northern Sawtooth in winter garb. Some of the steeper-sided benches between Meadow Creek and Highway 75 could be rated "more diffcult," but certainly can be negotiated by careful beginners. This area is used by snowmobilers, but

there is room for everyone. The only precautions necessary are to stay off the Stanley airstrip (planes do land there in winter) and don't go into the steep canyons at the head of Meadow and Goat Creeks without a guide.

Iron Creek road is skiable for the almost 5 kilometers (3 miles) from Highway 21 to the campground and trailhead. From the trailhead it's safe to ski another 3 kilometers (1.8 miles) into the bowl where the Iron Creek and Alpine Way trails are combined for a short distance. Check snow conditions and avalanche potentials before skiing up Iron Creek; some steep slopes along the road can slide. Only expert skiers in guided parties should attempt the climb to Alpine and Sawtooth lakes. Otherwise, this is all "easiest" skiing except for a few short steeper places along the road.

From the Stanley Lake crossroad there is excellent skiing in all directions: north and south in the meadows along Valley Creek, east into the ranch country of the Original Stanley Basin and west to Stanley Lake. The road to the lake is by far the most popular route from the crossroad for skiers and snowmobilers alike. Stanley Winter Sports Association occasionally grooms separate cross-country and snowmobile tracks to the lake. Part of the reason for the popularity is the open season for ice fishing on Stanley Lake. Beyond the lake, it's an easy ski of 3 kilometers (1.8 miles) through the meadows to

A guided group of skiers heads into the Sawtooth Wilderness.

Lady Face Falls, with its winter buildup of ice. There are also breath-taking views of Mt. McGown and the other peaks of the northern Sawtooths. The canyon above Lady Face Falls is very avalanche-prone. All of this area is "easiest" level skiing unless you want to try some of the slopes of Elk Mountain north of Stanley Lake. There is a road leading up the mountain from the lake and there is plenty of "more difficult" and "most difficult" skiing on the way down.

Gliding over snow-covered Elk Meadow on skis is much more pleasant than wading through it in the summer; just be sure to check the snow bridges over the narrow creek channels to be sure they will hold up. It's very hard to get out of one of those beaver trails if you fall in, skis and all. A full day or more of very pleasant skiing can be planned in the Elk Creek/Elk Meadow area with absolutely no avalanche danger unless you go far up the canyon above the meadow. For details of the trip up the road and into the meadow, see Backcountry Trip 12. Distance from the highway to the first meadow is 4 kilometers (2.4 miles), to the upper end of the big meadow, 5.5 more kilometers (3.3 miles). It's mostly level "easiest" skiing in scenic surroundings.

Many more meadows farther west along Highway 75 present excellent opportunities for untracked cross-country skiing.

16–White Cloud and Boulder Mountains

There obviously are a large number of places in the White Clouds and the Boulders to cross-country ski and snowshoe that I have not mentioned. Many of them are very beautiful and unique, but access is difficult and avalanche danger is high. Unless you are a very good skier, avalanche trained, and familiar with the country, you should go into these mountains only on guided tours. Cross-country skiing and snowshoeing are marvelous experiences; stay alive to enjoy them.

Germania Creek canyon from the air

Snowmobiling

Want to ski uphill at 50 miles an hour over deep smooth snow without even stretching your legs? You can, in the beautiful surroundings of the Sawtooth National Recreation Area, if you bring your own snowmobile. Snowmobiling is a thrilling sport as well as being another means of getting out onto the surface of the snow to see the winter landscape. There are also races and endurance contests testing the abilities of both machines and drivers but although they are certainly valid sports, they have relatively little to do with enjoying the surroundings. Fortunately, the SNRA has plenty of room, so far, for all kinds of over-the-snow activities, both mechanized and self-propelled.

To the ranchers and other permanent residents of the SNRA and Big Wood River Valley who live any distance away from the plowed highways, the snowmobile has become a necessity; it is the utility vehicle that replaces the pickup and the horse during the season of deep snow. It's reassuring to know there is a way to get to the highway over several miles of unplowed road if you need to, and carry back groceries and feed. It's also about the only way you can get hay out to cattle in 3 or 4 feet of new snow. That doesn't mean that it's all work and no play for the family snow machine; the natives like to have fun, too. Unlike some other major downhill ski resorts, Sun Valley and Elkhorn do not share in this enthusiasm. In fact, snowmobile use is prohibited in most of the residential areas. Mulligan of Sun Valley does offer guided snowmobile tours, however, as of the winter of 1986–87.

The marvelous ability of the snowmobile to transport people effortlessly for long distances over deep snow imposes serious responsibilities upon the operator of the machine in three areas: safety, respect for the environment, and consideration for the feelings and rights of other people.

THE SNOWMOBILE/CROSS COUNTRY SKI CONFLICT

The SNRA doesn't have much of a conflict as yet because there is still plenty of space and neither group imposes upon the other's territory to any great extent. With constantly increasing use by both factions, however, there may be confrontations, so the subject should be considered. To give credit where credit is due, snowmobilers never seem to complain about cross country skiers. In the unlikely event of a hundred or so skiers striding through the middle of a snowmobile race, that might change very quickly.

Skiers complain primarily about the noise the snowmobiles make. One of the greatest joys of cross-country skiing is to get away, temporarily, from the noise and stress of the everyday world. In the skier's opinion, the noise of snowmobiles destroys much of his reason for being where he is, and he might as well be skiing down a freeway. It's not a totally rational opinion, but it is very strongly felt by most skiers and the snowmobiler should be considerate of it.

Only a truly thoughtless and inconsiderate snowmobiler would drive his machine along a groomed cross-country track, thereby inconveniencing the skiers and causing the trail operator to have to re-groom and re-track. It does happen occasionally, though, possibly because the snowmobiler doesn't recognize what the track is or doesn't understand that he is doing a great deal of damage by driving along it.

SNOWMOBILES AND THE ENVIRONMENT

Unlike trailbikes and four-wheel-drive vehicles, snowmobiles do not tear up trails, cause erosion or destroy flora and fauna, provided they are operated responsibly. No responsible operator, of course, would drive over the tops of young evergreens, break down fences or chase animals.

REGULATIONS AND SAFETY REQUIREMENTS

The SNRA *Motorized Travel* map, available at the headquarters and the ranger stations and posted at trailheads and parking areas, delineates areas that are closed to snowmobiles for various reasons. A mimeographed handout map showing roads and trails open to travel in Sawtooth Valley and Stanley Basin is also available. The entire Sawtooth Wilderness is closed to snowmobiles as it is to all other motorized vehicles.

Because of the winter-time remoteness of backcountry areas in the SNRA, safety and survival precautions are of vital importance to snowmobilers traveling away from the cleared highways. Read the SNRA *Snowmobiling* folder and the Forest Service's *Winter Recreation Safety Guide*, paying particular attention to the sections on hypothermia, avalanche safety and rescue, survival equipment, and the requirement that everyone on a snowmobile trip be able to make the return trip on his own feet from wherever he is. Snowmobiles should not be used to transport young children or infirm persons into remote areas. Like all other winter backcountry travelers, snowmobilers should *never* go alone; that means there should be more than one machine.

SALES, SERVICE AND REPAIRS

There are only two snowmobile dealers in the area:

Super Sports, 2.5 miles south of Ketchum on Highway 75, near the railroad crossing and a quarter mile south of the Big Wood River bridge.

Don Cutler's agency at the Valley Creek Motel, one mile northwest of Stanley on Highway 21.

Both agencies offer complete service and repair facilities for most makes of machines. In addition, most of the filling station and garage mechanics in the area have had some experience with snowmobiles.

EVENTS

The big event of the winter is the 100-mile race sponsored by the Salmon River Snowmobile Club on a weekend in late February. This gruelling event consists of two 50-mile loops, paralleling and crossing Highway 21 on groomed trails between Stanley and Cape Horn. The start and finish of the race is at Stanley.

Stanley is also host to a "Fun Days" weekend, usually in January, which features shorter races and some contests for children. Other Idaho Snowmobile Associations hold somewhat impromptu meets and events at Baker Creek, Smiley Creek and the Valley View/Alturas site.

Snowmobiling Areas and Trails

Challenge issued and accepted at the Alturas snowmobile area

1–Baker Creek/Boulder Flats

A plowed loop of road between Highway 75 and the Big Wood River just north of the bridge at milepost 143 provides parking and access for Baker Creek to the south and the Boulder Flats to the north. This is the largest winter parking facility in the SNRA and one of the few offering toilets and a refuse container. The level flat inside the road loop is a well packed try-out, fun run and short race area. Baker Creek road junction is directly across from the parking loop in the wide flat at the mouth of the valley. The road is safe to travel at least 3 miles to the East Fork and for some distance beyond when avalanche conditions do not prevail. Side canyons and the steep upper canyon of Baker Creek are not safe at any time.

A quarter mile west of the parking facility, the Silver Creek road bridge gives access to the flats and rolling hills north of the Big Wood River. The first 1.5 miles of the Silver Creek canyon and the open hills on each side provide a variety of terrain for the thrill seeker, with relative safety from avalanches. The steeper slopes and narrow canyons higher up are dangerous, however.

All of this area is open to both snowmobilers and cross-country skiers, but, by mutual consent, it has become primarily a snowmobiling site. A few people do ski Baker and Silver creeks, however, so be on the lookout for them.

2–Upper Sawtooth Valley

Miles and miles of gently contoured hills and open meadows, looking like newly whipped cream, beckon as you descend the north side of Galena Summit. Parking is available at the Frenchman Creek bridge near milepost 163 on Highway 75 and farther north at the Valley Road junction.

The wide floor of the upper Salmon valley south of the highway is safe and fun to travel as far as the meadows above the Chemeketan campground 4.5 miles from the highway. Stay away from the steep slopes and gullies toward Galena Summit and test snow bridges over streams; it's better to get your feet wet than to mire your machine where you can't get it out. Frenchman Creek road is also safe to travel for 1.5 miles from the parking area, and the low ridge between Frenchman Creek and the Salmon will give you some practice running through trees if you want it.

Valley road junction, .5 mile south of Smiley Creek Resort on Highway 75, is the south end of 12.5 miles of groomed snowmobile trail running down the east side of the valley. The north junction with Highway 75 is at Champion Creek. A large area east of Valley Road is closed to all travel as winter habitat for deer and elk. Be respectful of private property throughout the Sawtooth Valley.

Smiley Creek Resort was closed during the winter of 1986–87 for the first time in many years. The owners are unsure, at the time of this writing, whether they will keep the resort open in future winters.

Smiley Creek road south of the resort can be safely traveled for a little more than 3 miles in scenic meadows and groves of timber to the point where the canyon narrows. Travel on up the canyon to the site of Old Vienna is unsafe. Instead, if you want to see and photograph historic ruins in the snow, drive 2.5 miles up the Beaver Creek road from Highway 75 to Old Sawtooth City.

Beaver Creek store is closed in the winter and there is no parking available there. Beaver Creek road is not especially scenic, but it does provide some excellent views of the southern Sawtooths. Description of Old Sawtooth City is included in Motor Trip 5. Sit quietly among the old cabins for a few minutes and try to imagine what it must have been like to "winter over" here back before the turn of the century. The valley above the old settlement is avalanche-safe for no more than another mile of travel, and then only in the center of the valley floor.

4–Alturas Lake

An 8.5 mile road loop from the parking area on the west side of Highway 75 one mile north of the Alturas Lake road junction includes delightfully varied terrain and sensational views of lake, creek and mountains. In addition there's a wide open flat west of the parking area for impromptu racing or speed trials. There are just enough bumps and dips for thrilling rides at high speeds. It's also an easy hop south to the Beaver Creek road described previously.

From the parking area near milepost 170, head north to the Valley View Summer Home road, then west for almost a mile to the bridge across Alturas Lake Creek. A tongue of timber runs along the creek where the bridge crosses, adding to the idyllic winter scene. Note that the creek is running fast enough not to be frozen over solid, and only the road bridges are safe crossings.

Just beyond the bridge in the edge of the trees there is a Y in the road. The right fork goes

Sawtooth Valley has plenty of wide-open snow

around a fence corner of private land, then north along the west side of the creek for 1.5 miles to intersect the Pettit Lake road. To follow the loop, turn left at the first **Y** and go a quarter mile southwest in the open to another **Y**. Turn left again at this one onto the Cabin Creek road. The right fork leads to private property at the Valley View Summer Home site. From the Cabin Creek **Y**, the road wanders south for 3 miles over open, rolling hills and through patches of timber to the north shore of Alturas Lake near the picnic area and boat ramp. During January and February, if the weather has been cold, it will probably be safe to venture out onto the ice for a short way to see the magnificent backdrop of snow-clad peaks at the head of the lake. Stay well away from the outlet, where the ice may be weak.

To see more of the scenery around the lake, follow the main road west past the Smokey Bear and North Shore campgrounds, but stop short of the point where the road is crowded between the lake and the steep ridge to the northwest. There is avalanche danger along this slope. Return along Alturas Lake road across the creek and almost to Highway 75 before running across the flat beside the highway back to the parking area. Busterback Ranch maintains a network of groomed cross-country ski trails on the flats and wooded benches directly west of the ranch between Highway 75 and Cabin Creek road. Snowmobiles do practically no harm by running directly across ski trails, but driving along the trails is pure vandalism. Please respect the rights and feelings of these other winter sports fans.

5–Decker Flat to Redfish Lake

Eleven-and-three-quarter miles of varied terrain and a multitude of scenic views of Sawtooth Valley, the Salmon River and the White Clouds are featured on this trip between the Hell Roaring road junction and the parking area at Redfish Lake road. The entire distance is essentially avalanche-free. You can also extend the trip on the north end to the Stanley Ranger Station parking lot, or on into Stanley and beyond, if you like. This is a round trip unless you have someone available to take your trailer to the other end.

Start from the intersection of Hell Roaring road with Highway 75, 4 miles south of Obsidian. There is limited parking at this junction and at the Fourth of July Creek road junction almost directly across the highway on the east side. If there is no room, you'll have to drive on up to Redfish, where there is a bigger parking area, and do the trip in reverse.

A quarter of a mile west of the highway, cross the bridge over the Salmon River and turn right at the **T** on the Decker Flat road leading north.

Beware of soft ice where streams run into the lake

211

The road runs close to the river for almost 1 mile around the end of the huge moraine north of Hell Roaring Creek, then turns slightly west and breaks out into wide-open Decker Flat. At the south end of the flat, the road forks into first two and then three branches. The track will probably have been groomed, so you will be able to follow the correct right-hand fork. The left fork runs into private property west of Decker Flat. If the track has not been groomed recently, and you can't find the roads in the flat, just head a little west of north across the flat for 3.3 miles to where another moraine juts close to the river and a campground sits beside Huckleberry Creek and the Bull Moose trailhead.

After crossing Huckleberry Creek at the campground, the road is again squeezed close to the river around the end of the moraine before entering another smaller flat. In the middle of this flat, and 1 mile north of the campground, come to a **Y**. Turn left on what is, from here north, the sheep driveway and look for where it goes uphill away from the river in sparse lodgepole pine and Douglas fir. There are good views of the fish hatchery across the river and of the White Clouds across the valley as you start up the hill.

The driveway and road climb gradually through thicker timber to the top of the very large moraine east of Redfish Lake. This is the moraine that dammed the lower end of Sawtooth Valley several thousand years ago until the river broke through it. The route wanders north through jumbled terrain for another .6 mile to drop down beside Highway 75 again just before reaching the Redfish road. You can end your trip here, return to Hell Roaring by the same route, or cross Redfish Lake Creek on the sheep bridge and proceed on north to the ranger station or Stanley.

6–Stanley Area

Snowmobilers are welcome in Stanley. It's not uncommon to see a number of machines parked in the motel parking lots without any trailers or pickups around. These belong to the people who have made the 50-mile trip from Lowman by way of Bear Valley and along the trails paralleling Highway 21. Some people claim it's the easiest way to get to Stanley in the winter.

Another writer has dubbed Stanley "snowmobile heaven," and he may well be right. It's hard to imagine another area with so much room to play and with such usually ideal snow and weather conditions. Except for the weekend of the 100-mile race, there are normally plenty of overnight accommodations during the winter season, but it's still a good idea to phone ahead for reservations. It's a long way to anywhere else.

Stanley and Stanley Basin
from above the Nip and Tuck road

All of the open country south of Stanley toward the ranger station and west toward the Sawtooths is generally open to snowmobiles. You need only respect private property and be on the lookout for a few fences. You can also go on south from the ranger station on a well-traveled trail to connect with the Redfish Lake road and, by way of Decker Flat as previously described, to all of the Sawtooth Valley.

The 15-mile, signed Nip and Tuck trail loop begins in the middle of Stanley on the north side of Highway 21. Look for the bridge across Valley Creek a quarter mile west of Highway 75. The trail goes across the bridge and up into the hills north of town to connect with the Nip and Tuck road at 1.5 miles near the site of the original settlement of Stanley. This much of the trail and another 1.5 miles of the Nip and Tuck road west to the top of the ridge is two-way traf-fic. Take a look at "picture postcard" Stanley nestled in the snow below and then, at a road fork, follow the orange signs on a one-way loop through the rolling hills for 6 more miles before returning the way you came. You can also get to this loop by taking the Nip and Tuck road out of Lower Stanley, but that part of the road isn't signed and may be a little hard to follow. There is little avalanche danger in these hills, so it's safe to venture off the road to try for an even better vantage point to photograph the magnificent northern Sawtooths, but be wary of wire fences. This is an especially spectacular trip in the late afternoon and evening to watch the sunset over the Sawtooth ridge. Then, as daylight fades and before turning on your lights for the return trip, you may see an awe-inspiring display of *Aurora Borealis* in the northern sky.

7–Highway 21 and Stanley Lake

Along the first 20 miles of marked trail leading to the Seafoam road beyond Cape Horn is just about everything a snowmobiler could ask for.

For the first leg of this journey, drive up Highway 21 2.5 miles to the plowed parking at Iron Creek road. The marked trail begins about a mile up Iron Creek road where the telephone line crosses the road, then follows the pole line over mostly forested rolling hills for 4 miles to Stanley Lake road near its junction with the highway. There is another plowed parking area here from which the heavily traveled road leads 3.5 miles west up the wide valley to the lake. Once there, you have a choice of chopping a hole through the ice to try for trout or doing some exploring around the lake and up the road that climbs to the saddle west of Elk Mountain.

At a little over 2 miles west of the highway on the Stanley Lake road, the marked snowmobile trail takes off north through the hills to eventually cross Elk Creek and, after 7 miles, cross the highway at Sheep Trail campground. There is a large cleared parking area at Sheep Trail campground with toilets and a refuse container.

The marked trail continues on the north side of Highway 21 through Trap Creek Narrows, then turns north on the Marsh Creek road to run 8 more miles past the Cape Horn guard station to the Seafoam road junction. None of this road is open to auto traffic. You are indebted to the Stanley Winter Sports Association for marking and grooming these trails.

Three miles south on the highway toward Banner Summit the Bear Valley road leads off to the west and almost 30 miles down to Lowman in the South Fork of the Payette canyon. There are no facilities along the way.

Directory

Information in this directory is as complete and accurate as we can make it as of the publication date. We hope not too much of it will be out of date when you read it. If you do run into problems, we suggest that you contact the SNRA Visitor Center, the Sun Valley/Ketchum Chamber of Commerce or the Stanley Chamber of Commerce.

Telephone area code for the entire state of Idaho is 208.

AIR TAXI AND CHARTER SERVICE

Augustus Airlines
P.O. Box 450
Sun Valley, Idaho 83353
Telephone 788-2927

Stanley Air Taxi
P.O. Box 30
Stanley, Idaho 83278
Telephone 774-2276

Sun Valley Aviation, Inc.
Hailey Airport
Hailey, Idaho 83333
Telephone 788-9511

Sun Valley Helicopter
Ski Guides, Inc.
P.O. Box 978
Sun Valley, Idaho 83353
Telephone 622-3108

Sun Valley Soaring (gliders)
Hailey Airport
Hailey, Idaho 83333
Telephone 788-3054

AUTOMOBILE RENTALS

Avis Rent-a-Car
Hailey Airport
Telephone 788-2382
  200 Sun Valley Road
  Ketchum
  Telephone 726-7305

Budget Rent-a-Car
1220 Airport Way, Hailey
Telephone 788-3660

Elkhorn Resort, Sun Valley
Telephone 622-3039

General Rent-a-Car
Ram Motors
202 N. Main Street, Hailey
Telephone 788-3688

Hertz Rent-a-Car
Sun Valley Mall
Telephone 622-3322

Hailey Airport
Telephone 788-4548

National Car Rental
Sun Valley Service Garage
Telephone 622-8221

Hailey Airport
Telephone 788-3841

Mountain Village Lodge
Stanley
Telephone 774-3661

Rent-a-Dent
Airport Way, Hailey
Telephone 788-4670

U-Save Auto Rental
931 N. Main Street, Ketchum
Telephone 726-3378

BACKPACKING EQUIPMENT AND SUPPLIES

Ketchum/Sun Valley area

Aspen Sports
Colonade Center, Sun Valley Road
Telephone 726-3361

Backwoods Mountain Sports
Highway 75 & Warm Springs Road
Ketchum
Telephone 726-8818

Elephant's Perch, The
220 East Avenue at Sun Valley Road
Ketchum
Telephone 726-3497

Snug Company, The:
Elkhorn
Telephone 622-9308

680 Sun Valley Road
Ketchum
Telephone 622-9300

Sun Valley Mall
Sun Valley
Telephone 622-9305

Stanley area

Sawtooth Mercantile
Telephone 774-3500

McCoy's Tackle Shop
Telephone 774-3177

CAMPGROUNDS

Contact SNRA or U.S. Forest Service for information about specific campgrounds in their respective areas.

Sun Valley KOA
Highway 75 So. of Ketchum
Telephone 726-3429

CROSS-COUNTRY SKI EQUIPMENT

(Most cross-country ski teaching and touring centers also sell and rent equipment.)

Aspen Sports
Colonade Center
Sun Valley Road
Telephone 726-3361

Backwoods Mountain Sports
Highway 75 & Warm Springs Road
Ketchum
Telephone 726-8818

Elephant's Perch, The
220 East Avenue at Sun Valley Road
Ketchum
Telephone 726-3497

Good Sports
No. Highway 75, Hailey
Telephone 788-2517

Snug Company, The
  Elkhorn
  Telephone 622-9308
  680 Sun Valley Road
  Ketchum
  Telephone 622-9300
  Sun Valley Mall
  Sun Valley
  Telephone 622-9305

CROSS-COUNTRY SKIING TEACHING AND TOURING CENTERS

Busterback Ranch
Star Route
Ketchum, Idaho 83340
Telephone 774-2217

Leonard-Ayer
P.O. Box 106
Stanley, Idaho 83278
Telephone 774-3389

Sun Valley Nordic Ski Touring Center
P.O. Box 272
Sun Valley, Idaho 83353
Telephone 622-4111

Sun Valley Trekking Company
P.O. Box 2200
Sun Valley, Idaho 83353
Telephone 726-9595

Wood River Nordic—Bigwood
Ski Touring Center
P.O. Box 3637
Ketchum, Idaho 83340
Telephone 726-3266

FISHING TACKLE

Chateau Drug
Giacobi Square, Ketchum
Telephone 726-5696

Good Sports
No. Highway 75, Hailey
Telephone 788-2517

McCoy's Tackle Shop
Stanley
Telephone 774-3377

Sawtooth Mercantile
Stanley
Telephone 774-3500

Silver Creek Outfitters
507 Main Street, Ketchum
Telephone 726-5282

Snug Company, The
Sun Valley Mall
Telephone 622-9305

FLOAT TRIPS

Idaho Guide Service
P.O. Box 1230
Sun Valley, Idaho 83353
Telephone 726-3358

Middle Fork River Company
P.O. Box 233
Sun Valley, Idaho 83353
Telephone 726-8888
  Stanley Summer Headquarters
  Highway 75, Stanley
  Telephone 774-2244

Middle Fork River Tours
P.O. Box 2368
Ketchum, Idaho 83340
Telephone 726-5666

Northwest River Company
P.O. Box 88
Stanley, Idaho 83278
Telephone 774-3334

Sevy Guide Service
P.O. Box 1527
Sun Valley, Idaho 83353
Telephone 788-3440

Sun Valley Rivers
P.O. Box 1776
Sun Valley, Idaho 83353
Telephone 788-9345

Two-M River Outfitters
P.O. Box 163
Sun Valley, Idaho 83353
Telephone 726-8844

Wild Rivers Idaho
P.O. Box 2599N
Sun Valley, Idaho 83353
Telephone 726-8097

FOREST SERVICE U.S.D.A. (OTHER THAN SNRA)

Boise Ranger District
7803 Warm Springs Avenue
Boise, Idaho 83707
Telephone 334-1572

Dutch Creek/Atlanta Ranger Station
Atlanta, Idaho 83601

Lowman Ranger District
Lowman, Idaho 83637
Telephone 259-3361

Sawtooth National Forest Headquarters
1525 Addison Avenue East
Twin Falls, Idaho 83301
Telephone 733-3990

GUIDES AND OUTFITTERS

Chilly Ranch Outfitters & Guides
P.O. Box 971
Sun Valley, Idaho 83353
Telephone 788-3341

Dennis Hill Outfitter & Guide
P.O. Box 465
Hailey, Idaho 83333
Telephone 726-7285

Epic Expeditions
P.O. Box 209
Sun Valley, Idaho 83353
Telephone 788-4995

Mystic Saddle Ranch
P.O. Box D
Stanley, Idaho 83278
Telephone 774-3591 or 774-3311

Sawtooth Lodge
Lowman, Idaho 83637
  or
1403 East Bannock Street
Boise, Idaho 83702
Telephone 344-6685 or 344-2437

Sawtooth Mountain Guides
Kirk & Dana Bachman
P.O. Box 18
Stanley, Idaho 83278
Telephone 774-3324

Smoky Mountain Outfitters
P.O. Box 478
Hailey, Idaho 83333
Telephone 788-2468

Sun Valley Outfitters
4th & Leadville
Ketchum, Idaho 83340
Telephone 622-3400

Sun Valley Wilderness Outfitters
P.O. Box 303
Sun Valley, Idaho 83353
Telephone 622-5019

LAW ENFORCEMENT

Ketchum, Sun Valley and Stanley have an emergency 911 number for police, fire and ambulance.

Police Dept., Ketchum
431 Main Street
Telephone 726-9333

Police Dept., Sun Valley
Sun Valley City Hall
Telephone 622-5345

Sheriff, Blaine County, Hailey
Telephone 788-2271

Sheriff, Custer County
  Stanley
  Telephone 774-3327
  Challis
  Telephone 879-2232

MEDICAL FACILITIES

Emergency telephone 911 in Ketchum, Sun Valley and Stanley

Blaine County Hospital
Highway 75 at
south side of Hailey
Telephone 788-2222

Moritz Community Hospital
Sun Valley
Telephone 622-3323

Salmon River Emergency Clinic
Stanley
Telephone 774-3565

MOTELS AND HOTELS

In Ketchum/Sun Valley area
contact Sun Valley/Ketchum
Chamber of Commerce
P.O. Box 2420
Sun Valley, Idaho 83353
Telephone 726-3423 or 726-4471

In Stanley area contact
Stanley Chamber of Commerce
P.O. Box 59
Stanley, Idaho 83278
Telephone 774-3591 or 774-2291

RESORTS AND GUEST RANCHES

Busterback Ranch
Star Route
Ketchum, Idaho 83340
Telephone 774-2217

Elkhorn Resort
Sun Valley, Idaho 83353
Telephone 622-4511

Idaho Rocky Mountain Ranch
HC64 Box 9934
Stanley, Idaho 83278
Telephone 774-3544

Redfish Lake Lodge
Stanley, Idaho 83278
Telephone 774-3536

Sawtooth Lodge
Lowman, Idaho 83637
No telephone at the lodge
    or
1403 East Bannock Street
Boise, Idaho 83702
Telephone 334-6685 or 344-2473

Smiley Creek Resort
Star Route
Ketchum, Idaho 83340
Telephone 774-3547

Sun Valley Resort
Sun Valley, Idaho 83353
Telephone 622-4111

SAWTOOTH NATIONAL RECREATION AREA

SNRA Headquarters and
Visitor Center
Star Route
Ketchum, Idaho 83340
Telephone 726-8291
*Use this mailing address for
all SNRA locations.*

SNRA Redfish Lake Visitor Center
Redfish Lake
Telephone 774-3376

SNRA Stanley Ranger Station
Highway 75
3 miles south of Stanley
Telephone 774-3681

Index